Circular Economy and Re-Commerce in the Fashion Industry

Archana Shrivastava
Jaypee Business School, JIIT, Noida, India

Geetika Jain
FMS, Amity University, Noida, India

Justin Paul
University of Puerto Rico, Puerto Rico

A volume in the Advances in Finance, Accounting, and Economics (AFAE) Book Series

Published in the United States of America by
    IGI Global
    Business Science Reference (an imprint of IGI Global)
    701 E. Chocolate Avenue
    Hershey PA, USA 17033
    Tel: 717-533-8845
    Fax: 717-533-8661
    E-mail: cust@igi-global.com
    Web site: http://www.igi-global.com

Copyright © 2020 by IGI Global. All rights reserved. No part of this publication may be reproduced, stored or distributed in any form or by any means, electronic or mechanical, including photocopying, without written permission from the publisher.
Product or company names used in this set are for identification purposes only. Inclusion of the names of the products or companies does not indicate a claim of ownership by IGI Global of the trademark or registered trademark.

                            Library of Congress Cataloging-in-Publication Data

Names: Shrivastava, Archana, 1968- editor. | Jain, Geetika, 1983- editor. |
   Paul, Justin, editor.
Title: Circular economy and re-commerce in the fashion industry / Archana
   Shrivastava, Geetika Jain, and Justin Paul, editors.
Description: Hershey, PA : Business Science Reference (an imprint of IGI
   Global), [2020] | Includes bibliographical references and index. |
   Summary: "This book examines best practices for assessing the
   technological landscape and for modelling sustainable business practices
   in the fashion industry"-- Provided by publisher.
Identifiers: LCCN 2019043461 (print) | LCCN 2019043462 (ebook) | ISBN
   9781799827283 (hardcover) | ISBN 9781799836445 (softcover) | ISBN
   9781799827290 (ebook)
Subjects: LCSH: Clothing trade--Economic aspects. | Clothing
   trade--Environmental aspects. | Sustainable development. |
   Fashion--Economic aspects. | Fashion--Environmental aspects.
Classification: LCC HD9940.A2 C48 2020 (print) | LCC HD9940.A2 (ebook) |
   DDC 381/.4574692--dc23
LC record available at https://lccn.loc.gov/2019043461
LC ebook record available at https://lccn.loc.gov/2019043462

This book is published in the IGI Global book series Advances in Finance, Accounting, and Economics (AFAE) (ISSN: 2327-5677; eISSN: 2327-5685)

British Cataloguing in Publication Data
A Cataloguing in Publication record for this book is available from the British Library.

All work contributed to this book is new, previously-unpublished material.
The views expressed in this book are those of the authors, but not necessarily of the publisher.

For electronic access to this publication, please contact: eresources@igi-global.com.

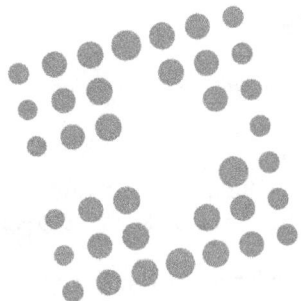

Advances in Finance, Accounting, and Economics (AFAE) Book Series

ISSN:2327-5677
EISSN:2327-5685

Editor-in-Chief: Ahmed Driouchi, Al Akhawayn University, Morocco

MISSION

In our changing economic and business environment, it is important to consider the financial changes occurring internationally as well as within individual organizations and business environments. Understanding these changes as well as the factors that influence them is crucial in preparing for our financial future and ensuring economic sustainability and growth.

The **Advances in Finance, Accounting, and Economics (AFAE)** book series aims to publish comprehensive and informative titles in all areas of economics and economic theory, finance, and accounting to assist in advancing the available knowledge and providing for further research development in these dynamic fields.

COVERAGE

- Microfinance
- Finance
- E-finance
- Behavioral Economics
- Economics of Intellectual Property Rights
- Statistical Analysis
- Interest Rates and Annuities
- Finance and Accounting in SMEs
- Economics of Migration and Spatial Mobility
- Investments and Derivatives

IGI Global is currently accepting manuscripts for publication within this series. To submit a proposal for a volume in this series, please contact our Acquisition Editors at Acquisitions@igi-global.com or visit: http://www.igi-global.com/publish/.

The Advances in Finance, Accounting, and Economics (AFAE) Book Series (ISSN 2327-5677) is published by IGI Global, 701 E. Chocolate Avenue, Hershey, PA 17033-1240, USA, www.igi-global.com. This series is composed of titles available for purchase individually; each title is edited to be contextually exclusive from any other title within the series. For pricing and ordering information please visit http://www.igi-global.com/book-series/advances-finance-accounting-economics/73685. Postmaster: Send all address changes to above address. Copyright © 2020 IGI Global. All rights, including translation in other languages reserved by the publisher. No part of this series may be reproduced or used in any form or by any means – graphics, electronic, or mechanical, including photocopying, recording, taping, or information and retrieval systems – without written permission from the publisher, except for non commercial, educational use, including classroom teaching purposes. The views expressed in this series are those of the authors, but not necessarily of IGI Global.

Titles in this Series

For a list of additional titles in this series, please visit:
http://www.igi-global.com/book-series/advances-finance-accounting-economics/73685

Handbook of Research on Accounting and Financial Studies
Luís Farinha (University of Beira Interior, Portugal) Ana Baltazar Cruz (School of Management, Polytechnic Institute of Castelo Branco, Portugal) and João Renato Sebastião (Polytechnic Institute of Castelo Branco, Portugal)
Business Science Reference • © 2020 • 487pp • H/C (ISBN: 9781799821366) • US $295.00

Emerging Tools and Strategies for Financial Management
Begoña Álvarez-García (Universidade da Coruña, Spain) and José-Pablo Abeal-Vázquez (Universidade da Coruña, Spain)
Business Science Reference • © 2020 • 357pp • H/C (ISBN: 9781799824404) • US $225.00

Recent Advances and Applications in Alternative Investments
Constantin Zopounidis (Technical University of Crete, Greece & Audencia Business School, France) Dimitris Kenourgios (National and Kapodistrian University of Athens, Greece) and George Dotsis (National and Kapodistrian University of Athens, Greece)
Business Science Reference • © 2020 • 385pp • H/C (ISBN: 9781799824367) • US $205.00

Growth and Emerging Prospects of International Islamic Banking
Abdul Rafay (University of Management and Technology, Pakistan)
Business Science Reference • © 2020 • 341pp • H/C (ISBN: 9781799816119) • US $215.00

Economics, Business, and Islamic Finance in ASEAN Economics Community
Patricia Ordoñez de Pablos (The University of Oviedo, Spain) Mohammad Nabil Almunawar (Universiti Brunei Darussalam, Brunei) and Muhamad Abduh (Universiti Brunei Darussalam, Brunei)
Business Science Reference • © 2020 • 374pp • H/C (ISBN: 9781799822578) • US $215.00

Handbook of Research on Theory and Practice of Global Islamic Finance
Abdul Rafay (University of Management and Technology, Pakistan)
Business Science Reference • © 2020 • 888pp • H/C (ISBN: 9781799802181) • US $445.00

For an entire list of titles in this series, please visit:
http://www.igi-global.com/book-series/advances-finance-accounting-economics/73685

701 East Chocolate Avenue, Hershey, PA 17033, USA
Tel: 717-533-8845 x100 • Fax: 717-533-8661
E-Mail: cust@igi-global.com • www.igi-global.com

Table of Contents

Preface xiv

Chapter 1
Sustainable Fashion 1
    Ruchi A. Saksena, National Institute of Fashion Technology, Chennai, India

Chapter 2
Determinants of Purchasing Intention for Re-Commerce in the Fashion Industry 10
    Nilesh Kumar, Amity University, Jharkhand, India

Chapter 3
Sustainability in the Fashion Industry 19
    Sana Vakeel, ITS Engineering College, Greater Noida, India
    Rashmi Kaushik, ITS Engineering College, Greater Noida, India

Chapter 4
Changing Customer Behavior in Sustainable Fashion Industry 31
    Mohamed Mohamed Elsotouhy, Faculty of Commerce, Mansoura University, Egypt

Chapter 5
Explaining Purchase Intention Towards Eco-Friendly Apparel: An Application of Theory of Planned Behavior 40
    Seemant Kumar Yadav, GLA University, Mathura, India
    Vikas Tripathi, GLA University, Mathura, India

Chapter 6
Recycling and Reuse of Fashion: A Way to Sustainable Environment 47
    Chand Prakash Saini, SGT University, Gurugram, India
    M. K. Nair, SGT University, Gurugram, India
    K. Tara Shankar, SGT University, Gurugram, India

Chapter 7
Influence of Micro-Celebrities on Generation Z: Perception, Customer Engagement, and Career Option 54
    Kanchan Chandar Tolani, Shri Ramdeobaba College of Enginneering and Management, India
    Ruchi Sao, Shri Ramdeobaba College of Engineering and Management, India

Chapter 8
Transmogrifying to Sustain Stimulating Potency 73
    Anant Deogaonkar, Shri Ramdeobaba College of Engineering and Management, India
    Sampada Santosh Nanoty, Maharaja Sayajirao University, India

Chapter 9
Thread of Sustainability: Crafting Fashion for Conscious Community and Conservation 80
    Nagma Sahi Ansari, National Institute of Fashion Technology, India
    Anannya Deb Roy, National Institute of Fashion Technology, India
    Sharmistha Banerjee, University of Calcutta, India

Chapter 10
Self-Construals Theory Applications for an Effective Communication of Sustainable Luxury 99
    Ludovica Gallo, LUISS Guido Carli, Italy
    Matteo De Angelis, LUISS Guido Carli, Italy
    Cesare Amatulli, University of Bari, Italy

Chapter 11
Recommercing Luxury Goods: A Market in Booming That Needs New Sustainability-Oriented Collaborative Strategies 117
    Floriana Iannone, Università degli Studi di Napoli "L'Orientale", Italy

Chapter 12
The Impact of Circular Economy on the Fashion Industry: A Research on
Clothing Share Services 142
    Tugce Aslan, Duzce University, Turkey
    Adem Akbiyik, Sakarya University, Turkey

Chapter 13
Customer Engagement by Fashion Brands: An Effective Marketing Strategy .. 161
    Samala Nagaraj, University of Hyderabad, India

Compilation of References 176

About the Contributors 198

Index 203

Detailed Table of Contents

Preface xiv

Chapter 1
Sustainable Fashion 1
    Ruchi A. Saksena, National Institute of Fashion Technology, Chennai, India

Fashion is undergoing a change in its very definition. The global fashion industry has grown at massive rates over the last decade and hence holds the power to influence a multitude of people. Sustainable fashion is one such concept that has influenced the design thinking of various creative heads across India and abroad. The awareness about sustainable fashion makes one realise several forms of sustainablity that can be adapted in a lifestyle. All strategies promoting more environmentally, socially, and ethically conscious production and consumption are important steps towards a more sustainable industry and, hence, a sustainable future. This chapter explores sustainable fashion.

Chapter 2
Determinants of Purchasing Intention for Re-Commerce in the Fashion Industry 10
    Nilesh Kumar, Amity University, Jharkhand, India

The re-commerce concept has gained huge attention from the consumer in the fashion market. India is a country with people from different cultural backgrounds and communities. Clothing is treated differently in India. Due to the important social significance of textiles, clothing is rarely thrown away. For this study, 200 university students and professors have been selected and their behavior analyzed. This study found that Indian consumers are always in need of uniqueness, and self-perception has an indirect impact on their purchase intention or buying behavior. Consumers with different levels of understanding, culture, and beliefs also showed differing preference structures. Results showed the intention of buying reused or recycled clothes mainly to match the lifestyle to satisfy the individual desires.

Chapter 3
Sustainability in the Fashion Industry 19
    Sana Vakeel, ITS Engineering College, Greater Noida, India
    Rashmi Kaushik, ITS Engineering College, Greater Noida, India

Rising awareness among consumers about reducing, recycling, and re-using garments has given birth to the concepts of reverse commerce (re-commerce) and re-fashioning in the apparel industry. Re-commerce in the fashion industry is booming just like any other re-selling business, which sells electronic items, furniture, and vehicles. The trend of fashion re-commerce is quite popular not just online, but also among the offline retail stores across the globe. Factors that have contributed to the growth of the re-commerce fashion industry include tough economic times, budget constraints, and increased awareness among consumers about keeping the planet green by reducing waste. Re-fashioning helps consumers in saving a lot of money while encouraging them for conscious consumption. Based on secondary sources data, the study focuses on motivation and barriers to fashion re-commerce. Sustainability is also an upcoming concept in the fashion industry. The authors discusses sustainability in the fashion industry with the help of a review of literature available for the same.

Chapter 4
Changing Customer Behavior in Sustainable Fashion Industry 31
    Mohamed Mohamed Elsotouhy, Faculty of Commerce, Mansoura
       University, Egypt

There is no doubt that sustainability has turned to a hot issue in recent years for its significant effect not only for the fashion industry but also for several fields. Nowadays, most organizations have shifted from traditional business models to sustainability-integrated business models. However, few studies have focused on changing customer behaviour towards adopting sustainability. In this chapter, the author focuses on presenting the damaging effects of the fashion industry in all phases of production and giving a view on how marketers stir consumers to embrace sustainable fashion in their own lives. This chapter concentrates on quality rather than quantity.

Chapter 5
Explaining Purchase Intention Towards Eco-Friendly Apparel: An
Application of Theory of Planned Behavior 40
    Seemant Kumar Yadav, GLA University, Mathura, India
    Vikas Tripathi, GLA University, Mathura, India

Textile manufacturing is one of the polluting industries contributing to approximately 1.2 billion tonnes of toxic greenhouse gases. Due to increasing consumer purchase index, companies are adopting unsustainable means like synthetic fiber and polyester, leaving tonnes of wastewater and other pollutants in order to fulfill customer demand. It leads to deterioration of the environment and causes serious health hazards. The present study addresses the issue of customer purchase intention towards environmentally friendly apparel by using the theory of planned behavior.

Chapter 6
Recycling and Reuse of Fashion: A Way to Sustainable Environment 47
    Chand Prakash Saini, SGT University, Gurugram, India
    M. K. Nair, SGT University, Gurugram, India
    K. Tara Shankar, SGT University, Gurugram, India

The chapter examines the role of recycling and reuse of fashion in order to achieve environmental sustainability. The chapter supports its conclusion by various reports that recycling of textile waste can be solutions to many environmental issues caused by fast fashion. However, textile recycling is an old term; in recent years, it has gained attention again due to fast fashion culture in significant parts of the world, which has resulted in overconsumption of textiles and led to waste generation. Waste recycling has become a multibillion industry. New ways are being created in terms of the development of sorting machines, design inputs, and innovative high-value products to make recycling a profitable proposition. The chapter also highlights how the second-hand market of clothes and the internet as a facilitator can help in reducing textile waste.

Chapter 7
Influence of Micro-Celebrities on Generation Z: Perception, Customer Engagement, and Career Option 54
    Kanchan Chandar Tolani, Shri Ramdeobaba College of Enginneering
        and Management, India
    Ruchi Sao, Shri Ramdeobaba College of Engineering and Management,
        India

A micro-celebrity is a person who has transformed from an ordinary person to a celebrity. Many organizations use micro-celebrities for advertising their products as they get to reach a larger audience easily. Micro-celebrities not only get popularity but also get to earn revenue; the desire for social media fame is found in many youths (Generation Z) today. The current study throws light on the perception of Generation Z towards micro-celebrities, identifies the influence of micro-celebrities on customer engagement, and explores micro-celebrity as an emerging career option for Generation Z. Major findings reveal that Generation Z follows micro-celebrities to stay updated with trends. Though association with micro-celebrities gives companies better customer reach, the influence of micro-celebrities on the purchase decision is uncertain. Many Generation Z individuals aspire to be micro-celebrities; however, when it comes to a career choice, some prefer to take it as a side hustle.

Chapter 8
Transmogrifying to Sustain Stimulating Potency 73
    Anant Deogaonkar, Shri Ramdeobaba College of Engineering and
        Management, India
    Sampada Santosh Nanoty, Maharaja Sayajirao University, India

This chapter focuses on exploring the practical implications of sustainability initiatives effectively through the efficient utility of technology by strengthening the marketing practices and ensuring the ease of sale. This is inevitable for standardizing the marketing practices that are globally acceptable.

Chapter 9
Thread of Sustainability: Crafting Fashion for Conscious Community and
Conservation 80
    Nagma Sahi Ansari, National Institute of Fashion Technology, India
    Anannya Deb Roy, National Institute of Fashion Technology, India
    Sharmistha Banerjee, University of Calcutta, India

This chapter aims to look into the current practices of fashion production and consumption and argues for a sustainable model. This model advocates the need of conscious creation and consumption, mindful connection with the community, and conservation of the ecology. It opens up conversations about fetishistic attitudes vs. sustainable practices and how production and consumption behaviors are manufactured in postmodern society. With interpretative epistemological stance, this chapter follows qualitative research methodology to develop an alternative model of fashion production and consumption. This alternative model, 'C3 Model of Art of Fashion', is the result of a qualitative study conducted amongst artisans, consumers, and entrepreneurs of Kantha.

Chapter 10
Self-Construals Theory Applications for an Effective Communication of
Sustainable Luxury 99
    Ludovica Gallo, LUISS Guido Carli, Italy
    Matteo De Angelis, LUISS Guido Carli, Italy
    Cesare Amatulli, University of Bari, Italy

The next generations of luxury buyers will be increasingly involved in social and environmental issues, gradually asking for more CSR accountability. Luxury maisons, despite recognizing sustainability as a business imperative, seldom communicate their initiatives due to the apparent incompatibility of the two worlds. Past research has demonstrated how the concurrent elicitation of conflicting concepts of self-enhancement and self-transcendence typical of sustainable luxury communication negatively impact brand evaluation. This study investigates how self-construal manipulation plays a role in mitigating the cognitive disfluency phenomenon arising from CSR communication by luxury brands. On a sample of Americans and Italians, three different priming conditions are tested: an independent prime, an interdependent (collective) prime, and a neutral prime. The results of the experiment reveal that eliciting the interdependent self-construal by emphasizing collective concepts prior to the CSR message exposure positively affects brand evaluation via an increase in information fluency.

Chapter 11
Recommercing Luxury Goods: A Market in Booming That Needs New
Sustainability-Oriented Collaborative Strategies 117
    Floriana Iannone, Università degli Studi di Napoli "L'Orientale", Italy

The aim of the work is to show that, in the luxury segment, retail operators are called to greater challenges imposed by the expansion of new competitive pressures especially driven by the dynamics of the demand trends increasingly oriented towards sustainability. The work provides a picture of the omnichannel strategies and of the practices adopted by the most important re-commerce players worldwide currently influencing the luxury brand choices in reassessing the opportunity offered by the re-commerce of the so-called 'gently-used' personal goods. The ultimate goal is to underline the need for new collaborative strategies for luxury brands in order to better organize the retailing activities in an omnichannel perspective, especially considering the opportunities opened by the theme of sustainability.

Chapter 12
The Impact of Circular Economy on the Fashion Industry: A Research on
Clothing Share Services 142
    Tugce Aslan, Duzce University, Turkey
    Adem Akbiyik, Sakarya University, Turkey

The fundamental changes in technology and globalization have changed consumer preferences along with the way people buy and consume. This change has profoundly affected new business models and consumption systems in all commercial markets, including the fashion industry in particular. Moreover, fashion businesses have begun to shift from traditional proprietary access business models to the sharing economy. The effect of the sharing economy or circular economy on the fashion industry is increasing day by day. Clothing sharing services, recycling, and re-use of used garments contribute to environmental sustainability and contribute to economic and social sustainability through sales revenue and employment. However, there is limited academic research on clothing sharing models. This research focuses on Dolap application, a clothing sharing service. It examines the role of trust in clothing sharing services from a consumer perspective. As a result of the analysis, it was found that trust in the platform positively and significantly affected the trust given to the service provider.

Chapter 13
Customer Engagement by Fashion Brands: An Effective Marketing Strategy .. 161
Samala Nagaraj, University of Hyderabad, India

No matter what changes time and technology bring to the world, fashion has its own way of adaptation. In the present times dominated by advanced technology and information, fashion enthusiasts, marketers, and industry are facing challenges and learning to adapt the new. With the increased options of selecting favorite fashion brands through largely available channels and information, fashion customers are equipped today with greater flexibility and understanding; this challenges brands to retain customers. Marketers are using new ways and platforms to engage customers. The chapter focuses on the effective marketing strategies adopted by fashion brands to engage customers. The chapter elaborately discusses the latest technologies and platforms used to engage customers. The chapter attempts to exemplify the effective engagement strategies followed by some of the successful fashion brands. It discusses new techniques in engaging like gamification and the use of advanced analytics for evaluation.

Compilation of References 176

About the Contributors 198

Index 203

Preface

United Nations (UN) has adopted the 2030 Agenda for Sustainable Development, comprising of seventeen Sustainable Development Goals (SDGs) emphasizing on five Ps – people, planet, prosperity, peace and partnership ("Fashion and the SDGs: what role for the UN?" 2018). The advancement of the fashion industry has a considerable effect on the accomplishment of the UN Sustainable Development Goals (SDGs) ("Threading the needle: Weaving the Sustainable Development Goals into the textile, retail, and apparel industry," 2018). This $2.5 trillion-dollar industry is the second highest user of water worldwide, consumes an estimated five trillion liters of water for dyeing processes a year and produces 20 percent of global water waste (Newburger, 2020). The sector is expected to contribute approximately 26 percent to global carbon emissions by 2050 ("Threading the needle: Weaving the Sustainable Development Goals into the textile, retail, and apparel industry," 2018). While the impact of the fashion industry is already significant today, it will further increase in future.

The advancement of the fashion industry has a considerable effect on the accomplishment of the UN Sustainable Development Goals (SDGs). Cotton farming alone is accountable for 24 percent of insecticides and 11 percent of pesticides ("Fashion is an environmental and social emergency, but can also drive progress towards the Sustainable Development Goals," n.d.). While the impact of the fashion industry is already significant today, it will further increase in future. By 2030, global middle class will grow up to 5.4 billion people leading to an increased demand for clothes and other goods that define middle-income lifestyles ("Circular Fashion - A New Textiles Economy: Redesigning fashion's future," n.d.).

The fashion industry that employs 70 million people along its value chain generates €2.5 trillion every year. But at the same time, it consumes ample amount of resources and has a deteriorating impact on the environment. Modern economic philosophy of "take, make, and dispose" relies on huge quantities of low-priced, easily available materials and energy. With the continuously increasing world population expected to cross 9 billion people and global garment manufacturing targets to increase by sixty percent by 2030 ("Circular Fashion - A New Textiles Economy:

Redesigning fashion's future," n.d.), this philosophy is crossing its physical limits. Consequently, fashion industry needs to lead the transition to a re-commerce which is eco-friendly and designs the products that last in society for as long as possible with bare minimum to no waste ("Refibra™ fiber – Lenzing's initiative to drive circular economy in the textile world, Lenzing," n.d.).

The apparel industry has the scale, reach, and technical expertise to deliver on target SDGs within the industry's sphere of influence in its interconnected global and local value chains. From the farm to the consumer, the textile, retail, and apparel production industry has an array of economic, environmental, social, and governance impacts. UN addresses the fashion industry in the areas of Sustainable Consumption and Production. It means buying and producing goods and services that do not harm the environment, society, and the economy ("Model of circular business ecosystem for textiles, VTT," n.d.). These challenges typically call for new theories, concepts, technological innovations, and methods regardless of whether they assume a micro or macro perspective.

With the growing concern towards economic sustainability, the participants of the fashion industry do agree that modern society has to develop through more innovative and sustainable ways ("Trending: New Sustainable Fashion Collections, Connections, CEO Agenda," 2018). This entails how modern producers manufacture and consume fashionable goods such as shoes, clothing, garments, and accessories ("Sustainable Consumption and Production in the Proposed Sustainable Development Goals," 2014). At major clothing giants, corporate social responsibility (CSR) managers today openly converse how they work to realign their existing business practices, production methods, and store concepts towards enhanced sustainability ("Circular Fashion - A New Textiles Economy: Redesigning fashion's future," n.d.). This includes efforts dedicated to improve almost all stages of the product's life namely designing, raw material acquisition & production, manufacturing, transportation, storage, sales & Promotion, and final sale, to use, reuse, repair, re-create and recycling of the merchandise and its components ("Extending the lifecycle of apparel and footwear, Playing for our Planet: How Sports Win from Being Sustainable," n.d.).

In order to contribute to the UN Sustainable Development Goals, we present a comprehensive study to address sustainable fashion industry. This book is an attempt to explore and propose solutions, best practices to Sustainable Development Goals in the fashion industry. The book endeavours to provide a transnational platform to explore the experiences of multinational investors, researchers, academicians, and policymakers as they confront these issues in various verticals of fashion industry in different countries, which offers best-practice guidelines for assessing the technological landscape and for modelling sustainable business practices in the fashion industry. The book throws light on what manufacturers, retailers, brands and consumers can do to secure value and create competitive advantage in today's business environment and reach the SDGs. The book explores on new business opportunities for suppliers, brands and retailers across the fashion industry. They can rethink on designing, production and distribution and move towards shared business and social objectives.

The book endeavors to provide a transnational platform to explore the experiences of multinational investors, researchers, academicians, and policymakers as they deliberate these issues in various verticals of fashion industry which would offer best-practice guidelines for modeling sustainable business practices in the fashion industry.

The various emerging views on sustainable fashion reflected in the collection of chapters contributed by researchers, academicians, and practitioners from all over the world. The book presents a global perspective and addresses the need of an international audience.

We are grateful to IGI Global for giving us this wonderful opportunity to bring together various perspectives across the world. These peer-reviewed chapters are easy to comprehend. We endorse the 'Circular Economy and Re-Commerce in the Fashion Industry' for all-time learning and recommend it to all libraries. Kudos to the contributors and the publisher for disseminating such a relevant book in today's time!

ORGANIZATION OF THE BOOK

The book is organized into 13 chapters. A brief description of each of the chapters follows:

Chapter 1 reviews the transformation that the Global Fashion Industry is currently going through to achieve sustainable fashion. The author discusses various forms of sustainable fashion production and consumption that have grown over the last decade.

Chapter 2 sets the scene for discussion on circular economy. The author examines the determinants of purchase intention of used fashion cloths. It also investigates the challenges and drivers to implement sustainability in fashion design.

Chapter 3 considers various aspects of changing customer behavior towards fashion sustainability. The author discusses an integrated approach to achieve fashion sustainability across varied cultures.

Chapter 4 focuses on the role of marketers in directing customers to sustainable fashion through creating awareness. This chapter tried to postulate a cyclic integrated process from marketers prospective for marketing sustainable fashion.

Chapter 5 identifies factors affecting purchase intention of eco-friendly apparels in Indian context. The study applies theory of planned behavior to assess the consumer's intention and hence behavior towards eco-friendly apparels.

Chapter 6 addresses the issue of increasing fashion waste. Authors suggested various tools for solving the problem and popularizing the diversion of fashion.

Chapter 7 focuses on understanding the concept of micro-celebrity and its influence on the generation Z. The authors attempt to understand the influence of micro-celebrities on customer engagement.

Chapter 8 focuses on exploring the practical implications of sustainability initiatives effectively through the efficient utility of technology by strengthening the marketing practices, ensuring the ease of sale.

Chapter 9 introduces readers to various perspectives on conspicuous consumption of fashion and a sustainable model of production and consumption with a specific way termed as art of fashion. The chapter deals with how fashion industry needs to build a sustainable base in order to preserve, conserve and march towards a holistic growth.

Chapter 10 reviews self-Construals theory applications for an effective communication of sustainable luxury. The authors propose a solution to possible negative outcomes stemming from luxury sustainability communication.

Chapter 11 presents a picture of the strategies and the practices adopted by the important re-commerce players worldwide. Authors emphasize the need for luxury brand of new collaborative strategies in organizing the retailing activities in an omnichannel perspective, especially considering sustainability perspective.

Chapter 12 analyses role of trust in online or mobile clothing sharing services in the sharing economy. The authors present a research model to examine the role of trust in sharing economics platforms.

Chapter 13 focuses on the effective marketing strategies that are adopted by fashion brands in the market setting. The chapter offers a complete picture relating to the customer engagement that is done in the prevailing fashion industry.

REFERENCES

Circular Fashion - A New Textiles Economy. Redesigning fashion's future. (n.d.). Retrieved from https://www.ellenmacarthurfoundation.org/publications/a-new-textiles-economy-redesigning-fashions-future

Extending the lifecycle of apparel and footwear, Playing for our Planet: How Sports Win from Being Sustainable. (n.d.). Retrieved from https://www.uefa.com/MultimediaFiles/Download/uefaorg/General/02/55/63/72/2556372_DOWNLOAD.pdf

Fashion and the SDGs: what role for the UN? (2018, March). Conference session presented at International Conference Center, Geneva, Switzerland.

Fashion is an environmental and social emergency, but can also drive progress towards the Sustainable Development Goals. (n.d.). Retrieved from https://www.unece.org/info/media/news/forestry-and-timber/2018/fashion-is-an-environmental-and-social-emergency-but-can-also-drive-progress-towards-the-sustainable-development-goals/doc.html

Model of circular business ecosystem for textiles, VTT. (n.d.). Retrieved from https://www.vtt.fi/inf/pdf/technology/2017/T313.pdfhttps://www.vtt.fi/inf/pdf/technology/2017/T313.pdf

Newburger, E. (2020, February 8). *'Clothing designed to become garbage' — Fashion industry grapples with pollution, waste issues.* Retrieved from https://www.cnbc.com/2020/02/07/new-york-fashion-week-how-retailers-are-grappling-with-sustainability.html

Refibra™ fiber – Lenzing's initiative to drive circular economy in the textile world, Lenzing. (n.d.). Retrieved from http://bit.ly/337357v

Sustainable Consumption and Production in the Proposed Sustainable Development Goals. (2014, June 16). Retrieved from https://spaces.oneplanetnetwork.org/system/files/scp_in_the_sdgs_iacg.pdf

Threading the needle: Weaving the Sustainable Development Goals into the textile, retail, and apparel industry. (2018, July). Retrieved from https://assets.kpmg/content/dam/kpmg/cn/pdf/en/2018/12/threading-the-needle-key-highlights.pdf

Trending: New Sustainable Fashion Collections, Connections, CEO Agenda. (2018, March 29). Retrieved from https://sustainablebrands.com/read/product-service-design-innovation/trending-new-sustainable-fashion-collections-connections-ceo-agenda

Chapter 1
Sustainable Fashion

Ruchi A. Saksena
National Institute of Fashion Technology, Chennai, India

ABSTRACT

Fashion is undergoing a change in its very definition. The global fashion industry has grown at massive rates over the last decade and hence holds the power to influence a multitude of people. Sustainable fashion is one such concept that has influenced the design thinking of various creative heads across India and abroad. The awareness about sustainable fashion makes one realise several forms of sustainablity that can be adapted in a lifestyle. All strategies promoting more environmentally, socially, and ethically conscious production and consumption are important steps towards a more sustainable industry and, hence, a sustainable future. This chapter explores sustainable fashion.

SUSTAINABLE FASHION

What started as a means to express oneself and further getting adapted by the masses, fashion is undergoing a change in its very own definition. The Global Fashion Industry has grown at massive rates over the last decade and hence holds in its power to influence a multitude of people. Sustainable Fashion is one such concept that has influenced the design thinking of various creative heads across India and abroad.

Our Common Future

In the 1980s, the United Nations set up the Commission on Environment and Development, also known as the Brundtland Commission.

DOI: 10.4018/978-1-7998-2728-3.ch001

The outcome of this order was a comprehensive document entitled "Our Common Future", also called the Brundtland Report. According to the report, sustainable development is development which "meets the needs of the present generation without compromising the ability of future generations to meet their own needs." *("Sustainability," 1987)*

The Commission led to a successful unification of environmentalism with social and economic concerns on the world's development agenda. Sustainability revolves around the concepts of moving forward ecologically, socially and environmentally that altogether find ways towards a long lasting prosperity.

Sustainability comes down to the kind of future we are leaving for the next generation. The desperate need for sustainability in fashion has been recognized over the past decade and has made its appearance among the work of various designers in their own understanding of the word sustainable. As designers become more and more aware of the changing environmental and economical conditions of the world, the products offered by the same are becoming more and more multi-dimensional- advanced in utility and durability at once.

Circular Fashion

Green Strategy, a consultancy firm based in Stockholm, Sweden, specializes in sustainability and circularity issues in fashion. They help their local and global clients to achieve their sustainability objectives based on key sustainability principles, circular thinking, best practice, and latest research. Green Strategy has identified seven main forms of more sustainable fashion production and consumption, as seen in the figure below.

Dr. Anna Brismar, the founder of Green Strategy created the seven forms of sustainable and circular fashion in 2012 and then updated in 2016. Ideally, all aspects of the figure above come together for every new garment produced.

With the kind of technology that exists in the 21st century, it enables the industry to predict the fashion requirements: trends, demands, etc. well ahead of its need. Each garment must be produced according to the demand or should be a custom-make (Number 1), of supreme quality and lasting design (Number 2), in an environment-friendly manner (Number 3) keeping in mind the various socially, ethically accepted norms which keeps our culture and heritage alive through the production process (Number 4). The product, once out for use must have a long life through good care, repair and redesign, if required (Number 5). Down the line, when the product is no longer desired, it can be handed into a secondhand shop, donated to charity or handed over to friends, relatives or perhaps a swap-shop, to prolong its active life (Number 6 and 7). When it reaches the end of its life, the garment should be returned for recycling of the textile material, which can hence be reused in the manufacturing

Sustainable Fashion

of new clothes or other textile products. Ideally, instead of buying newly produced clothes, one should consider renting, borrowing or swapping clothes (Number 6), or to buy secondhand or vintage (Number 7) *(Green Strategy, 2019, para3)*.

Figure 1. Seven main forms of sustainable fashion production and consumption

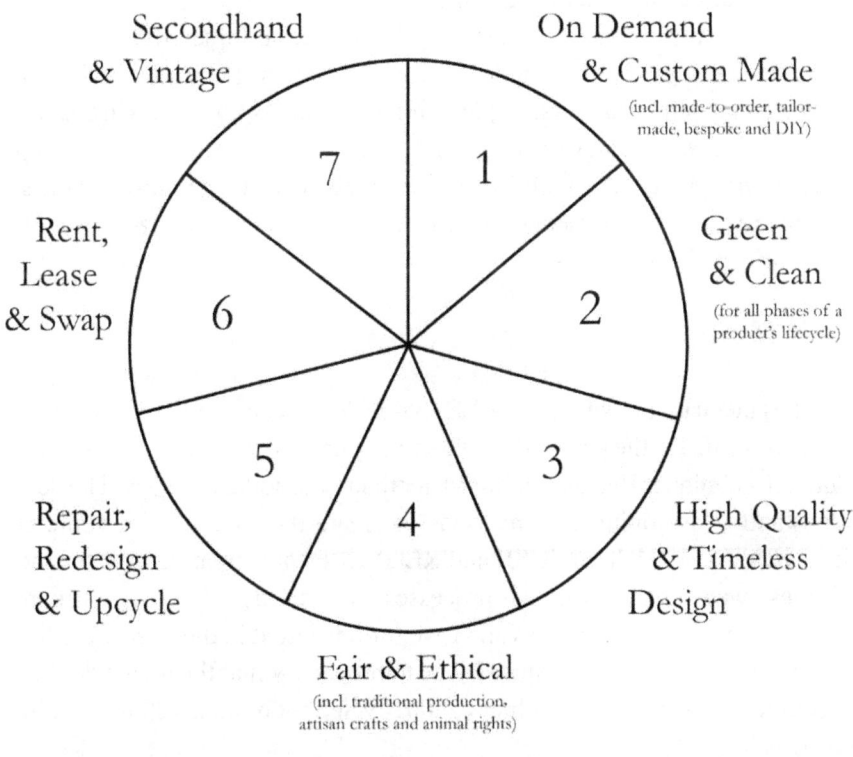

This figure covers sustainability from both the producer's as well as the consumer's perspective. Ideally, the products in the fashion industry should undergo this line of production and consumption. But this, unfortunately, is not the case and practically, is not 100% possible. That is why, even when the labels are unable to achieve full sustainability, every step in the way counts for a better tomorrow. Even as individuals, people now seek opportunities to renew their wardrobes in the most sustainable and ethical ways possible often using: "Second hand & Vintage", "Repair, Redesign & Upcycle" or "Rent, Loan & Swap". A part of the community that prefers newly manufactured clothes without history and who choose to stay true to a particular style, "On demand" and "High quality & Timeless design" are likely to be most befitting. Whether one prefers to renew the wardrobe often or more sporadically, "Green & Clean" and "Fair & Ethical" are important choices when indulging in new garments *(Green Strategy, 2019, para 4-5)*. Efforts towards sustainability may entail a relatively higher price tag, nevertheless, these environmentally and socially/ethically conscious decisions by the global community will round up to major contributions towards sustainability.

Sustainable fashion stands to be a highly debatable topic worldwide. Fashion and textile sectors have a multitude of processes when it comes to delivering the final product to their customers. Implementing sustainable practices in every step of production requires extensive research and planning. Numerous clothing companies are undergoing changes in their business models to further improve their supply chains that reduce environmental impacts, employ good social practices and boost the economy in all their steps.

Less is More

LEVI's has taken up in its WATER<LESS® INNOVATIONS to reduce the amount of water consumed in the production of denim by up to 96%. The brand has employed production techniques that use far less water than traditional methods. The designers are constantly developing new methods to create the same denim while cutting back on water (REDUCE, REUSE and RECYCLE) and creating new finishes that require less water than traditional processes. As recorded, Levi's uses more than 20 water-saving finish techniques and is very transparent in their practices for other labels across the globe to be inspired. The numbers say that the iconic denim brand has saved more than 1.8 billion liters and recycled more than 129 million liters of water *(Levi's, 2018)*.

By 2020, Levis' goal is for 80% of all its products to be made using Water<Less® innovations.

Reusing the Refuse

Textile manufacturing has a range of processes- washing/drying, warp preparation, weaving, dyeing, printing, finishing, quality and process control, and warehousing. The major wastes generated by this sector are fibre wastes which depending on the material can take as much as 5 months for cotton or even 200 years for polyester fibers to degrade *(Australian Industry Group, 2016)*. Wet finishing processes use up to 200 litres of water per kilogram of fibre, which makes water wastage the largest waste by volume.

When processed fabrics are put in garment production, around 16-20% of solid fabric goes to waste as post cutting/stitching waste, defected and end-of-the-line fabrics. Out of the produced garments, 1.5-2% of these are rejected because of damages. Some production houses undertake efforts to down-cycle these pieces of fabrics into rugs/bags,etc.

Doodlage, a clothing brand based in Delhi, India, aims to create well-finished premium clothes out of the waste fabric. The waste keeps increasing by the day which gives way to further innovative solutions to utilise the 'refused' fabrics'. Segregation of the waste fabric helps in this process. A part of this wastage is shredded which gets translated into textured panels. These textured pieces are then converted into their range of home decor collections. This is an initiative of the brand towards RECYCLING, an important aspect of sustainability. Doodlage also uses recycled cotton polyester, corn, eucalyptus and banana fabrics in its production, not just as a costumer attraction but also as an alternative solution to conventional cotton *(Doodlage, 2019).*

Vegan Clothing

Steps towards sustainability require a thorough and thoughtful approach. As mentioned, the production process for any garment is an extensive process. A number of initiatives are undertaken to bring about solutions which satisy both social and environmental needs of this era. Sustainable lifestyles have a deep connection with organic living. When it comes to looking at this from production point of view, a number of brands invest in undergoing an organic and fair process. Organic and fairtrade refers to preventing use of genetically modified seeds, synthetic pesticides or fertilisers, using natural pest control in the process of farming for the textile fiber. Further, no child labour, no price exploitation- paying fair wages to the farmers and labourers involved in the cultivating process, no farmer suicides (a relatively common and unfortunate practice in India). These practices translate into happier lives, healthier communities and a nicer planet for all of humanity *(No Nasties, n.d.).*

No Nasties, a brand based in Goa, India, focuses on producing clothing which has a production cycle that not just focuses on environmentally friendly ways but is also socially thoughtful about their farmers who are involved in the process. These efforts lead to better lifestyles of everyone who is associated with the brand, starting from the farmer and his land until the customer who gets a product that is ethically made and makes one feel good on the outside, and the inside.

Another label based in Pondicherry, *Upasana*, works on similar social and environmental causes. The concept of conscious sustainable fashion is what drives these kind of brands to design creatively, in an effort to solve problems, which is, in-fact, the main purpose of design. Any problem, be it post-tsunami trauma, farmer suicides, garbage littering, weavers losing their job, Upasana looks at social issues as a space to exercise for change. In an effort to elevate the devastated lives of the fisherwoman after a Tsunami on the banks of Bay of Bengal in Tamil Nadu, Upasana employed these women to make 'Tsunamika dolls' out of their waste fabrics which were used as decorative items(keychains, hangings, etc). Other efforts included- Kapas (organic cotton project with families of Madurai); Small Steps (compact bags as an alternative to plastic bags); Varanasi Weavers (a project with the weaving communities of Varanasi) and Paruthi (India's local organic brand to support India's organic farming community) *(Upasana, 2015)*.

In many ways, sustainable fashion is also the new luxury. When buying luxury items, consumers tend to thoroughly think through before making a purchase. It is of course an investment to own such products. A number of luxury brands have acknowledged the 21st century's environmental issues, and have taken up the responsibility through collective action and common objectives to combat greenhouse gasses and emphasize sustainability in the industry.

Stella McCartney

The label under the designer's name has always been dedicated towards developing a line of ethical luxury fashion. In a partnership with Kering, Stella McCartney launched her own fashion house in October 2001. The designer's beliefs and principles have a huge impact in her curations. Being a vegetarian, Stella McCartney does not use any leather or fur in her designs. The label has also invested in sustainable fabrics using cutting-edge technology: reengineered cashmere, recycled nylon ECONYL®, recycled poylester, organic cotton and lines of Skin-Free Skin and Fur-Free apparel. Her collections include women's and men's ready-to-wear, accessories, lingerie, eyewear, fragrance and kids.

Clevercare, a five-step labeling system was developed by Stella in 2014 to help consumers care for and prolong the life of the clothing through mindful garment care. This increases awareness regarding carbon footprint that every human practices leaves back on the planet. The label in this effort reduces their environmental footprint at every point of the design process *(Stella McCartney, n.d.)*. Every measure that the brand takes towards sustainability is also regularly measured and audited to stay ahead in their competition against climate change.

The brand is also a member of the Ethical Trading Initiative. Most of their suppliers still remain to be the small businesses are artisans in Europe. Stella McCartney collaborates with numerous NGOs and environmental conservation organizations as well, including Wildlife Works and Parley for the Oceans.

von Holzhausen

The brand offers an assortment of essentials, easy to wear bags and accessories in timeless colour ranges, at prices targeting a luxury market. In its initial years, the brand created its products from both animal leather and its animal-free alternative. As the designer, Vicki von Holzhausen later realised that the leather tanning industry is the second most polluting industry in the world with a high amount of water pollution, the brand decided to switch over to using solely vegan leather. In the Malibu based designer's views, the leather based industry does not reflect the brand's core mission and hence the use of alternative leather would be a 100% sustainable and ethical *(Decker, 2017)*.

Technik–leather is a 100% animal free material which is exclusively designed under von Holzhausen to have the feel of traditional leather combined with an extended durability of an engineered performance fabric. The manufacturing processes used focuses on conservation of raw materials, toxic-free solutions, and a minimal dependency on natural resources *(von Holzhausen, 2017)*. The numbers say that 99% of solvents used in processing of the material are recaptured and recycled.

The design sense of the brand focuses on fabricating fashion that has a high functionality quotient along with a style statement. Realizing that the consumers are becoming more and more concerned with the welfare of animals and the environment as a whole, von Holzhausen recognizes that leather is no longer a luxurious resource as compared to a well-made animal-free alternative. She believes in giving her clients the aspirational look and feel of a beautifully designed product with added benefits of a longer lifespan and environment friendly production and existence.

The brand also follows transparent pricing in accordance with its ethical standards. It gives 10% of the profits from each purchase back to their local, Los Angeles community. It has also had a partnership with the charity, Hope Gardens, a part of Los Angeles' largest homeless shelter, Union Rescue Mission, since its inception in 2015.

Aforementioned fashion-conscious consumers seem to care that they purchase sustainable styles. In a study conducted by McKinsey & Company in collaboration with Business of Fashion in 2018, 66% of shoppers among millennials say that they are willing to spend more on brands that prioritize their sustainability initiatives. It is, of course, necessary to understand the impact of less sustainable sartorial choices *(BOF, McKinsey & Company, 2018)*. The Ellen MacArthur Foundation, an NGO committed to facilitating the creation of a global circular economy across industries, cites in its A New Textiles Economy: Redesigning Fashion's Future report that 73% of 53 million tons of garments produced every year end up in landfills or incinerated *(Ellen MacArthur Foundation, 2017)*. This statistic is quite enough to initiate sustainable choices from both the sides, the producer and the consumer.

The awareness about "sustainable fashion" makes one realise about the several forms of sustainability that can be adapted in a lifestyle. All strategies promoting more environmentally, socially and ethically conscious production and consumption are important steps towards a more sustainable industry and hence, a sustainable future.

REFERENCES

Australian Industry Group. (2016, October 3). *Waste Saving Fact Sheet*. Retrieved from http://cdn.aigroup.com.au/Environment/14_Textiles_Waste_Reduction_Factsheet.pdf

BOF, McKinsey & Company. (2018). *The State of Fashion*. Retrieved from https://www.mckinsey.com/~/media/McKinsey/Industries/Retail/Our%20Insights/The%20influence%20of%20woke%20consumers%20on%20fashion/The-State-of-Fashion-2019.ashx

Decker, V. (2017, April 26). Vicki von Holzhausen Makes Vegan Leather Luxurious With Her Handbag Brand von Holzhausen. *Forbes*. https://www.forbes.com/sites/viviennedecker/2017/04/22/vicki-von-holzhausen-makes-vegan-leather-luxurious-with-her-handbag-brand-von-holzhausen/#3ddd44a9247d

Doodlage. (2019). *Eco Checklist – Doodlage*. Retrieved from https://www.doodlage.in/eco-checklist/

Ellen MacArthur Foundation. (2017). *A new textiles economy: Redesigning fashion's future*. Retrieved from https://www.ellenmacarthurfoundation.org/publications

Future O. C. Report of the World Commission on Environment and Development. UN Documents. (n.d.). Retrieved from http://www.un-documents.net/ocf-02.html

Green Strategy. (2019). *Seven Forms of Sustainable Fashion*. Retrieved from https://www.greenstrategy.se/sustainable-fashion/seven-forms-of-sustainable-fashion/

Levi's. (2018, March 22). *Sustainable Clothing & Eco-Friendly Brand Initiatives | Levi's® US*. Retrieved from https://www.levi.com/US/en_US/features/sustainability?ab=aboutusLP_sustainability_031918

McCartneyS. (n.d.). *Circularity*. Retrieved from https://www.stellamccartney.com/experience/us/sustainability/circularity-2/

Nasties, N. (n.d.). *What is Fair Trade?* Retrieved from https://www.nonasties.in/pages/fairtrade

Sustainability. (1987). Retrieved from https://sustainabledevelopment.un.org/content/documents/5987our-common-future.pdf

Upasana. (2015). *About Us*. Retrieved from https://www.upasana.in/pages/about-us

von Holzhausen. (2017). *About our Vegan Technik-Leather*. Retrieved from https://vonholzhausen.com/pages/technik-leather

Chapter 2
Determinants of Purchasing Intention for Re-Commerce in the Fashion Industry

Nilesh Kumar
Amity University, Jharkhand, India

ABSTRACT

The re-commerce concept has gained huge attention from the consumer in the fashion market. India is a country with people from different cultural backgrounds and communities. Clothing is treated differently in India. Due to the important social significance of textiles, clothing is rarely thrown away. For this study, 200 university students and professors have been selected and their behavior analyzed. This study found that Indian consumers are always in need of uniqueness, and self-perception has an indirect impact on their purchase intention or buying behavior. Consumers with different levels of understanding, culture, and beliefs also showed differing preference structures. Results showed the intention of buying reused or recycled clothes mainly to match the lifestyle to satisfy the individual desires.

INTRODUCTION

First it is important to understand the concept of circular economy by which the development of re-commerce concept does exist. Circular economy is the most recent attempt to conceptualize the integration of economic activity and environmental well-being in a sustainable way (Rani N., Yaduvanshi, Myana & Saravan, 2016). The circular economy emphasizes the redesign of processes and the recycling of materials that contribute to more sustainable business models. The much-criticized

DOI: 10.4018/978-1-7998-2728-3.ch002

linear economy approach produces products from finite reserves and throws waste at landfills. An early approach to practical sustainability was considered and demonstrated as an "economy in loops" of resource saving, waste prevention and product life extension. Re-commerce or reverse commerce refers to the process of selling previously owned, new or used products, primarily electronic devices or media such as books, through physical or online distribution channels to companies or consumers who want to repair, if necessary, and reuse, recycle or resell them afterwards (Ellen MacArthur Foundation, 2015).

The pre-consumer textile waste in India has a number of applications based on the fibre composition. Cotton waste has a number of applications such as paper making, surgical products such as bandages and pillows, Open End spinning, automotive industry, tissue paper production or in the non-woven industry, litter, manure for mushrooms and more. Cotton waste is also exported from India to other countries after it has been cleaned and the required standard has been reached. VP Udyog Limited, Kolkata, India is an exporter of refined camel noil and cardboard cotton waste, yarn waste, stocking waste from India to countries such as England, France, Malaysia, Thailand, China, Taiwan, Hong Kong and Singapore. Anandi Enterprises of Tirupur, India produces and exports certified recycled dyed and blended yarns and recycled fabrics of cotton and polyester. Industries like these produce pollution-free waste with a wide range of applications in key industries (Bairagi, 2014).

The Indian textiles industry is extremely varied, with the hand-spun and hand-woven textiles sectors at one end of the spectrum, while the capital intensive sophisticated mills sector at the other end of the spectrum. The decentralised power looms/ hosiery and knitting sector form the largest component of the textiles sector. The close linkage of the textile industry to agriculture (for raw materials such as cotton) and the ancient culture and traditions of the country in terms of textiles make the Indian textiles sector unique in comparison to the industries of other countries. The Indian textile industry has the capacity to produce a wide variety of products suitable to different market segments, both within India and across the world.

Second-hand stores are becoming more and more popular nowadays, not only because of the vintage trend, but also because of what it represents: recycling something that has been used and generally of good quality, avoiding the accumulation of unwanted clothing (Ethitude, 2017).

Textile or clothing waste is generally categorized as waste before consumption or after consumption. The pre-consumer waste consists of by-product material from the yarn, textile and clothing industry. Textile waste after consumption mainly comes from household sources and consists of clothing or textiles that the owner no longer needs as it was (Kapila et al, 2019)

India's textiles sector is one of the oldest industries in Indian economy dating back several centuries. India's overall textile exports during FY 2017-18 stood at

US$ 39.2 billion in FY18 and is expected to increase to US$ 82.00 billion by 2021 from US$ 31.65 billion in FY19 (up to Jan 19) (IBEF, n.d).

Textile waste after consumption is recycled in the industrial sector and in almost every Indian household. Recycling of wool and acrylic waste after consumption in India, Panipat, in northern India, is the world's largest hub for textile recycling and produces recovered "sloppy" woollen yarns and blankets from used winter clothing.

The main purposes of this research were following: (1) To understand and identify the determinants of purchase intention of used fashion cloths. (2) To identify the challenges and drivers to sustainability of fashionable clothes. (3) To examine the extent of use of resources. The findings of this research can enhance the understanding of current practices of implementing sustainability in fashion design.

BACKGROUND

The revaluation of pre-worn clothing and accessories, historically reviewed, includes a series of practices, from simple methods for de-clothing and re-using the raw material, perhaps to turn to the less worn side, as would have been done in the Middle Ages, to the complex scaffold of professions in the nineteenth century (Allerston, 1999). These industries recycle all kinds of clothing, with a machine-like economy, through specialist and discreet skills. Perhaps the most technologically advanced was the production of "sloppy" cloth in the north of England from rags of wool, cotton and indeed all fibers (except silk) that became the basic fabric for ready-to-wear clothing production in 1834.

In the mid-nineteenth century and the beginning of the twentieth, with the arrival of ready-to-wear and its standardized sizes, second-hand clothing lost its appeal and gradually became an export product to African countries.

With the emergence of "sloppy" (low quality recycled wool fabric used as blankets by American and British soldiers during the First World War), a trend of poorly recycled clothing began.

During the Second World War, various second-hand markets appeared in Europe, such as the famous resin market in Italy. The market began selling stolen or abandoned items and clothing from American soldiers as they walked through the city and eventually became one of the best known vintage markets. Even today, markets such as resin offer many of the most important vintage markets in Europe or the United States.

Fashion is inherently the most change-intensive category of consumer products and the fast fashion trend is spreading rapidly in the fashion industry. The current dominant fashion company necessarily embraces trends, even if they are initially undesirable. This phenomenon is predominant in the fashion industry as a requirement for survival in trend-sensitive fashion markets.

The complexity of purchasing materials and textile production processes makes it a challenge to distinguish between what is considered sustainable material. Various natural raw materials and fibers appear to be "organic", but they can be contaminated during material extraction and fiber-to-fabric production processes within the current textile production system, including bleaching, dyeing, printing and finishing. A single material can contain both organic and technical components. Western consumption patterns encourage excessively that leads to a negative impact on global sustainability. Implementing textile recycling increases global sustainability. Two major issues related to the global nature of textile recycling are: (1) textile waste is created and disposed of globally, and (2) a large part of the used clothing market is in developing countries where annual wages are sometimes lower than the cost of one outfit in the United States (Challa, 2007). For many people in developing countries it is necessary to be able to receive surplus clothing from industrialized countries. The Indian fashion scenario is known for its cultural heritage, elegance and colour. It brings out the subtlety and beauty that countless decades have endured. Because it is not only comfortable, refined and aesthetically beautiful, but it has also evolved over time. The fashion industry in India is an amalgamation of dynamic conventions and is making a huge flight in today's global scenario. From ethnic to western, salwar kameez to high-street fashion; the fashion industry in India has definitely undergone a transformation. Needless to say, the fashion industry in India has been favoured by thousands of years of rich tradition and knowledge such as the fashion of sewn garments that has existed in India since ancient history.

The textile industry in India is one of the largest segments of the Indian capital goods sector. According to the report of the Indian Brand Equity Foundation (IBEF), "India is the second largest textile exporter in the world. In addition, favourable demographics and rising income levels are believed to be the main drivers of growth for the Indian textile and clothing industry in the coming years".

METHODOLOGY

Sample and Sampling: The sample of the present study consist 200 university students, professors and staffs. They were selected through judgemental sample technique. It was based on the chance of selection. The data collection was conducted in Ranchi with local consumers. This state as the geographical context of inquiry appears to be relevant in terms of fashion consumption. It allows us to learn how dynamic is the market of a small city where every individual is after a unique product. So the survey was conducted through questionnaire which includes personal data questions as well and it was conducted in a university at Ranchi.

Each sample was asked questions for 10-15 minutes in order to collect the relevant data.

Table 1. Description of observed data

Data Observed	Options	% (Percentage)
Gender	Male	50%
	Female	50%
Occupation	Student	72%
	Professor	18%
	Staff	10%
Marital Status	Single	56%
	Married	15%
	Widowed	1%
	In a Relationship	28%
Age	21-30	79%
	31-40	17%
	41-50	4%
Education	Doctorate	8%
	PG	20%
	UG	72%
Income	No Income	57%
	Less than 5000	15%
	5001 to 20000	13%
	20001 to 35000	10%
	35001 to 50000	5%

The data processing was carried out with observation method where the behaviour of each sample is studied. Data analysis was carried out with the examination of all the answers and discussions.

MAIN FOCUS OF THE CHAPTER

The fashion industry is one of the most resource-consuming companies associated with extremely complex global supply chain networks and rapid cycles of production and consumption processes. The fashion industry faces many challenges, such as the important natural resources needed in the textile and clothing production process, the use of chemicals during cultivation, and the dyeing of textiles or surface treatments, labour exploitation and other social challenges within the supply chain. Self-concept, the perception of an individual about himself, is a fundamental determining factor for all human behaviour. Provide perceptions about self-motivating behaviour, control and direction to the wishes and goals of the individual (Hur & Cassidy, 2019). Consumer purchase intention, an important predictor of current buying behaviour, refers to an outcome or criteria assessment of consumers regarding website quality, information search, and product evaluation. Clothing serves many purposes: it can help us protect against different types of weather and can improve safety during dangerous activities such as walking and cooking. It protects the wearer against rough surfaces, rash causing plants, insect bites, splinters, thorns and spines by forming a barrier between the skin and the environment. Clothing can insulate against cold or heat. They can also provide a hygienic barrier, keeping infectious and toxic materials away from the body. Clothing also offers protection against harmful UV radiation.

The most obvious function of clothing is to improve the comfort of the wearer by protecting the wearer against the elements. In warm climates, clothing offers protection against sunburn or wind damage, while in cold climates the thermal insulation properties are generally more important. Shelter usually reduces the functional need for clothing. For example, coats, hats, gloves and other superficial layers are normally removed when entering a warm house, especially if one lives or sleeps there. Similarly, clothing has seasonal and regional aspects, so thinner materials and fewer layers of clothing are generally worn in warmer seasons and regions than in colder ones.

Clothing fulfils a series of social and cultural functions, such as individual, professional and sexual differentiation and social status. In many societies, norms about clothing reflect norms of modesty, religion, gender, and social status. Clothing can also act as a form of decoration and an expression of personal taste or style (Kumari, 2012).

Purchased apparels are being reused, recycled or resell in the market. The concept of reusing cloth does exist in Indian market. Used clothes were earlier sold in the local market which was called chow bazaar and now with use of internet platform the product are sold online with the reach of million people (Thamizhvanan & Xavier, 2013). The main determinants of the purchase intention of used clothes are follows:

1. Utilisation.
2. Interest.
3. Perception.
4. Need for uniqueness.
5. Attitude.

It was found that the students were Interested or we should say that they are comfortable wearing the used clothes on the other hand university professors or staffs seems to be less interested or they were in discomfort for wearing the used clothes. In terms of utilisation as the survey is done in the university where employees are more into simple clothes than fashionable clothes so the utilisation of fancy clothes were less on the other hand the university students showed their utilisation and the vulnerable age of the students and lack of freedom in the family to wear fashion clothes they were too inclined to buy these clothes which are comparatively lower in price. Perception includes the Individuals who have a strong desire to be unique often express their individuality through personalized products such as clothing and accessories. The interest in clothing is multidimensional and consists of five components or dimensions: concern about physical appearance, experimentation with the appearance, increased awareness of clothing, improvement of personal safety and improvement of individuality (Rani & Gupta, 2013). The nature of these dimensions indicates that people are interested in clothing because they want to look different and express their individuality. These individuals who want to show their individuality through clothing do not necessarily have to conform to others with regard to their appearance .In fact, choosing clothing is considered a behaviour that seeks uniqueness, where clothing serves as an aid to expand or reflect one's unique self. Consumers can plan to buy a certain brand because they find that the brand offers the right functions, quality or emotional benefits. High-quality perception can lead to consumers recognizing the differentiation and superiority of a certain brand and thus this encouraged them to choose that alternate option over these expensive brands and then they intend to buy these fashionable clothes from the sellers who sell used clothes at the lower price Simply put, other aspects of the use clothes are the same and consumers can buy these used clothes with higher quality.

CONCLUSION

There is a great need of studies related to purchase intention and the uses of used clothes on the population. Therefore, this study identified factors influencing of purchase intention towards used fashionable clothes. Self-concept and need for uniqueness directly influenced clothing interest and indirectly influenced purchase intention .Perceptions, attitudes, and experiences need for uniqueness play an important role for buying a product but in terms of clothing there are few more points are being considered by the individual which are level of comfort, price, and psychological aspects. Use of second hand clothes that has become trend now and this satisfy the unique need of users. India is a country of multiculturalism and the enormous diversity is reflected in the variation of traditional clothing and clothing styles that vary from state to state, which is rarely seen elsewhere in the world. It has been travelling from one subculture to another for centuries and traces of stylish Indians can be discovered from the time of Harappa and MohenjoDaro. With the advent of globalization, many changes have taken place in the Indian fashion industry. Clothing interest and emotional value were other important variables that directly influenced buying intent. The students and employees age between 20- 30 shows much interest for these clothes as it is attracting and this could be related to their status in the premises or the friends group on the other hand the age group of 35- 50 with good salary were least interested for these clothes as they found the price similar in online fashionable clothes app. This is a matter of comfort also as people are now more conscious for hygiene and status. So the study shows the students are intended towards these cloths due to price affordability, usability and interest.

REFERENCES

Allerston, P. (1999). *Reconstructing the Second-Hand Clothes Trade in Sixteenth and Seventeenth Century Venice*. Academic Press.

Bairagi, N. (2014). Recycling of Textile in India. *Journal of Textile Science and Engineering*.

Challa, L. (2007). *Impact Of Textiles And Clothing Industry On Environment: Approach Towards Eco-Friendly Textiles*. https://www.fibre2fashion.com/industry-article/1709/impact-of-textiles-and-clothing-industry-on-environment

Ellen MacArthur Foundation. (2015, November 26). *Towards a Circular economy: Business rationale for an accelerated transition*. Author.

Ethitude: A little history of second hand clothes. (2017, January 19). https://medium.com/@ethitudeblog/a-little-history-of-second-hand-clothes

Hur, E., & Cassidy, T. (2019). Perceptions and attitudes towards sustainable fashion design: Challenges and opportunities for implementing sustainability in fashion, International Journal of Fashion Design. *Technology and Education, 12*(2), 208–217. doi:10.1080/17543266.2019.1572789

Kapila, P., Dhillon, B. S. (2019, March 8). *Management of post consumer textile waste*. Academic Press.

Kumari, P. (2012). Changing Purchase Behaviour of Indian Customers. *ArthPrabandh: A Journal of Economics and Management, 1*(8), 35-41.

Rani, M., & Gupta, R. (2013). Determinants of consumer buying behaviour: A study of readymade garments. *International Journal of Research in Commerce & Managemment, 4*(4), 49–52.

Rani, N., Yaduvanshi, R., Myana, R., & Saravan. (2016). Circular Economy for Sustainable Development in India. *Indian Journal of Science and Technology, 9*(46), 1-9. Retrieved from https://www.researchgate.net/publication/312125734_Circular_Economy_for_Sustainable_Development_in_India

Thamizhvanan, A., & Xavier, M. J. (2013). Determinants of customers' online purchase intention: An empirical study in India. *Journal of Indian Business Research, 5*(1), 17–32. doi:10.1108/17554191311303367

Chapter 3
Sustainability in the Fashion Industry

Sana Vakeel
ITS Engineering College, Greater Noida, India

Rashmi Kaushik
ITS Engineering College, Greater Noida, India

ABSTRACT

Rising awareness among consumers about reducing, recycling, and re-using garments has given birth to the concepts of reverse commerce (re-commerce) and re-fashioning in the apparel industry. Re-commerce in the fashion industry is booming just like any other re-selling business, which sells electronic items, furniture, and vehicles. The trend of fashion re-commerce is quite popular not just online, but also among the offline retail stores across the globe. Factors that have contributed to the growth of the re-commerce fashion industry include tough economic times, budget constraints, and increased awareness among consumers about keeping the planet green by reducing waste. Re-fashioning helps consumers in saving a lot of money while encouraging them for conscious consumption. Based on secondary sources data, the study focuses on motivation and barriers to fashion re-commerce. Sustainability is also an upcoming concept in the fashion industry. The authors discusses sustainability in the fashion industry with the help of a review of literature available for the same.

DOI: 10.4018/978-1-7998-2728-3.ch003

INTRODUCTION

The idea of sustainability is not new for us but the sustainable fashion is a new idea taking shape now a days. During the starting phase of 90's only innovators entered and changed existing phenomenon of fashion industry and explored the opportunities which later on became norms of this industry. Motive behind all the ideas was the thought that through the clothing one can maintain social and cultural diversity and can be a motivational factor for new business models.

A rapid growth of Consumerism and globalization are two leading factors of new fashion industry, consumers of now a days are obsessed with the latest fashionable clothes and accessories which can be available only because of mass production and this mass production of clothes and fashion accessories accelerated the growth of fashion industry. We all, as a supplies also as a consumer always look for low cost products with speedy and free delivery facilities. We as a customers are already capable enough to collect and cross check all the information regarding the required products and their alternatives.

It take a lot of efforts to differentiate between ethical and unethical brands while making the purchases from the global market, as the customers have already realized that most of the companies are not following the ethical practices when it comes to the production and this realization proved to be an excellent beginning towards motivating customers to search for more reliable and sustainable options in the fashion industry, with the urgent need of a new marketing practices to have a more reliable and stronger and positive relationship between brand quality, credibility and the consumers.

Objectives of the Study

R1: To narrow down definition of sustainable fashion and finalize its importance in the sustainability movement and to differentiate between fast and sustainable fashion.

R2: How exactly consumers are going the get benefits because of sustainable fashion and what are the marketing techniques companies can use to attract the new customers.

Sustainability: This term was first in 1987 when the World Commission on Environmental Development explained that 'sustainable development is the process to meetswith the needs of current generations without decreasing the potential of future generations to meet their own needs' (Berfield, 2015).

Sustainability can be any step taken towards to maintain an ecological balance between producing, supplying, and purchasing goods and the preservation and maintenance of natural resources.

There is no conflict among researchers and activists on the term sustainability but they are still not able to describe a full proof process as of yet. Sustainability as an activity has gained traction in the business world all the entrepreneurs are trying to find out the solutions that concludes as ecologically friendly clothes and accessories thatconsumers actually preferring over non-sustainable counterparts.

Definition of Sustainable Fashion

Sustainable fashion implies ethics, durability and the reuse of products. A single definition of sustainable fashion is difficult to finalise because of the absence of current industry standard. The whole idea of sustainable fashion moves around a various terms like eco-friendly, ethical trade, sustainable, slow, eco etc. (Cervellon & Wernerfelt, 2012), attempting to emphasize on and make a correction in the variety of perceived wrongs in the fashion industry including animal cruelty, environmental damage and worker exploitation (Bin, 2014)

All the above terms are used interchangeably and frequently for different Objectives just because of the ambiguity, for example, Choi et al. (2012) defines 'ethical fashion' as 'fashionable clothes that incorporate fair trade principles with sweatshop free labour conditions while not harming the environment or workers by using biodegradable and organic cotton', whereas Cervellon and Wernerfelt (2012) use 'green fashion' to refer to much the same set of issues.

Objectives of Sustainable Fashion

Motive of the sustainable fashion is to result in a slow production process and utilization of garments on the global scale (Flower, 2009). The key component of sustainable production is the 'replacement of harmful chemicals with environmentally friendly materials' as well as the reduction of 'waste and resource consumption through apparel recycling' (Flower, 2009).

To ensure the sustainable fashion it is important to draw a proper guideline for ethical production and consumption.

KEY ELEMENTS REQUIRED TO ACCELERATE THE GROWTH OF SUSTAINABLE FASHION

To emphasize on quality then on quantity with a change of customer mindset by motivating them to prefer low but high quality products.

Second is follow the production process that "don't exploit natural and human resources just to have maximum speed of manufacturing".

Third is to enhance usability of products just to ensure longer product lifecycle.

In Academics, very few researches has been conducted on slow fashion, however with the growth of more sustainable companies and consumer interest, there is a hope that sustainable fashion will take a front seat sooner. There are many positive effects of adopting a more sustainable fashion system and educated consumers are learning to make more socially conscious purchasing decisions. Without a point of reference it is difficult to qualify the current relationship between consumers and sustainable brands; the research that has been done so far, however, provides a framework that could be used to increase consumer understanding of the negative effects of fast fashion, and the possibility of the development of a sustainable apparel model.

Steps in the Sustainable Direction –lot of sweatshop scandals came into picture between the era of 1980s and 1990s and this was the reason behind the first anti-fur campaign also, it created a lot of social pressure on fashion industry and merchandisers to ensure a better and ethical production process in their factories. Everyone related to this industry was getting interested in sustainable fashion. Well known personalities of the industry emphasized on fair trade practices to produce ethical products. First fashion show with the theme of ethics was organized in paris in year 2004. The fashion trend towards sustainability also reached to large scale brands, such as H&M with its organic Conscious Collection and MUJI's fair trade products (Lion, Macchion, Danese & Vinelli, 2016).

Consumers and Sustainable Fashion

Only few researchers tried to investigate the motivational factors driving consumers towards sustainable fashion, most of them just concentrated on supply chain and few on customer response towards sustainable fashion Choi et al. (2012) purposefully sample sustainable fashion consumers, focusing on how 10 highly vocal online activists define themselves as sustainable fashion consumers. Very few research have been conducted on Sustainable fashion, however research in the broader context of ethical consumption suggests personal values play a pivotal role in ethical decision-making (Park & Kim, 2016).

Various Researches on consumer purchasing behaviour concluded that the requirement of ethical production process in fashion industry is increasing among the consumers. Consumers are nowconsidering the social consequences of their purchasing behaviour, especially when human are getting exploited in the factories during the production processes. Human resources working at Sweatshophas been identified as one of the most important ethical concerns when making clothing decisions (Dach & Allmendinger, 2014). Most of the researchers concentrated only on perception of sustainable fashion by the general population, with less emphasis on actual consumers of sustainable fashion.

Choi et al. (2012) conducted 39 interviews with frequent consumers to create a link between purchased products and purchasing criteria and personal values. During the interviews, clothing that was taken as a sustainable product by consumers was required to compare in both durability and style. The outcome of these interviews was that consumers wanted to be confident in what they were. All the consumers were looking to full-fill their need for self-esteem through comfort and looking good. Just because of using sustainable fashion, consumers can have both psychological and physical satisfaction which will help the consumers feel good about themselves. Consumers also made it clear that their looking good is not determined by the others but by themselves only. The second thing they were looking for was self-expression which can achieve by unique style and sense of individuality. The Participant described the term self-expression as something through which one can describe himself/herself without saying anything.

Consumers were very much ready to buy the clothes made up of natural materials just to save the environment. This emphasizes the importance of using natural materials as it is an important attribute to the consumers, also that they preferred the clothes which are made through the environment friendly process. Consumers were feeling good just because of doing well for their environment.

McNeill and Moore (2015) conducted a survey to find out consumers' attitudes toward the use of sustainable fashion and identify the impact of the 'fast fashion' on these attitudes. All consumers in the study cited fashion and clothing as having a certain level of importance to them. However, where some customers noted that fashion was important but in an ethical way and that they believed all consumption should be meaningful, others felt that fashion's importance was centred on 'fitting in' and the social norms of fashion consumption.

McNeill and Moore (2015) conducted a survey to conclude the key elements of consumer's attitudes and perception towards sustainable fashion and their consumption pattern of clothing and accessories, it allows for a certain level of subjectivity when it comes to the most successful method for attracting customers to a new sustainable fashion company. Several elements of their results are able to be used to draw further conclusions about consumer behavior and patterns, and what fuels any person to make an investment in fashion -- as customers increase their awareness of the negative implications of their addictions to fast fashion, their consuming habits have a tendency to change (Bin, 2014).

Jägel et al. (2012) study is a rare example of motivation driven research into sustainable fashion (or even ethical consumption generally). They explore hypothetical and future purchases covering a range of 'sustainability' issues on consumers who self-report having performed at least one of the following: recycling clothing, boycotting a company and buying eco or fair trade clothing. They report a relatively high incidence of ethical values such as social justice, equality and supporting the environment as underpinning their hypothetical consumption behaviours.

Consumers were motivated to do finalizes their purchase in an ethical way. For example, consumers wants to support the environment by reducing the waste. Also they are motivated because they are reducing risks for other in society through buying products that are not made by exploiting human and natural resources. Yet, they are also looking for individual benefits such as comfort, individuality, looking good and various aspects of design in sustainable fashion. Being Sustainable does not mean compromise with quality and premium pricing strategies. One may lose its brand image in case of approaching the segment with low quality product with less prices. So it is always advisable to have good quality with good prices with durable, natural material so that sustainable suppliers can meet with the competition of the segment.

One more issue to be addressed is how actually brands defines the term "Sustainability", few were saying it is eco friendliness of any Brand and few said that it is a fair trading practices followed by Brand.

To attract the new customers, durability of materials, natural materials and health benefits should be considered on priority basis, except that they should be motivated to buy branded products only as they fulfil the consumer's egotistical need and talk about value and premium prices, consumers are capable to pay. Consumers can be educated about reducing need in an ethical way through the public relation and market communication channels.

Sustainable Marketing Practices

An upcoming requirement to find out the most sustainable marketing practices to attract future consumers towards brands or products in the fashion is being recognized. Identity marketing is one step takent owards global business strategy to create a "link between consumer and certain brands" (Bhattacharjee, Berger & Menon, 2014). Studies show that often explicit identity-marketing messages are not as effective in connecting a particular brand to a consumer's identity (Bhattacharjee, Berger & Menon, 2014). By a comparison of efficacy within message content, the messages that "specifically define identity expression are more likely to reduce purchase likelihood than those that merely suggest a relevance of a product towards the consumer's particular demographic and lifestyle" (Bhattacharjee, Berger & Menon, 2014). This particular research, despite its potentially large sample size, continuous implementation, and plausible analysis has an evident drawback -- it does not delve deeply into specific marketing approaches used by brands to target their key demographics, whether it be by age, race, gender, level of education, etc., it leaves an ambiguous and generalized definition of identity marketing and its potential potency. Research of consumer behavior is crucial to understanding consumer response to feeling defined by brands rather than feeling free to make the choice based on their specific needs (Choi, Lo, Wong, Yee & Chan, 2012).

Brand transparency is one more major component of sustainable fashion marketing. It is important that consumers should know where and how the clothes are being prepared and what the raw materials, used to prepare them is. So many researches have been conducted to conclude how and why a particular consumers is likely to respond to a particular brand and message explicit.

Yan et al. (2012) concluded these two variables by conducting a research where he distributed a questionnaire to 342 college students with questions asked whether they would prefer to brands known as "environmentally friendly." They just hoped to attract students towards products that were honest about their production, materials, and level of sustainability. The results concluded that terms like eco, green, natural, organic, and sustainable were not helping to grow the product sales. He concluded that the most effective strategy for drawing more attention towards environmentally friendly apparel goods was to follow a multifaceted approach that emphasize on selling points such as brand name, comfort, quality, low price, etc, instead of talking about a single eco-product strategy. The research concluded that attitude toward brand, eco-fashion involvement, and environmental commitment were strong predictors of intention to purchase an environmentally friendly apparel brand.

With this, it can be concluded that for apparel merchandisers to build more positive attitudes towards brands, they should provide all the information about environmentally friendly brands in their marketing communication. Through this marketers can attract students who are interested in purchasing environmentally friendly products, but who are not following to a green lifestyle always. Further, marketers may be able to reach those who are not thinking about purchasing environmentally friendly products by raising awareness and knowledge of the benefits associated with their products and brands, which may help to establish a sustainable market for eco-fashion (Dong et al., 2013).

Sustainable Manufacturing Practices

Sustainability in the industry is an upcoming issue as both corporate managers and academics emphasizing the need of adding sustainability into corporate strategy just tocreate competitive advantages and to reduce sustainability problems' (Egels-Zanden, 2015).

Although Several researches suggested how sustainability can be integrated with, there are few that particularly follow corporate attempts to add sustainability into their company mission.

The company works on the goal of adding social sustainability into strategy by creating a corporate ideal that emphasizes on slow production as well as "full transparency" (Egels-Zanden, 2015). Nudie Jeans Co. talked about worker rights by only sourcing from democratic countries with acceptable working conditions, disclosing all manufacturing practices both within and out of the company to the consumers, and fostering a corporate culture based on fully transparent marketing practices (Egels-Zanden, 2015).

There are very bright chances of companies following the policy of complete transparency, consumers could potentially respond to well to brand honesty or with confusion. Without the understanding of harmful raw materials and exploiting working conditions, consumers may not be able to differentiate between the companies who disclose little to no information and those who choose to disclose all of it. An ethnographic approach in future studies, along with first hand observations and interviews would be beneficial in increasing the understanding of feasible marketing, production, and consumption strategies -- there is hope, however, that as more sustainable companies emerge, non-sustainable companies may follow their lead and create a shift in the current corporate culture.

Sustainability and Low-Cost Business Models

Corporate sustainability is not directly related with agood brand image or improved control over supplier relationships, but it can help to minimize the "downside risk of the business model" (Lueg, Pedersen & Clemmensen, 2015). This can be ensured by "creating necessary contracts that goes beyond traditional shareholder value, moving risk towards suppliers, and improving leadership by motivating management and employees, and payiong more attention to critical issues" (Lueg, Pedersen & Clemmensen, 2015). Corporate sustainability adds to increased shareholder value as a more effective control over suppliers, and provide a framework that could potentially introduce 'mandatory disclosure of suppliers or to establish an industry-wide comply-or-explain code of conduct.'

The rise of globalization and the ability to generate apparel faster to meet consumer demand has created a low cost business model that is far from ethically charged, however, there is no information that suggests that the model cannot be regenerated tobemore sustainable.

Lue, Pedersen and Clemmensen (2015) conducted a case study on the role of corporate sustainability in a large Scandinavian clothing and apparel company (SCAC). The essential role of a Scandinavian setting in this study is a condensed example of sustainability in what is generally considered to be a more politically and governmentally flexible environment. The implication is that sustainability actually adds value to a low cost business model. Although the goal of the SCAC is not necessarily altruistic, it does offer the potential to "triple the bottom line of economic, social, and environmental company performance" as well as to meet the stakeholders' expectations for production (Lueg, Pedersen & Clemmensen, 2015). Although it has been proven that there are little to no negative effects of corporate sustainability, this study highlights the distinct gap in research. However, it is evident that a further understanding of the value of sustainability and the effects of modern fashion practice (including production, branding, etc.) could have a great impact on the future of the globalized fashion industry.

Methodology

Sustainable fashion has already got a great attention from academics, brands, and consumers, still scope of further research is still there because of limitations enforced by the globalization and normalization of "fast fashion." Just to understand and enhance current research, I started it by literature review, one more element of my research revealed that very few researches has been conducted on the study of corporate sustainable practices. There is currently limited research about the success of marketing strategies for sustainable fashion. To formulate the multifaceted approach that several studies suggest, including highlighting major selling points such as brand name, comfort, quality, low price, etc., there needs to be observation of both completely ethical and sustainable fashion companies as well as those beginning to adopt a more transparent approach to their production and distribution practices. Egels-Zanden (2015) provides a particularly excellent model of this method through his observation of a one hundred percent transparent sustainable fashion company. His simple approach to examining a functioning corporate strategy provides tangible evidence towards the notion that corporate culture can shift. By specifically referencing the ethical and sustainable ways the company produces and sells their product and cross-comparing it with the growth of the company, Egels-Zanden succeeds in presenting a concrete example of an effective marketing, production, and consumption strategy. As a starting point for my own research I can use the values of measurement Egels-Zanden employed to conduct my own research focusing on sustainability and strategy in a changing corporate culture. To conduct my own analysis of the benefits and losses of complete brand transparency I would need to observe a specific marketing approach (potentially a multi-faceted marketing approach) by a single company.

Along with interviewing someone either employed at or running an ethical fashion company, I look forward to conducting interviews with sustainable fashion designers with either their own lines (which they may sell online or in store). To narrow what is a largely broad topic often too intermingled with the hegemony of the environmentalist movement, I will need to begin with a smaller, more qualitative approach so that I may understand how designers were first introduced to sustainable fashion, what materials they use to create their clothing, and what they hope will be the future of the sustainable fashion industry. With further elaboration from those actively working and keeping up with the field I may be able to gain a level of expertise that can only be acquired through personal experience.

CONCLUSION

Sustainable fashion is an emerging concept in the fashion industry with the potential to grow exponentially as consumers are becoming more knowledgeable about unethical treatment of human resources and harmful to environment production practices of the fast fashion industry. By decreasing the consumption and production patterns, the fashion industry can be converted into more sustainable industry for the future. In order to achieve the results the movement desires, consumers must be faced with the realization that the non-transparent, fast fashion giants they actively subscribe to are not making a positive social or environmental impact. With educated consumers, companies can develop multi-faceted marketing approaches that look beyond basic keywords for example- "green" or "eco-friendly" and attract customers towards the quality of the product, comfort, and brand name. Sustainable fashion could potentially change the way people consume and the way companies produce, with the correct balance of the two, an incredibly positive socially and environmentally beneficial effects would ensue.

REFERENCES

Berfield, S. (2015). Making Ethical Chic. *Bloomberg Businessweek*, (4454), 56.

Bhattacharjee, A., Berger, J., & Menon, G. (2014). When identity marketing backfires: Consumer agency in identity expression. *The Journal of Consumer Research, 41*(2), 294–309. doi:10.1086/676125

Cervellon, M. C., & Wernerfelt, A. S. (2012). Knowledge sharing among green fashion communities online: Lessons for the sustainable supply chain. *Journal of Fashion Marketing and Management, 16*(2), 176–192. doi:10.1108/13612021211222860

Choi, T. M., Lo, C. K., Wong, C. W., Yee, R. W., & Chan, T. Y. (2012). The consumption side of sustainable fashion supply chain. *Journal of Fashion Marketing and Management*.

Dach, L., & Allmendinger, K. (2014). Sustainability in Corporate Communications and its Influence on Consumer Awareness and Perceptions: A study of H&M and Primark. *Procedia: Social and Behavioral Sciences, 130*(15), 409–418. doi:10.1016/j.sbspro.2014.04.048

Egels-Zandén, N., Hulthén, K., & Wulff, G. (2015). Trade-offs in supply chain transparency: The case of Nudie Jeans Co. *Journal of Cleaner Production, 107*, 95–104. doi:10.1016/j.jclepro.2014.04.074

Flower, G. (2009). Sustainable appeal: The slow fashion movement. *Alive: Canadian Journal of Health & Nutrition*.

Jägel, T., Keeling, K., Reppel, A., & Gruber, T. (2012). Individual values and motivational complexities in ethical clothing consumption: A means-end approach. *Journal of Marketing Management, 28*(3-4), 373–396. doi:10.1080/0267257X.2012.659280

Lion, A., Macchion, L., Danese, P., & Vinelli, A. (2016, April). Sustainability approaches within the fashion industry: The supplier perspective. *Supply Chain Forum International Journal (Toronto, Ont.), 17*(2), 95–108.

Lueg, R., Pedersen, M. M., & Clemmensen, S. N. (2015). The role of corporate sustainability in a low-cost business model–A case study in the Scandinavian fashion industry. *Business Strategy and the Environment, 24*(5), 344–359. doi:10.1002/bse.1825

McNeill, L., & Moore, R. (2015). Sustainable fashion consumption and the fast fashion conundrum: Fashionable consumers and attitudes to sustainability in clothing choice. *International Journal of Consumer Studies, 39*(3), 212–222. doi:10.1111/ijcs.12169

Park, H., & Kim, Y. K. (2016). An empirical test of the triple bottom line of customer-centric sustainability: The case of fast fashion. *Fashion and Textiles*, *3*(1), 25. doi:10.118640691-016-0077-6

Shen, B. (2014). Sustainable fashion supply chain: Lessons from H&M. *Sustainability*, *6*(9), 6236–6249. doi:10.3390u6096236

Shen, D., Richards, J., & Liu, F. (2013). Consumers' awareness of sustainable fashion. *Marketing Management Journal*, *23*(2), 134–147.

Yan, R. N., Hyllegard, K. H., & Blaesi, L. F. (2012). Marketing eco-fashion: The influence of brand name and message explicitness. *Journal of Marketing Communications*, *18*(2), 151–168. doi:10.1080/13527266.2010.490420

Chapter 4
Changing Customer Behavior in Sustainable Fashion Industry

Mohamed Mohamed Elsotouhy
https://orcid.org/0000-0002-2444-6141
Faculty of Commerce, Mansoura University, Egypt

ABSTRACT

There is no doubt that sustainability has turned to a hot issue in recent years for its significant effect not only for the fashion industry but also for several fields. Nowadays, most organizations have shifted from traditional business models to sustainability-integrated business models. However, few studies have focused on changing customer behaviour towards adopting sustainability. In this chapter, the author focuses on presenting the damaging effects of the fashion industry in all phases of production and giving a view on how marketers stir consumers to embrace sustainable fashion in their own lives. This chapter concentrates on quality rather than quantity.

INTRODUCTION

Sustainability has received much attention recently due to its ability to protect our environment from pollution caused by fashion industry. Producing and marketing a huge amount of fashion items have negative impacts on our environment (Thorisdottir & Johannsdottir, 2019). To be more specific, artisan tailors evolved the fashion industry in favor of multinational enterprises before its spread over various countries and continents (Pedersen, Gwozdz & Hvass, 2016). Fashion makes people more

DOI: 10.4018/978-1-7998-2728-3.ch004

satisfied emotionally and socially as they use it to express themselves to their peers (Bertram & Chi, 2018).The industry becomes more complicated, international and fragmented and its core turned to the notion of continual consumption of new stuff while discard the old ones (Kozlowski, Bardecki & Searcy, 2012). The advent of fast-fashion changed the nature of fashion; meaning that to be fit in your social, individual must stay fashionable and wearing new trend clothes (Bertram & Chi, 2018).Recent fashion industries with more available resources, a short-life cycle, and over-consuming of a product have unfavorable impacts on society (Pedersen et al., 2016). Each year over 90 million of garments throw up in garbage, in UK alone people use 1.5 to 2 million tons of textile, while1.2 million tons of them go to landfills (DEFRA 2007). When these clothes cumulate over time, this in turn can causes fatal pollution in a long-term. One of the most effective ways to treat this issue is through sustainability.

Over 30 years ago, World Commission on Environment and Development stated that sustainable development will meet the needs of the present without harming any of future generation's needs (World Commission on Environment and Development, 1987). Sustainability means the balance among economic, social, and environmental needs of today with the need of upcoming generations (Wang et al., 2019).Since then, sustainable has turned to be a common trend in almost all arena and applied for products, services, and other approaches (Evans & Peirson-Smith, 2018). Focusing on sustainability in clothing, researchers started to treat fashion industry pollution through concentrating on sustainability. Kozlowski et al. (2012) paper provided a conceptual and analytical framework through conflating life cycle and stakeholder analyses as a way to develop responses for the fashion industry. Corporates with innovative business models are more likely to adapt sustainability, both of innovative business model and sustainability are found in organizations which have flexibility and discretion values in its root (Pedersen et al., 2016). Study of Yang, Song and Tong (2017) concluded that the most crucial areas in this field are disposal fashion in sustainable retailing, fast and slow fashion, green branding, and eco-labeling which focus on secondhand fashion, reverse logistic, and emerging opportunities in e-commerce. Regarding customer response, Grappi, Romani and Barbarossa (2017) analyzed how customer evaluates or responses to brands after Greenpeace's 2011 Detox campaign which aimed to reducing toxic chemicals in the fashion industry. They found that customer's evaluation of brand blame plays a mediating role between their attitudes toward brand and purchase intentions. The lack of comprehension of key green terminology in communication among user is problematic in fashion brand marketers, while these messages are often unclear; it leads to user frustration rather than positive decision making and action (Evans & Peirson-Smith, 2018). Jacobs et al. (2018) focused on two sides in sustainable clothes, one of them is about changing the attitudes and values towards sustainability, the other is about focusing on how firms make durable clothes available in their retail stores. Major researches focused on the same research domain which is theoretically broke up to fragmented approach that prevents the ability to address the systemic nature of sustainability, Thomas (2018) paper treated this problem by adapted critical realism as a meta-theoretical framework to corporate, link and extend the sustainability marketing field. However, although customer attitudes towards sustainable clothes have been grown more and more favorable in the past few years, the role of marketers in introducing clothes with environmental and socially responsible is still lagging behind (Jacobs et al., 2018). This chapter focuses on the pollution caused by fashion industry, and how can marketers affect the customer behavior to adapt sustainability.

This chapter focuses on the role of marketers in direct customer to sustainability through creating awareness. This awareness can, in turn, lead to actions of doing sustainable activities. It also concentrated on post-purchasing processes which are vital for marketing sustainable fashion. This cyclic and integrated process (figure 1) is necessary for the success of altering customer behavior to addict sustainable clothes. It starts with viewing the negative environmental effects of the fashion industry, then it moves to discuss how can marketers change customer behavior towards sustainable clothes, before it ending with the conclusion.

The Fatal Effects of Fashion Industry

The quality of life is in its countdown as a result of consumption practices which effect on climate changes, lack of resources, poverty, and biodiversity damages (Thomas, 2018). Regarding the impact on environment, clothing, textiles, and footwear came fourth in the list of industries which held by the European Environmental Agency in 2014 after housing, transports, travel, and food (Pal & Gander, 2018). The World Bank stated that textile manufacturing alone emits 72 toxic elements; thirty of them cannot be purified in the purification process (Anguelov, 2016). Jia, Govindan, Choi and Rajendran (2015) stated that the production processes of textile have huge negative effects on our environment; these effects are toxic chemical usage, wasteful use of water and energy, and using dangerous materials. The pulse of the Fashion Industry in 2017, stated that the world is suffering from water paucity, as the fashion industry alone uses 79 billion cubic metres annually (Pal & Gander, 2018). Thorisdottir and Johannsdottir (2019) asserted that the fashion industry is one of the most polluting in the world, so they affirmed that firms should integrate between sustainability practices and business models of the fashion industry. As a result to this, H&M showed its effectiveness to environmental pollutions caused by its fast-fashion through adapting the eco-friendly programs (Yang et al., 2017). Anguelov (2016) illustrated the damaging effects of every phase in the textile process which are spinning, weaving, and finishing. In the first phase which is spinning, it creates noise and dust pollution. Regarding the weaving process when starch added to the fabric to make it more strong and stiff, it causes using a huge amount of water and then pours it in wastewater with a large amount of starch. In the mixing process, there is heat used intensively and heated water finally ended in local watersheds. Although the wet process is the most vital phase in production, it still one of the most phases that using water to dyeing and finishing, as well as the using of petrochemicals. Furthermore, the accumulation of these fabrics in landfills and then getting rid of it by burning can diffuse carbon dioxide which affects our climate through global warming. Global Footprint Network in 2017, showed that only 20 per cent of clothes have been recycled or reused, while the rest percentage ended in landfills (Pal & Gander, 2018). The problems not only environmental but also there are social problems such as unfair working practices which included child worker, low wages, and psychological problems due to the price pressures and hard work for a long time (Pedersen et al., 2016). Social costs also appear in labor exploitation and health damage from side effects of unsafely products (Anguelov, 2016). Regarding occupational problems, there are respiratory issues due to the accumulation of cotton dust and air particulates, and exhausting work which leads to musculoskeletal risks (Bick, Halsey & Ekenga, 2018).

Changing Customer Behavior Towards Sustainable Fashion

The changing in behaviors arises from the change in values and attitudes, as Bendell and Kleanthous (2007) and De Beers (2008) said that altering in values and attitudes is necessary for changing behavior towards sustainable fashion by stirring social values away from what we wear(prominent) to what is our responsibility for the environment (Gordon, Carrigan & Hastings, 2011). Although values are difficult to change in the short term, marketers could establish context-specific events which can provide customers with particular information about sustainable issues in fashion clothes (Jacobs et al., 2018).Gordon et al. (2011) illustrated this process by mentioning what During London Fashion Week 2009 Defra did when they launched a sustainable clothing plan which concentrated on diminishing the impact of disposable fashion and its cumulating in landfills on environment and society. To assure the success of sustainability in the fashion industry, marketers should give up the traditional-integrated marketing strategy based on sustainability and look forward to embedding sustainability in the marketing mix (Kumar et al., 2012).The starting point to achieving responsible consumption is by adapting it as a way of life, so marketers stir the awareness of customers about the negative effect of consumption and its effects on the environment and society (Kumar, 2018). Jacobs et al. (2018) gave practical solutions for creating demand for sustainable clothes. They said that marketers should introduce the organization's transparency about sustainability and ecological benefits of products for customers, for example, personal benefits of sustainable clothes (skin tolerance and self-esteem) for customers with highly self-enhancement values. Another example is to give a narrative story about environmental causes such as the high consumption of water and how can this effect on our quota of water (Evans & Peirson-Smith, 2018).Therefore, marketers should play their role in creating awareness in order to facilitate the adaptation of sustainability by customers in the long term until it turns to a lifestyle.

Regarding customer purchasing actions, Evans and Peirson-Smith (2018) suggested that marketers should concentrate on offering tangible concepts, applicable features, and create a specific theme which can be embedded in promotional messages to assuring moving customers to take sustainable action. Some fashions brands adapted sustainable deeds such as reusing, recycling and reselling to catalyzing customers towards sustainable action practices (Pedersen et al., 2016). For instance, M&S adapted "learning by doing" strategy when creating a partnership with Oxfam to use its raw materials in recycling discarded clothes and reselling them in markets as a new practice in encouraging customers to participate in actions (Morgan, 2015). One more example, which has been narrated by Havass, (2014) is the collaboration between Filippa K and American Eileen Fisher when they motivate customers to take action by bringing back their used clothes to present them in second-hand stores. Moreover, technology is playing a critical role in this regard nowadays via online resell with providing various channels to resell used clothes, a better example of this model is Patagonia's online resell podium in cooperation with eBay (Pedersen et al., 2016). Marketers have to not concentrate on one way to afford sustainably clothes. They need to increase or allocate sections for sustainable clothes in retails stores to attract customers who not prefer to shop online, or sometimes they need to create alliances with credential retailers to reduce costs (Jacobs et al., 2018).

Finally, it is crucial to benefit from active customer through encouraging them to participate alongside with marketers in deploying sustainable fashion by offering them an ethical or sustainable fashion (Evans & Peirson-Smith, 2018). In marketing, consumers are not just been targeted to consume products, but also to participate in the post-purchase process. So, marketers should include customers in the co-production of achieving and marketing sustainability through engaging in servicing, disposal, recycling, and reselling products (Kalva, 2017). In doing so, customers will unconsciously turn to marketers talking about their experience in doing favorable activities that are beneficial for the environment and society and try to motivate others to do these activities. Although Jacobs (2018) asserted that, there is a great demand for improving clothes' durability rather than Fashion exterior shape, which in turn lead to creating big distance gap between two purchasing actions, it is essential to keep in touch with customers and build customer relationship. In order to expand customer's base and stimulating them in cooperation in the sustainability process, marketers should offer unique benefits. These benefits such as present organic fabrics or durability-oriented clothes besides activate inactive markets (Jacobs, 2018). The integration among these processes, which are awareness, action, and relationship, is necessary for turning customer's brain from the uncompleted sustainable brain to fully saturated brain. Customers also should play their own role in mitigating pollution caused by the fashion industry. Although the idea of fast-fashion builds on "more for less", customer should throw away this idea and adapt "less for more", especially in high-income countries (Bick, Halsey & Ekenga, 2018). In the same vein, it does not depend only on companies and marketers, customers also have to play their role in creating awareness and actions among them through the establishment of associations, putting banners, and deploy brochures about the effects of clothes on human, animals, and biodiversity. Finally, governments should also play a role here by putting strict regulations for companies and individuals and make sure that everyone should stick with it. This pollution not only does effect on us but also on the next generations, as we will witness on and already we witnessed new weak generations with lung and body problems.

Figure 1. The cyclic and integrated process of altering customer behavior to addict sustainable clothes

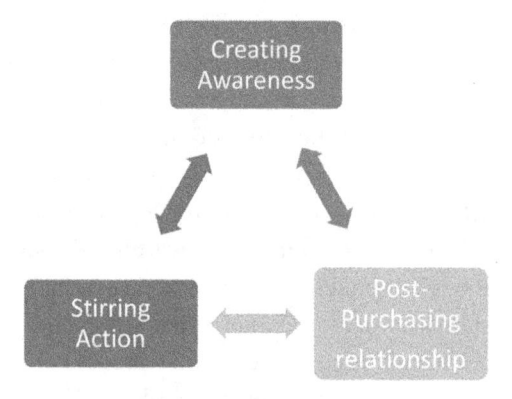

CONCLUSION

As discussed above, directing customer behavior to adopt sustainability in the fashion industry has received much attention from scholars in almost all fields. A large number of researches treated this issue from different points; the integrated process of changing customer behavior has not to pose yet. This chapter tried to postulate a cyclic integrated process from marketers prospective to overcome these untreated issues. Reviewing the literature in this field, the chapter concluded that every phase leads to the next. The awareness in its core concentrated on introducing information about the negative effect of the fashion industry which stimulates customers blame. The second phase is moving customer from knowledge to action, by making them participate in activities like recycling and reselling which diminishing the sense of blame and make them self-satisfied. The final phases, which also lead to first phase by bringing others to the circle, is a post-purchasing phase. This phase based on creating a relationship with customers through embedded them in the process so that they can transport their experience into their friends, relatives, and neighbors. So the process remains in circulation indefinitely. This present chapter completes what researchers ended with, as it putting one brick in the big building of marketing sustainability which is the trending subject in the whole world. What makes this study unique; it is concentrating on creating an integrated approach which can adapt in any field and in any culture. Antecedent studies focused on the effects of the fashion industry on environment, social, and economic aspects to try to come up with a holistic view of sustainability. Some researchers studied the luxury industry, operations, stakeholder, innovation, and business models. Others focused on consumer interpretations, customer reaction, green thinking, and sustainability marketing. This chapter took a general overview of marketing sustainability to change customer behavior with the neglect of other factors affect these subjects. This chapter opens the way for future researches in this subject to testing the influence of this integrated approach on other subjects and how can other factors mediate or moderate its impact.

REFERENCES

Anguelov, N. (2015). *The dirty side of the garment industry: Fast fashion and its negative impact on environment and Society*. CRC Press. doi:10.1201/b18902

Bendell, J., & Kleanthous, A. (2007). *Deeper Luxury*. https://www.wwf.org.uk/deeperluxury

Bertram, R. F., & Chi, T. (2018). A study of companies' business responses to fashion e-commerce's environmental impact. *International Journal of Fashion Design. Technology and Education, 11*(2), 254–264.

Bick, R., Halsey, E., & Ekenga, C. C. (2018). The global environmental injustice of fast fashion. *Environmental Health, 17*(1), 92. doi:10.118612940-018-0433-7 PMID:30591057

De Beers. (2008). *Luxury: Considered*. http://www.debeersgroup.com

DEFRA. (2007). *Maximising reuse and recycling of UK clothing and textiles.* London: Department for Environment, Food and Rural Affairs.

Evans, S., & Peirson-Smith, A. (2018). The sustainability word challenge: Exploring consumer interpretations of frequently used words to promote sustainable fashion brand behaviors and imagery. *Journal of Fashion Marketing and Management, 22*(2), 252–269. doi:10.1108/JFMM-10-2017-0103

Gordon, R., Carrigan, M., & Hastings, G. (2011). A framework for sustainable marketing. *Marketing Theory, 11*(2), 143–163. doi:10.1177/1470593111403218

Grappi, S., Romani, S., & Barbarossa, C. (2017). Fashion without pollution: How consumers evaluate brands after an NGO campaign aimed at reducing toxic chemicals in the fashion industry. *Journal of Cleaner Production, 149*, 1164–1173. doi:10.1016/j.jclepro.2017.02.183

Jacobs, K., Petersen, L., Hörisch, J., & Battenfeld, D. (2018). Green thinking but thoughtless buying? An empirical extension of the value-attitude-behaviour hierarchy in sustainable clothing. *Journal of Cleaner Production, 203*, 1155–1169. doi:10.1016/j.jclepro.2018.07.320

Jia, P., Govindan, K., Choi, T. M., & Rajendran, S. (2015). Supplier selection problems in fashion business operations with sustainability considerations. *Sustainability, 7*(2), 1603–1619. doi:10.3390u7021603

Kalva, R. S. (2017). A Model for Strategic Marketing Sustainability (Marketing mix to Marketing matrix). *National Conference on Marketing and Sustainable Development,* 7-23.

Kant Hvass, K. (2014). Post-retail responsibility of garments–a fashion industry perspective. *Journal of Fashion Marketing and Management, 18*(4), 413–430. doi:10.1108/JFMM-01-2013-0005

Kozlowski, A., Bardecki, M., & Searcy, C. (2012). Environmental impacts in the fashion industry: A life-cycle and stakeholder framework. *Journal of Corporate Citizenship,* (45): 17–36.

Kumar, B. (2018). Sustainability Marketing and Its Outcomes: A Discussion in the Context of Emerging Markets. In *Strategic Marketing Issues in Emerging Markets* (pp. 327–341). Singapore: Springer. doi:10.1007/978-981-10-6505-7_30

Kumar, V., Rahman, Z., Kazmi, A. A., & Goyal, P. (2012). Evolution of sustainability as marketing strategy: Beginning of new era. *Procedia: Social and Behavioral Sciences, 37*, 482–489. doi:10.1016/j.sbspro.2012.03.313

Morgan, E. (2015). 'Plan A': Analysing business model innovation for sustainable consumption in mass-market clothes retailing. *Journal of Corporate Citizenship*, *2015*(57), 73–98. doi:10.9774/GLEAF.4700.2015.ma.00007

Pal, R., & Gander, J. (2018). Modelling environmental value: An examination of sustainable business models within the fashion industry. *Journal of Cleaner Production*, *184*, 251–263. doi:10.1016/j.jclepro.2018.02.001

Pedersen, E. R. G., Gwozdz, W., & Hvass, K. K. (2018). Exploring the relationship between business model innovation, corporate sustainability, and organisational values within the fashion industry. *Journal of Business Ethics*, *149*(2), 267–284. doi:10.100710551-016-3044-7

Thomas, N. J. (2018). Sustainability marketing. The need for a realistic whole systems approach. *Journal of Marketing Management*, *34*(17-18), 1530–1556. doi:10.1080/0267257X.2018.1547782

Thorisdottir, T. S., & Johannsdottir, L. (2019). Sustainability within fashion business models: A systematic literature review. *Sustainability*, *11*(8), 2233. doi:10.3390u11082233

United Nations World Commission on Environment and Development. (1987). *Our common future*. Oxford: Oxford University Press.

Wang, H., Liu, H., Kim, S. J., & Kim, K. H. (2019). Sustainable fashion index model and its implication. *Journal of Business Research*, *99*, 430–437. doi:10.1016/j.jbusres.2017.12.027

Yang, S., Song, Y., & Tong, S. (2017). Sustainable retailing in the fashion industry: A systematic literature review. *Sustainability*, *9*(7), 1266. doi:10.3390u9071266

Chapter 5
Explaining Purchase Intention Towards Eco-Friendly Apparel:
An Application of Theory of Planned Behavior

Seemant Kumar Yadav
 https://orcid.org/0000-0001-7295-1866
GLA University, Mathura, India

Vikas Tripathi
GLA University, Mathura, India

ABSTRACT

Textile manufacturing is one of the polluting industries contributing to approximately 1.2 billion tonnes of toxic greenhouse gases. Due to increasing consumer purchase index, companies are adopting unsustainable means like synthetic fiber and polyester, leaving tonnes of wastewater and other pollutants in order to fulfill customer demand. It leads to deterioration of the environment and causes serious health hazards. The present study addresses the issue of customer purchase intention towards environmentally friendly apparel by using the theory of planned behavior.

INTRODUCTION

Textile manufacturing is one of the polluting industry contributing approximately 1.2 billion tonnes of toxic greenhouse gases. According to Mckinsey (2016), due to increasing consumer purchase index companies are adopting unsustainable means like synthetic fiber and polyester leaving tons of waste water and other pollutants

DOI: 10.4018/978-1-7998-2728-3.ch005

in order to fulfills customers demand. As polyester and other synthetic materials are produced from crude oil, the emission for production is reported much higher causing threats to the environment. The customer's search for the latest design clothing had induced the cloths of shorter timeframe leading the excessive manufacturing and wastage both. According to an estimate due to improper recycling of polyester and other synthetic clothes approximately 60% of such items gets disposed off into the open environment in the form of landfill (Rogelj *et al.*, 2018). The recent environment disasters like hazardous air quality, global warming, irregular pattern of heavy rainfall in one part of the world and historic high temperature in the other part of the world has grabbed the attention of world at the front of climate change issues and now consumers are getting more conscious about the products they are using and its impact on the environment. In the fashion industry it pioneered the termed like sustainable fashion/ecological fashion/green fashion/ethical fashion or organic fashion concepts. One of the recent incident of Indian national capital Delhi, where whole city becomes hostile due to extremely poor air quality and there was an emergence like situation. Similarly, one of the oldest city of India, Chennai is witnessing the worst ever situation of water crisis just like it was faced by the South African City Cape town in 2018.Due to these environmental disaster, the companies and consumer both are exhibiting the serious concerned about the wellbeing of the environments. The companies like No Nasties, Doodlage is utilizing recyclable material to produce clothing. The Raymond group, India's leading textiles manufacturer has introduced 'Ecovera' range of garments made up from the specific R|Elan™ Green Gold fibers. These fibers are the product of recycling process of consumer's waste PET bottles. In conjunction with the company's effort of sustainable manufacturing it is also equally important to understand the customer's behavior towards the purchase intention of ecofriendly apparels. As far as developing the understanding about consumers behavior towards eco-friendly products is concern the matured literature is available in American and European countries (Kumar & Ghodeswar, 2015) but as far as Asian countries are concern it is very less (Chen & Chai, 2010).The absence of consumer's behaviors insight about eco-friendly consumption, will make it more difficult for the firm's to device the appropriate strategies (Kim & Chung, 2011).

The gist of the preceding discussion demands the study to assess the consumer's behaviors against the eco-friendly products and identify the factors leading or inhibiting them to behave as an environment friendly consumers. The study is situated in world's fastest growing economy, India which also represents a great deal of Asian countries also. In the study the most prominently used Theory of Planned behavior was used assess the consumer's intention and hence behavior towards eco-friendly apparels.

FRAMEWORK

Eco-Friendly Purchase Intention and Theory of Planned Behavior

The basic genesis of eco-friendly purchase intention indicates an individual's willingness to purchase such products which do harm environment by any means (Jaiswal 2012; Chen & Chang 2012). There are various researchers who investigated the eco-friendly purchase intention from different perspectives. Hartmann et al. (2005) examines the emotional brand, D'Souza *et al.* (2006) posit eco-labels, Park and Ha (2012) advocate social factors, Brick and Lewis (2016) mentioned demographic factors, Tang and Lam (2017) repots personality traits as the predictor of consumers purchase intention of eco-friendly products.

The preset study utilizes the well-grounded theory of planned behavior *TPB* (Ajzen, 1991) to understand the consumer's behavior. The TPB posit a linkage between the individual's beliefs and evaluative criteria, necessary to explain the behavior. TPB identifies Attitude, perceived behavioral control and subjective norms as the antecedents of intention. The perceived behavioral control indicates one's belief about availability of resources and other mediums which provides capability to behave in a specific manner (Ajzen, 1985). The Attitude components indicates the one's positive or negative evaluation of an object/incident which may be translate as intention to behave in a certain way (Ramayah et al., 2010). The subjective norms represent norms of one's social environment which provides a basis of the formation behavioral intention.

The adoption of TPB is made in the field of eco-friendly apparels with the viewpoint that a person with positive attitude towards eco-friendly products, having resources and capability to purchase eco-friendly products, concerned with the societal norms which supports environment friendly actions will be having intention to purchase eco-friendly apparels also.

Figure 1. Conceptual framework

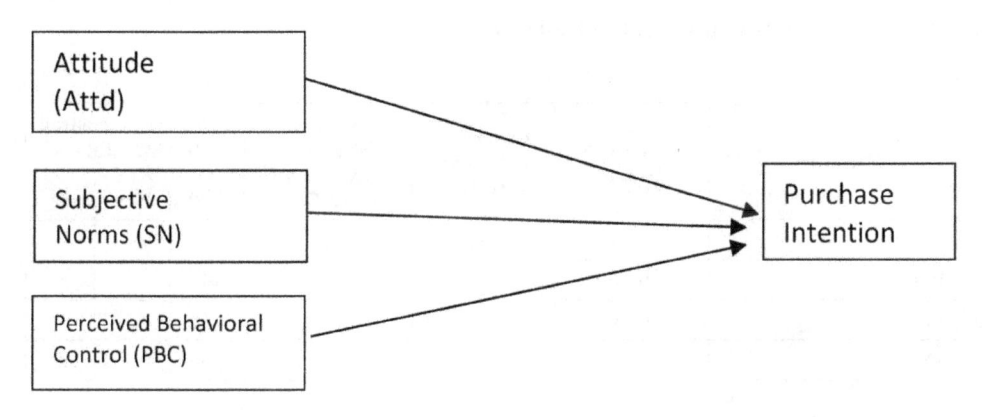

```
┌─────────────────┐
│ Attitude        │──────────────┐
│ (Attd)          │              │
└─────────────────┘              ▼
┌─────────────────┐      ┌──────────────┐
│ Subjective      │─────▶│ Purchase     │
│ Norms (SN)      │      │ Intention    │
└─────────────────┘      └──────────────┘
┌─────────────────┐              ▲
│ Perceived Behavioral│───────────┘
│ Control (PBC)   │
└─────────────────┘
```

Accordingly, we are hypothesizing that:

H1: Attitude towards eco-friendly apparels affects it purchase intention.
H2: Subjective norms affects purchase intention of eco-friendly apparels.
H3: Behavioral control affects purchase intention of eco-friendly apparels

Sample and Data Collection

The data for the study was collected through a structured questionnaire. It was consisting of Attitude (6 items) (Armitage *et al.*, 1999), subjective norms (3 items) (Armitage *et al.*, 1999), perceived behavioral control (6 items) (Armitage & Conner, 1999) and purchase intention (3 items) (Armitage *et al.*, 1999). All the items were measured at 5 point Likert scale. The referral sampling technique was used to for the purpose of data collection. Within the time frame of approximately three months, 345 respondents were contacted and finally 100 respondents were found eligible for the data analysis. Respondents were consisting of 50% of female and 50% male. In terms of the age group 56% of respondents belonged to the below 25 years' age category, 30% to the between 25 to 30 years' category and 14% were belongs to the above 35 yrs.

ANALYSIS AND OUTPUT

The measurement and structural model were estimated by using partial least square structural equation modelling (PLS-SEM). The PLS-SEM is suitable in conditions where the sample size is relatively small and there is lack of information of the data distribution (Hair *et al.*,2014).The scale's reliability was assessed by Cronbach's alpha and composite reliability (Table 1).

Constructs	Cronbach's Alpha	Composite Reliability (CR)	Average Variance Extracted (AVE)	Heterotrait Monotrait (HTMT) Ratio		
				Attd	PBC	PI
Attd	0.8	0.87	0.57			
PBC	0.94	0.95	0.77	0.72		
PI	0.84	0.9	0.75	0.89	0.55	
SN	0.51	0.74	0.5	0.36	0.21	0.87

The internal consistency measures of each construct Chronbach's alpha was above 0.7, except SN = 0.51 but the CR for the constructs were found above the minimum threshold limit of 0.7. Additionally, the AVE for all the constructs were also find satisfactory against the minimum threshold of 0.5. These outcome indicates the establishment of convergent validity of the scale.

Further the HTMT criteria was used to assess the discriminant validity Table 1). The HTMT ratio below 0.9 indicates the establishment of discriminant validity (Hair *et al.*,2014).

The structural model assessment indicates the value of R^2 of the dependent variable "purchase intention", has a value of 0.79. The t value for the individual coefficient are obtained via bootstrapping procedure consisting 500 subsamples. As the result, the hypothesis H1 and H2 were accepted while the hypothesis H3 was rejected. Attitude has a positive and significant impact on the purchase intention (β=0.62; p<0.05). Similarly, subjective norms also have a positive and significant impact on the purchase intention (β=0.47; p<0.05). But perceived behavioral control has a positive but insignificant impact on the purchase intention (β=0.06; p >0.05)

DISCUSSION AND CONCLUSION

This study attempted to identify factors affecting purchase intention of eco-friendly apparels in Indian context. The study deploys Attitude, Subjective Norms and Perceived Behavioral Control as the predictors of purchase intention. The research found a significant positive relationship between attitude and purchase intention, therefore H1 was supported. The output reconfirmed the significant role of attitude on consumers purchase intention. Among the three predictors the Attitude's regression coefficient was the most significant which posit its dominance role in expanding the purchase intention. Further, the study also reports the positive and significant effect of subjective norms on purchase intention. It confirms that consumer's purchase intention is not only influenced by their attitude but also by their social environments and a customer perceiving greater social pressure and patronage will exhibit a greater intention to purchase eco-friendly apparels. The subjective norms also provide a reference point to make any decisions because in situation when an individual is lacking required information to make any decision then they sought this information from their concerned sources and hence the role of their social group plays a significant role. The insignificant role of PBC indicates the lack of availability of resources and other mediums which provides capability to an individual as far as purchasing of ecofriendly apparels is concern. The high pricing, inadequate distribution and lack of manufacturing at wider level inhibits the proper control of consumer while making such decisions. Hence the hypotheses H3 was not supported.

To gear up the purchasing of ecofriendly apparels it is important to educate consumers about the wellbeing of environments and there is need to change the people's attitudes towards the environment. But it equally important to provide reasonable opportunity to consumers to purchase eco-friendly apparels. It includes the reasonable pricing, product availability and production of quality products. If manufacturer will provide lucrative alternative in favor of eco-friendly products against the traditional products, then the customer will be more prone to purchase the eco-friendly apparels.

REFERENCES

Ajzen, I. (1985). From intentions to actions: A theory of planned behavior. In *Action control* (pp. 11–39). Berlin: Springer. doi:10.1007/978-3-642-69746-3_2

Ajzen, I. (1991). The theory of planned behavior. *Organizational Behavior and Human Decision Processes, 50*(2), 179–211. doi:10.1016/0749-5978(91)90020-T

Armitage, C. J., Armitage, C. J., Conner, M., Loach, J., & Willetts, D. (1999). Different perceptions of control: Applying an extended theory of planned behavior to legal and illegal drug use. *Basic and Applied Social Psychology, 21*(4), 301–316. doi:10.1207/S15324834BASP2104_4

Armitage, C. J., & Conner, M. (1999). Distinguishing perceptions of control from self-efficacy: Predicting consumption of a low-fat diet using the theory of planned behavior 1. *Journal of Applied Social Psychology, 29*(1), 72–90. doi:10.1111/j.1559-1816.1999.tb01375.x

Brick, C., & Lewis, G. J. (2016). Unearthing the "green" personality: Core traits predict environmentally friendly behavior. *Environment and Behavior*, *48*(5), 635–658. doi:10.1177/0013916514554695

Chen, T. B., & Chai, L. T. (2010). Attitude towards the environment and green products: Consumers' perspective. *Management Science and Engineering*, *4*(2), 27–39.

Chen, Y. S., & Chang, C. H. (2013). Greenwash and green trust: The mediation effects of green consumer confusion and green perceived risk. *Journal of Business Ethics*, *114*(3), 489–500. doi:10.100710551-012-1360-0

D'Souza, C., Taghian, M., & Lamb, P. (2006). An empirical study on the influence of environmental labels on consumers. *Corporate Communications*, *11*(2), 162–173. doi:10.1108/13563280610661697

Hair, J. F. Jr, Sarstedt, M., Hopkins, L., & Kuppelwieser, V. G. (2014). Partial least squares structural equation modeling (PLS-SEM). *European Business Review*.

Hartmann, P., Ibáñez, V. A., & Sainz, F. J. F. (2005). Green branding effects on attitude: Functional versus emotional positioning strategies. *Marketing Intelligence & Planning*, *23*(1), 9–29. doi:10.1108/02634500510577447

Jaiswal, N. (2012). Green products: Availability, awareness and preference of use by the families. *Indian Journal of Environmental Education*, *12*, 21–25.

Kim, H. Y., & Chung, J. E. (2011). Consumer purchase intention for organic personal care products. *Journal of Consumer Marketing*.

Kumar, P., & Ghodeswar, B. M. (2015). Factors affecting consumers' green product purchase decisions. *Marketing Intelligence & Planning*, *33*(3), 330–347. doi:10.1108/MIP-03-2014-0068

Park, H., & Cho, H. (2012). Social network online communities: Information sources for apparel shopping. *Journal of Consumer Marketing*, *29*(6), 400–411. doi:10.1108/07363761211259214

Ramayah, T., Ahmad, N. H., & Lo, M. C. (2010). The role of quality factors in intention to continue using an e-learning system in Malaysia. *Procedia: Social and Behavioral Sciences*, *2*(2), 5422–5426. doi:10.1016/j.sbspro.2010.03.885

Rogelj, J., Popp, A., Calvin, K. V., Luderer, G., Emmerling, J., Gernaat, D., ... Krey, V. (2018). Scenarios towards limiting global mean temperature increase below 1.5 C. *Nature Climate Change*, *8*(4), 325–332. doi:10.103841558-018-0091-3

Tang, C. M. F., & Lam, D. (2017). The role of extraversion and agreeableness traits on Gen Y's attitudes and willingness to pay for green hotels. *International Journal of Contemporary Hospitality Management*.

Chapter 6
Recycling and Reuse of Fashion:
A Way to Sustainable Environment

Chand Prakash Saini
SGT University, Gurugram, India

M. K. Nair
SGT University, Gurugram, India

K. Tara Shankar
SGT University, Gurugram, India

ABSTRACT

The chapter examines the role of recycling and reuse of fashion in order to achieve environmental sustainability. The chapter supports its conclusion by various reports that recycling of textile waste can be solutions to many environmental issues caused by fast fashion. However, textile recycling is an old term; in recent years, it has gained attention again due to fast fashion culture in significant parts of the world, which has resulted in overconsumption of textiles and led to waste generation. Waste recycling has become a multibillion industry. New ways are being created in terms of the development of sorting machines, design inputs, and innovative high-value products to make recycling a profitable proposition. The chapter also highlights how the second-hand market of clothes and the internet as a facilitator can help in reducing textile waste.

DOI: 10.4018/978-1-7998-2728-3.ch006

Copyright © 2020, IGI Global. Copying or distributing in print or electronic forms without written permission of IGI Global is prohibited.

1. INTRODUCTION

Fashion is a word all are obsessed with, whenever one talks about fashion, trend, fast fashion, the other party immediately jumps into the discussion to give every insight of one's understanding. We, all around the globe want to be recognised by our style, and fashion adds to our style, for the same we wish to have new apparel, accessories every time we make our social presence. Also, this presence should be without repeating the ones we have already been into. As a marketer, this is an excellent opportunity for grabbing the market share, as a consumer also this act as a differentiator but if the same is to be noticed for society at large, this is not a very motivating phenomenon. The apparent reason is that adverse effects on the environment and a large number of manufacturers of low-price garments are involved in the production. The report estimates India's apparel market will be worth $59.3 billion in 2022, making it the sixth-largest in the world, and comparable to the UK ($65 billion) and Germany ($63.1 billion), according to data from McKinsey's Fashion Scope (2019). The aggregate income of the addressable population (individuals with over $9,500 in annual income) is expected to triple between now and 2025 (McKinsey & Company 2019). The reason behind the same is waste fashion material which no individual wants to use, i.e. dress material once used are neither reused nor recycled in 75% of the cases IPCC (2000).

Adverse effects of non-recycling can be explained by depletion of natural resources, production of solid waste, generation of wastewater, exploitation of labour amount of noxious chemical being used and cause of economic problems by a genetical modification of seeds (UNEP, 2007).

1.1 Fashion as an Indiscriminate Disposable Habit

Stiff competition in the fashion industry has led the manufacturers to produce clothes at an increasingly lower price which motivates the customer to buy it and to use only once (Claudio, 2007). Some of the industry experts call the 'fast fashion' as same that of fast food. The worst that this 'fast fashion' has done is that it has motivated the customers of fashion neither to use nor to dispose of. This all result in higher consumption of fashionable goods, and at present, it is a double-edged sword, favourable for the economy but dangerous for the environment, as it has increased the problem of textile disposal (Jana, 2006).

1.2 Types of Textile Waste

Following are the three types…

1.2.1 Pre-Consumer Textile Waste

Manufacturing waste during the processing of fibres (both natural and synthetic) and production of finished yarn and textile usually produces waste parallel, which is termed as Pre-consumer textile waste. Pre-consumer textile waste is usually "clean waste". In most of the cases pre-consumer textile waste is usually "Clean waste", most of the firms either manage the disposal of the same themselves or pay fee against the dumped part of the waste.

1.2.2 Post-Consumer Textile Waste

As the name suggests this type of waste is created when any garment or household textile is no longer in use and customer decide to discard because of any of the reasons like worn out, size issue, out of fashion. This category allows identifying and selecting the garment which can easily be reused or recycled and much of which can be sold to third world nation. Another smart way to reduce can be shredding into fibre and to use the fibre in similar products.

1.2.3 Industrial Textile Waste

Commercial waste generated from the waste of hospitals, carpet and curtain industries are considered as commercial and industrial waste. This waste is "Dirty waste" and is the real cause of the environmental problem.

2. RECYCLING OF TEXTILE WASTE

Textile waste can be recycled or reused. The strategy can be to convert them into low value or value-added products or promoting the users to sell it further, i.e. Second-hand fashion industry. Motivation can be provided to the users to do the same by the following methods

2.1 Convenience

The convenience of location and access is essential when diverting clothes for recycling and reuse. Some of the efforts needed to increase convenience are:

1. Recycling bins.
2. POS collection.
3. Collection at corporate.

4. Establishing transfer stations.
5. Events.
6. NGOs doing it at the doorstep.
7. Mobile Apps.

2.2 Spreading Awareness

1. Government Initiatives.
2. Educating the public.
3. NGO's contribution.
4. Student Awareness Program.

2.3 Returns on Experience

1. Sharing experience.
2. Acknowledging the donors.
3. Benchmarking area, state-wise.

3. USE OF THE INTERNET TO RESOLVE THE PROBLEM

The Internet can be used as an essential tool for solving the problem of increasing fashion waste and popularising the diversion of fashion (Varsha & Khare, 2012). Already there has been a significant amount of emphasis and awareness programs

Figure 1. ThredUP resale report
Source: Resale Report ThredUP (2019)

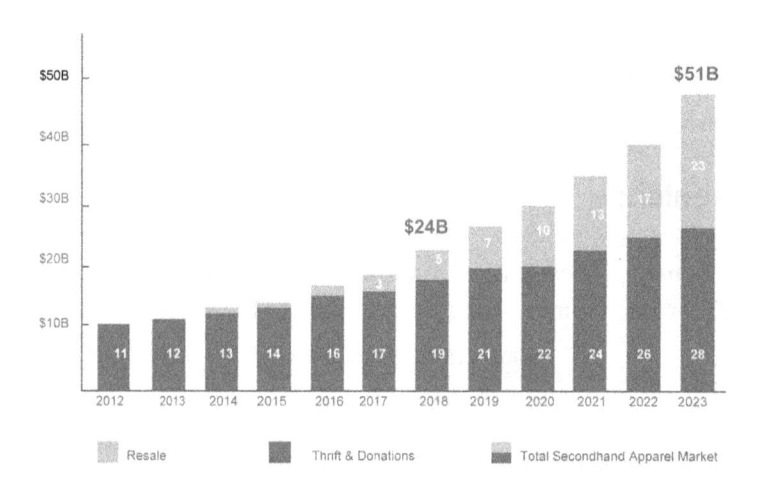

are being run for recycling, reusing and donating the used fashion clothes, but the internet and various apps are doing well in this context. It is beneficial for both the first user as well as for the second user. One fulfils the want of fashion at a reduced price, while the other party can fulfil their financial requirements. Selling, renting of used clothes over apps is gaining momentum as from the resale report ThredUP (2019) Secondhand Market Will Reach $51B in 5 Years.

As per the same report, Millennials and Gen Z will be driving the growth of the Second-hand fashion market.

If everyone bought one used item instead of new this year, we would SAVE:

Figure 2. Savings from buying used items
Source: Resale Report ThredUP (2019)

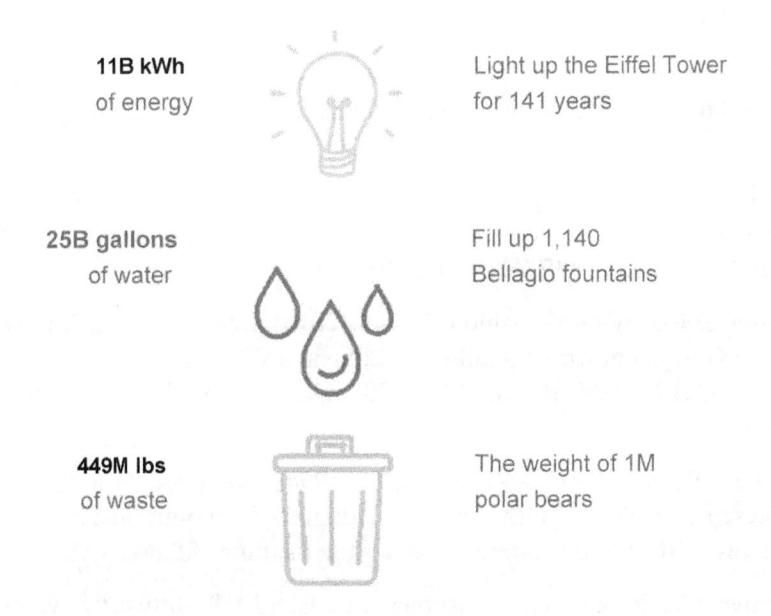

11B kWh of energy		Light up the Eiffel Tower for 141 years
25B gallons of water		Fill up 1,140 Bellagio fountains
449M lbs of waste		The weight of 1M polar bears

CONCLUSION

It is evident from the above discussion that fast fashion is creating challenges for the environment by creating waste both in the production and post-purchase stage. Changing trends in usage and selling of second-hand fashion can be a solution to the environmental problem caused by fast fashion. If the used fashion can be reused, it can reduce waste by almost 70%. In future textile recycling would be an important industrial activity as textile manufacturing.

The government and the public have an equal responsibility to maintain a sustainable environment. The government can take initiative like partnering with NGOs. There shall be awareness programs to reduce or not to produce waste through non- degradable items: a new venture degree diploma and degree course to be launched in universities and colleges. Awareness implementation, as well as execution, has to be in an equally parallel path is the only way to protect the environment from breathing freely.

REFERENCES

Claudio, L. (2007). Waste couture: Environmental impact of the clothing industry. *Environmental Health Perspectives, 115*(9), A448–A454. doi:10.1289/ehp.115-a449 PMID:17805407

Inter-Governmental Panel- IPCC. (2000). *Climate Change Special Report on Emission Scenarios*. https://www.ipcc.ch/site/assets/uploads/2018/03/emissions_scenarios-1.pdf

Jana, M. H. (2006). Digging for Diamonds: A Conceptual Framework for understanding Reclaimed Textile Products. *Clothing & Textiles Research Journal, 24*(3), 262–275. doi:10.1177/0887302X06294626

Mc Kinsey & Co. State of Fashion Report. (2019). https://www.mckinsey.com/~/media/McKinsey/Industries/Retail/Our%20Insights/The%20State%20of%20Fashion%202019%20A%20year%20of%20awakening/The-State-of-Fashion-2019-final.ashx

Nousiainen, P., & Talvenmaa-Kuusela, P. (1994). *Solid textile waste recycling*. Paper presented at the Globalization–Technological, Economic, and Environmental Imperatives, 75th World Conference of Textile Institute, Atlanta, GA.

Perspectives on Retail and Consumer Goods. (2019) https://www.mckinsey.com/~/media/McKinsey/Industries/Retail/Our%20Insights/Perspectives%20on%20retail%20and%20consumer%20goods%20Number%207/Perspectives-on-Retail-and-Consumer-Goods_Issue-7.ashx

Prosperity Without Growth. (2011). *The transition to a sustainable economy*. Sustainable Development Commission. http://www.sd-commission.org.uk/data/files/publications/prosperity_without_growth_report.pdf

ThreadU. R. R. (2019). https://www.thredup.com/resale

UN Report. (2013). *World population projected to reach 9.6 billion by 2050*. https://www.un.org/en/development/desa/news/population/un-report-world-population-projected-to-reach-9-6-billion-by-2050.html

UNEP. (2007). *Global Environmental Outlook 4.* http://wedocs.unep.org/handle/20.500.11822/7646

Varsha, G. (2012). Value Creation in post-consumer apparel waste: a study of urban-rural dynamics in India. NIFT.

WWF. (2010). *Living Planet Report.* https://wwf.panda.org/knowledge_hub/all_publications/living_planet_report_timeline/lpr_2010/

Chapter 7
Influence of Micro-Celebrities on Generation Z:
Perception, Customer Engagement, and Career Option

Kanchan Chandar Tolani
Shri Ramdeobaba College of Enginneering and Management, India

Ruchi Sao
Shri Ramdeobaba College of Engineering and Management, India

ABSTRACT

A micro-celebrity is a person who has transformed from an ordinary person to a celebrity. Many organizations use micro-celebrities for advertising their products as they get to reach a larger audience easily. Micro-celebrities not only get popularity but also get to earn revenue; the desire for social media fame is found in many youths (Generation Z) today. The current study throws light on the perception of Generation Z towards micro-celebrities, identifies the influence of micro-celebrities on customer engagement, and explores micro-celebrity as an emerging career option for Generation Z. Major findings reveal that Generation Z follows micro-celebrities to stay updated with trends. Though association with micro-celebrities gives companies better customer reach, the influence of micro-celebrities on the purchase decision is uncertain. Many Generation Z individuals aspire to be micro-celebrities; however, when it comes to a career choice, some prefer to take it as a side hustle.

DOI: 10.4018/978-1-7998-2728-3.ch007

INTRODUCTION

The most important feature of a global society is the increasing use of the Internet (Toronto, 2009). The use of internet has increased tremendously in the past decade. The excessive use of internet services is impacting the mental and social lives of individuals to a large extent (Kim & Haridakis, 2009).

Mobile phones and Internet services have become an integral part of everyone nowadays. Also internet services are easily available at an affordable price (Leena, Tomi & Arja, 2005; Coogan & Kangas, 2001).

Rapid technological advancement and the extensive use of the Internet have led to increasing use of social media by people on their day to day basis. People make use of social media to remain in contact with friends, family and the outside world. It connects people to the world outside. Consumers and companies are extensively using the internet and social media to connect and collaborate. (Jones, 2010). Social media has become a platform for creating and trading user-developed content (Kaplan & Haelein, 2010). According to Nielson (2012), individuals who use the internet tend to spend most of their time on social media than any other website. People use various social media platforms on a regular basis such as Facebook, Snapchat, Instagram, Twitter, YouTube, online blogs, etc. Instagram is rated as the most used social media out of all (Raice & Spencer, 2012).

The extensive use of social media by consumers had made it an important marketing tool used by companies today. (Michaelidou, Siamagka & Christodoulides, 2011). Marketers are largely using social media to create awareness about their brands among users. (Barreda, Bilgihan, Nusair & Okumus, 2015). Organizations are also using social media platforms to endorse their products to their target consumers. Many researchers in the area of marketing support the argument that the use of social media as an advertisement tool is a necessary strategy to survive in the dynamic market today (Pradiptarini, 2011; Frey & Rudloff, 2010; Nikolova, 2012).

This growing trend has led to the creation of an online economy. Many micro-celebrities get to earn revenue from these endorsements on social media. Micro-celebrities is a popular practice these days among internet users. It is an emerging trend that involves sharing user-generated content on social media and creating a fan base for oneself. They create their content strategically so that people get entertained and also, their audience size increases gradually. Some researchers call the fan base of these micro-celebrities as a networked audience (Marwick & Boyd, 2010). The Networked audience is basically the viewer of the content created by these micro-celebrities and follow their content regularly.

BACKGROUND

Micro-celebrities are social media produced celebrities (Khamis et al., 2017). Micro-celebrity involves direct dialogue with the fans using social media, thus it is considered as a more authentic and reliable type of the traditional celebrity (Senft, 2008). Various other names used for micro-celebrities are "Internet celebrity", "YouTube celebrities", "YouTube stars", "Web stars", "Internet famous" (Gamson, 2011; Burgess & Green, 2009; Senft, 2008; Tanz, 2008; Jerslev, 2016).

In the past century, being a celebrity was an extra ordinary thing. A common person could not even think of dreaming to become one. However, in this present century with the emergence of social media, the scenario has had a sea change. Micro-celebrity is also defined as a person who has transformed form an ordinary person to a celebrity (Turner & Rojek). It is considered as becoming a media person from a non-media person. (Couldry, 2004). Micro-celebrities are regular users of social media who get famous among all other users (Khamis et al., 2016). These are those people who make use of social media platforms for becoming famous and indulge in creating content which helps them generate a fan base (Clarewells, 2014). It is an online performance aimed at presenting oneself as a celebrity (Marwick, 2013). Micro-celebrities create content in various areas such as fashion, health, and fitness, beauty, humor, technology, gaming, food, inspiration (Van Hoof & Verhoeven, 2014). In recent years there has been an increase in micro-celebrity right from bloggers, glamour models, and social media coaches.

These social media celebs not only receive popularity and fame by their content but they also get to earn money. As companies are actively using social media platforms for promoting their products, they prefer collaboration with these micro-celebrities (Van Hoof & Verhoeven, 2014). It's been years when marketing has broadened the scope from direct to indirect marketing. In a highly competitive market, companies are choosing various strategies to have a larger market share. One such measure is reaching out to popular micro-celebrities on various social media platforms (Kolarova, 2018).

The use of micro-celebrities helps companies in directly connecting to the consumers. As these micro-celebrities have a huge fan base thus their content is viewed and shared by many. By associating with these micro-celebrities, marketers get to reach to this larger audience easily (Elberse & Verleun, 2012). According to Indian firms, use of micro-celebrity for marketing products is very useful in customer engagement and reach (Bhattacharya, 2019). It also helps marketers in creating more positive "word of mouth" publicity (Barreda, Bilgihan, Nusair & Okumus, 2015). It enable organizations to engage their customers and helps them in making their brands strong (Mangold & Johnston, 2014).

According to a study conducted by Khim-Yong Goh, Cheng-Suang Heng, Zhijie Lin on retail chain outlet's user-generated and marketer-generated content (UGC and MGC), engagement with respect to brand communities on social media leads to a positive increase in purchase expenditure. It was also observed that UGC has a greater impact than the MGC on the purchases made by the consumers at large. Advertisements from various companies selling the same product may often put the consumers in a dilemma. The consumers often resort to reviews and feedback given in the form of blogs or video blogs by users or micro-celebrities which are perceived to be more authentic and reliable by the former. The consumers can have a belief that marketer-generated content may be deceptive with the intention to increase sales; unlike consumers whose intentions are just to give an honest review. Micro celebs may also create polls which are perceived to be highly reliable by the end-users before making a decision for purchase.

A study conducted on the same lines, suggest that majority of consumers have positive attitude toward the social influencers. The major reason for this is the authenticity and trustworthiness of the micro-celebrities. Many consumers consider these micro-celebrities to be more reliable than the traditional celebrities (Jargalsaikhan, 2016).

A similar experiment was conducted by Maria Kolarova, 2018 to compare the effectiveness of traditional celebrities and micro-celebrities as influencers for consumers, it was observed that that micro-celebrities are more effective influencers for consumers as compared to the old traditional celebrities. In addition to it, experience and trust factor of micro-celebrities enhances the effectiveness for the desire to purchase in consumers thereby making them loyal with the brand. Thus companies are increasingly using these social influencers for marketing their commodities and are ready to give them good amount of compensation for the same.

Companies research and identify the micro-celebrities of the relevant field and pay them compensation for endorsing their commodities in their videos or blogs or websites. By associating with these micro-celebs companies attempt to develop a direct connect with their target audience (Cultureshop, 2015).

According to a survey, majority of firms in India are spending 5% to 7% of their marketing budget on micro-celebrities (Bhattacharya, 2019). Thus this makes the micro-celebrities not only famous but also rich. Moreover to become a micro-celebrity you need not have an educational degree. The good thing about "micro-celebrity" as a concept is that regardless of whether you have achieved something prominent or not if you can entertain the audience with your content and get many followers, you can still become a celebrity and earn money (Boyd & Marwick, 2011). The desire for social media fame has been witnessed in many youths today. Youngsters today wish to get content faster, focus on privacy, like to stay connected, un-used to waiting, prefer selective sharing, passionate about social issues and attracted to influencers. This generation is known to be having a span of attention of around 18 seconds. Youngsters today grasp information fast and lose interest in anything very quickly and thus love watching short-lived content. The new generation, which is affecting the environment globally is Generation Z. These are young and smart individuals born from 1993 to 2005 (Taylor & Keeter, 2010).

Born after Millennials, Generation Z has such unique characteristics and traits that they have now become an important matter of study for researchers, anthropologists, and trend analysts (Williams, 2015).

There are various names allocated to this unique generation by multiple researchers. Generation Z individuals are also referred to as Digital Natives, I-Generation, Net-Gen, Generation 2020, Internet Generation, Screensters, Zeds, Tweens, Baby Bloomers and Generation 9/11 (Prensky, 2001; Williams, Page, Petrosky & Hernandez, 2014).

Though Millennials is also called as a tech-savvy generation, generation Z are digital natives in a true sense as they are born and are living in an era of digitalization. It is the first generation which is witnessing such ready access to advanced technology (Prensky, 2001).

This generation is well versed with new technology and devices. They are used to living in a world that is connected 24/7. Easy and affordable availability of smartphones has made it very convenient for the new generation to access social media and other platforms. This is not true for only the rich individuals belonging to this generation. Children who belong to middle-class families also own a smartphone. Technology and internet services are available at a very affordable price, which has made it easier for everyone belonging to the new generation to use it (Rideout et al., 2010)

Social media has become a very significant part of the everyday lives of these youngsters. In a survey conducted by Palley (2012), it was seen that these new generation individuals are not only habituated to use social media regularly but they are also emotionally attached to it. Many of the respondents of the study said that they cannot imagine spending even a day without their smartphones and internet facility.

Generation Z individuals spend one-quarter of their time on social media platforms. They are extremely good at multitasking and can use multiple social media apps at one time. They prefer to get any information instantaneously and are not used to waiting. According to Generation Z, "Smart is the new cool" (Cohen, 2007; Gorrell, 2008).

Thus, the easiest way to capture the attention of this generation is to master the techniques of social media. The key to engaging Generation Z is to use social media platforms.

This generation has very high social needs, as they are born in the age of social media they like to have social acceptance and appreciation for every single thing that they perform. Peer review and acknowledgment is very crucial for them. They like to be connected to people who have similar interests in music, fashion, games, etc. But what makes them different is that they wish to be connected to individuals of same likings on social media platforms. Thus, in contrast to traditional friends groups or friend circle, these youngsters have online communities, WhatsApp groups, fan clubs, and blogs. This driving need also creates a need to have fame. For this generation gaining popularity is more important than earning a lot of money. They would prefer fame over money. Thus, this generation tends to be more attracted to social influencers and social media celebs.

As the new generation is tech-savvy, wants success fast and desires to become popular. Micro-celebrities emerges as a new and unique career option for the new generation youths.

Thus the current study focuses on understanding the concept of micro-celebrity and its influence on the generation Z. The study attempts to understand the influence of micro-celebrities on customer engagement. It also aims at finding out whether the young individuals today consider this as a good career option.

MATERIAL AND METHODS

This study is undertaken to understand the concept of micro-celebrity and to analyze it as a career option for the young generation. For this purpose, a pilot study was conducted with the help of interviews of 15 people belonging to Generation Z. With the help of a pilot study and literature review, the questionnaire of the study was formulated. Participants of the study belonged to generation Z. Snowball sampling technique & convenience sampling was used to identify the sample. The total number of participants was 165. The data was analyzed using descriptive statistics.

RESEARCH IMPLICATIONS

Micro-celebrity is a person who has transformed from an ordinary person to a celebrity. Many organizations use micro-celebrities for advertising their products as they get to reach a larger audience easily. Micro-celebrities not only get popularity but also get to earn revenue, the desire for social media fame is found in many youths (Generation Z) today. The current study throws light on the perception of generation Z towards micro-celebrities, identifies the influence of micro-celebrities on customer engagement and explores micro-celebrity as an emerging career option for generation Z. The findings of the study will be useful for the marketers and policy makers to better understand Generation Z and their perceptions about micro-celebrities. It will also help the companies to understand the influence of these micro-celebrities on customer (Generation Z) engagement. Thus it will enable them to make suitable marketing strategies.

DATA ANALYSIS

Social Media Networks Used

In the ever-changing scenario on the technology front, there are many social media networks used. The hashtag is the new trend which is there to stay for sure. As per the responses, figure 1 demonstrates the usage of the same by the new generation. Instagram followed by WhatsApp messenger are the most widely used networks. Some of the most important features of Instagram are video, stories, push notifications for favorite accounts and geo tagging. In WhatsApp, the most important feature is the concept of mute notifications wherein one can have complete control over privacy. The traits of generation Z believe more in visuals thereby creating stories with an option of privacy.

Reasons for Following Micro-Celebrity

The growth in the industry of micro-celebrities has numerous reasons. Most of the respondents tend to follow micro-celebrities to stay updated and learn new trends. Figure 2 shows the various reasons for following micro-celebrities.

Popular Categories of Micro-Celebrity

The industry of micro-celebrities is diverse. Micro celebs are sharing their life journey through social media in the areas of motivation, health, fashion, travel and many more through images, boomerang or videos. Figure 3 represents the areas in which generation Z prefers to follow micro-celebrities; top being fashion bloggers and least digital marketing bloggers.

Most Followed Micro-Celebrities

The number of micro-celebrities is growing very rapidly. In the popular category of micro-celebrities discussed, there are few names which are famous amongst the generation Z. As generation Z is more into stories and short lived content, Sandeep Maheshwari who is a motivational / inspirational speaker is the most followed one. He connects to the audience as he himself has struggled in his life, failed and emerged as a celebrity. Generation Z can relate to him and follow as he sounds real and the audience can relate to him. Figure 4 shows the most followed micro-celebrities of many.

Figure 1. Social media networks used

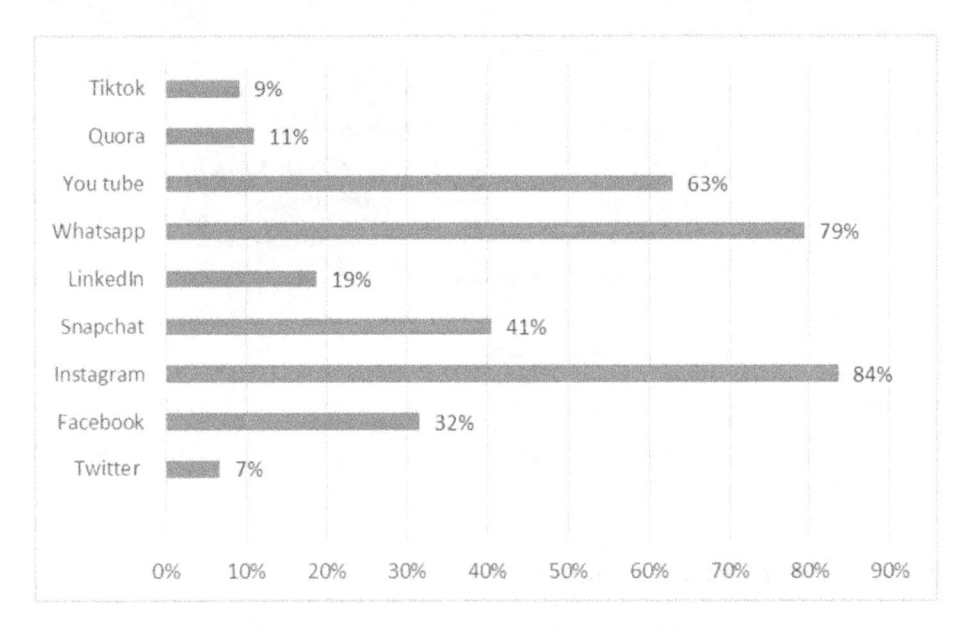

Platform	%
Tiktok	9%
Quora	11%
You tube	63%
Whatsapp	79%
LinkedIn	19%
Snapchat	41%
Instagram	84%
Facebook	32%
Twitter	7%

Figure 2. Reasons for following micro-celebrities

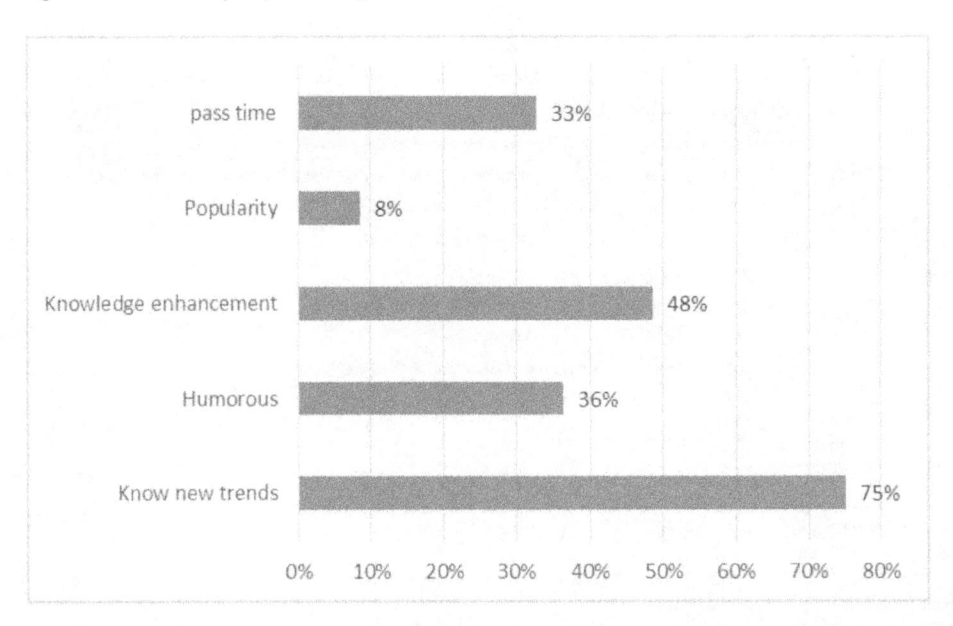

Reason	%
pass time	33%
Popularity	8%
Knowledge enhancement	48%
Humorous	36%
Know new trends	75%

Figure 3. Popular categories for micro-celebrities

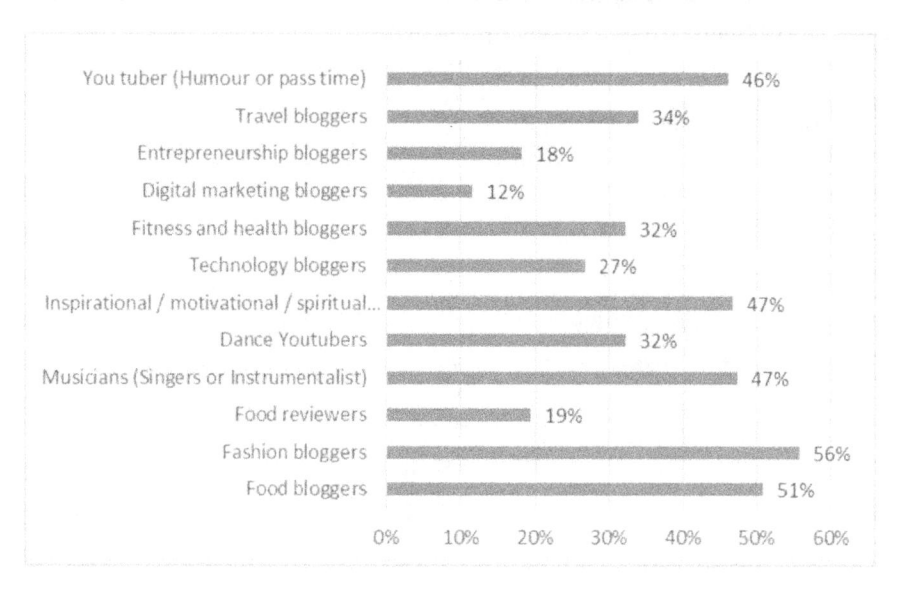

Category	%
You tuber (Humour or pass time)	46%
Travel bloggers	34%
Entrepreneurship bloggers	18%
Digital marketing bloggers	12%
Fitness and health bloggers	32%
Technology bloggers	27%
Inspirational / motivational / spiritual...	47%
Dance Youtubers	32%
Musicians (Singers or Instrumentalist)	47%
Food reviewers	19%
Fashion bloggers	56%
Food bloggers	51%

Figure 4. Most followed micro-celebrities

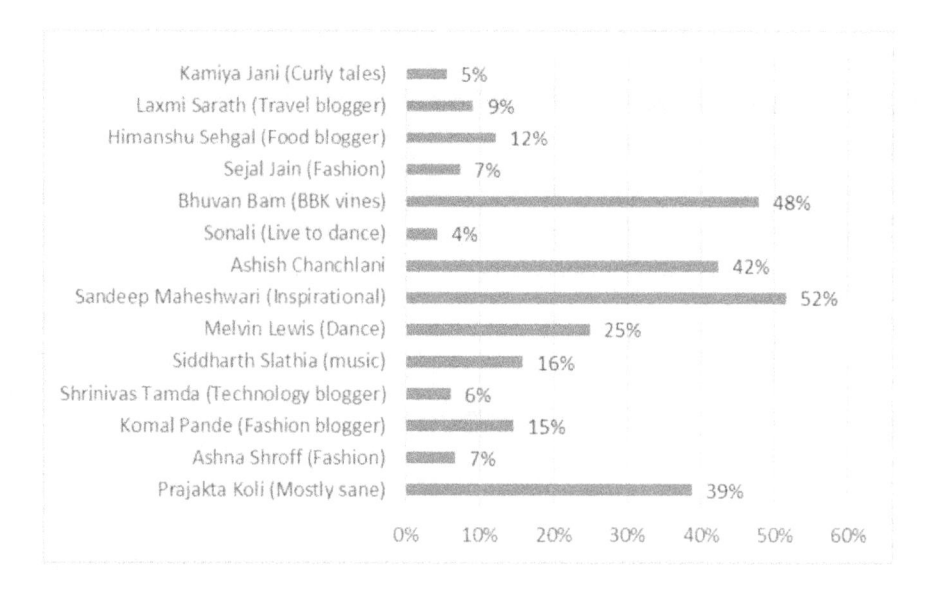

Micro-celebrity	%
Kamiya Jani (Curly tales)	5%
Laxmi Sarath (Travel blogger)	9%
Himanshu Sehgal (Food blogger)	12%
Sejal Jain (Fashion)	7%
Bhuvan Bam (BBK vines)	48%
Sonali (Live to dance)	4%
Ashish Chanchlani	42%
Sandeep Maheshwari (Inspirational)	52%
Melvin Lewis (Dance)	25%
Siddharth Slathia (music)	16%
Shrinivas Tamda (Technology blogger)	6%
Komal Pande (Fashion blogger)	15%
Ashna Shroff (Fashion)	7%
Prajakta Koli (Mostly sane)	39%

Figure 5. Purchase decisions taken

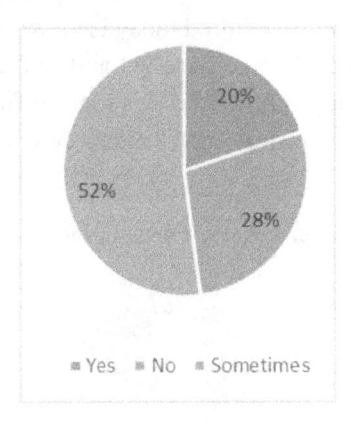

[Pie chart: Yes 20%, No 28%, Sometimes 52%]

Purchase Decisions Taken

Micro-celebrities are untainted in the industry and do not have any big team to work for them. So, the opinions given by them may sound more realistic and relatable. Due to this, the connection established between the brand and the audience can be really unique. The reel may look unrealistic due to the glam quotient which is not present in the micro celebs. They endorse many products thereby influencing the viewers. The researchers attempted to identify whether the choices of certain micro celebs and their endorsements are considered while making a purchase decision. The responses show that 20% of the participants make decisions on the recommendation of a micro celeb and 52% sometimes make a decision under the influence of micro-celebrities.

Usage of Brands Endorsed by Micro-Celebrity by Them

Some of the micro-celebrities see endorsements and tie-ups as a business model. However, there may be situations where the brand endorsed is not being actually used by them. The parameter tries to capture responses from the respondents about the perception with respect to usage of endorsed brands by micro-celebrities. The perception of respondents is represented in figure 6.

Aspiration to be a Micro-Celebrity

With growing fame and name of micro-celebrities, many youths today aspire to become one. The youngsters have a different idea with respect to the life they want to live. There has been a major shift in the way celebrities are born in entertainment industry. Gone are the days where it was mandatory to have a godfather. With the dawn of internet, the only thing required today is knowledge, talent and proper use of social media. Micro celebs are self-crafted and self-choreographed. This trend creates a desire in many youngsters to become a social influencer. Figure 7 represents the number of respondents aspiring to be a micro-celebrity.

Figure 6. Usage of brands endorsed by micro-celebrity by them

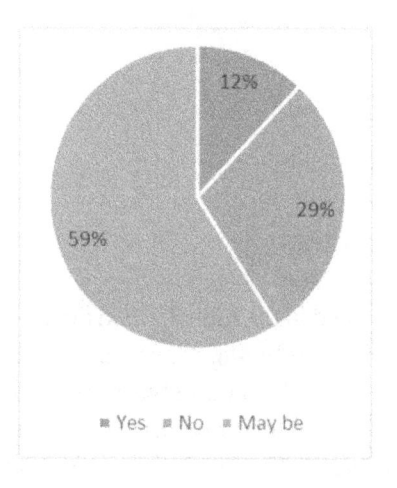

Figure 7. Aspiration to be a micro-celebrity

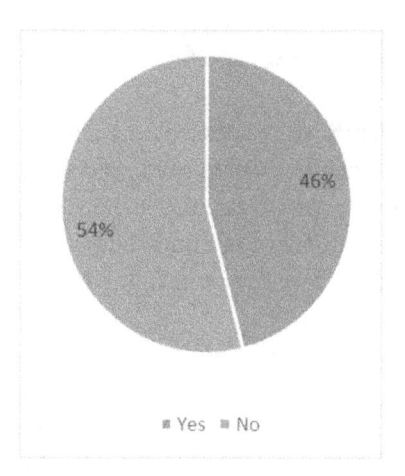

Figure 8. Micro-celebrity as a career option

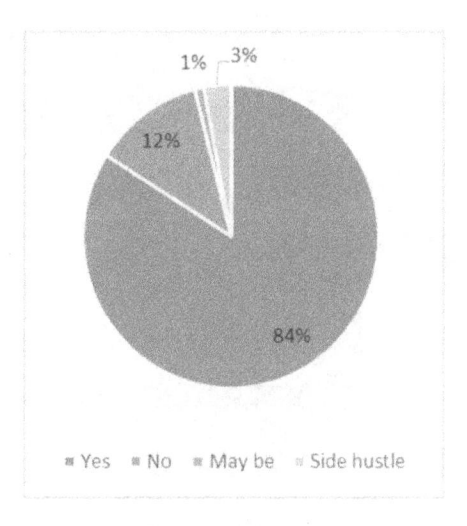

Micro-Celebrity as a Career Option

Choosing a life where the youngsters can live their passion sounds to be an amazing option. However, if the same is clubbed as a career choice, the respondents had a different mindset. Figure 8 represents the choice of respondents with respect to a career option.

Reasons for Choosing to be a Micro-Celebrity as a Career

No doubt, working for passion and fun are two of the most important criteria that they foresee. Generation Z is expressive and do not go by the old school of thought. They like to stay free and express their opinions before a set of people. Being a micro celeb certainly gives such a platform. Figure 9 represents various reasons for choosing to be a micro-celebrity as a career option. The topmost reason identified by respondents is as being a micro-celebrity allows one to follow their passions.

Reasons for Not Choosing to be a Micro-Celebrity as a Career

One of the pitfalls in this type of career can be fame which lasts for a shorter duration of time. Figure 10 represents various reasons for not choosing to be a micro-celebrity as a career option. One of the strongest reasons identified for not choosing being a micro-celebrity is a career is as it is not a stable career option.

Figure 9. Reasons for choosing being a micro-celebrity as a career

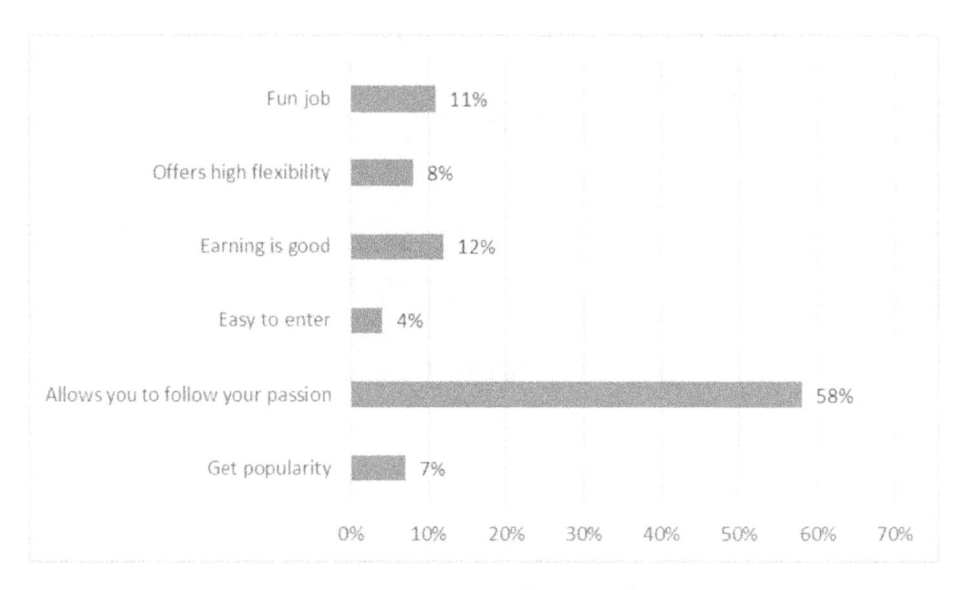

Reason	%
Fun job	11%
Offers high flexibility	8%
Earning is good	12%
Easy to enter	4%
Allows you to follow your passion	58%
Get popularity	7%

Figure 10. Reasons for not choosing being a micro-celebrity as a career

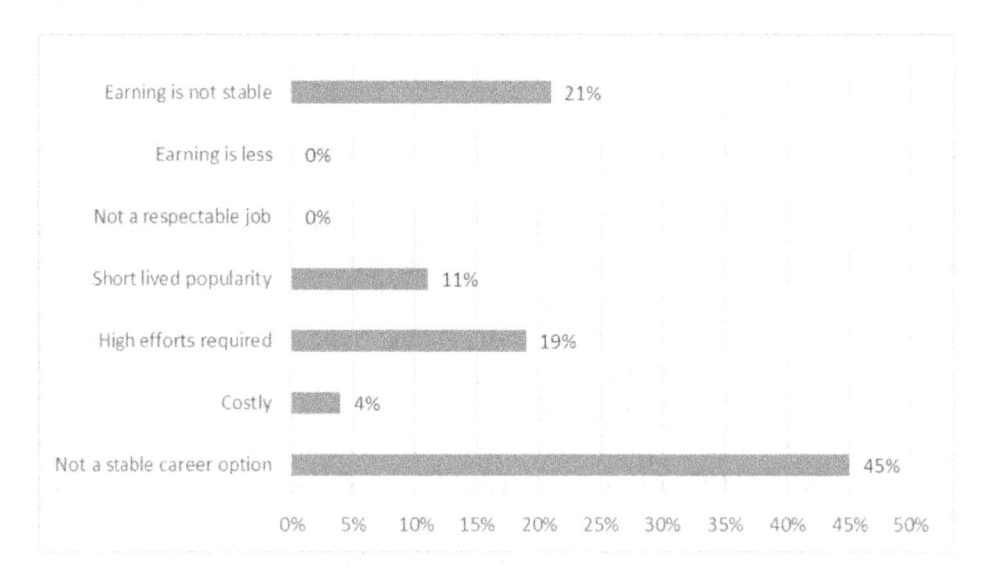

Reason	%
Earning is not stable	21%
Earning is less	0%
Not a respectable job	0%
Short lived popularity	11%
High efforts required	19%
Costly	4%
Not a stable career option	45%

FINDINGS AND CONCLUSION

The current study is divided into three segments. The first segment focuses on understanding the perception of generation Z towards micro-celebrities. The second segment identifies the influence of micro-celebrities on customer engagement. In the third segment of the research, an attempt is made to explore micro-celebrity as an emerging career option.

The first segment of the study reveals that generation Z today are aware of micro-celebrities and are also following many of them. The main reason for following these micro-celebrities for the majority of youngsters is that they get to know about new trends. Some youngsters follow them because they find their content humorous and some feel that it aids in their knowledge enhancement.

While a few youngsters follow these micro-celebrities just to pass time. Micro-celebrities create content in various areas such as fashion, health, and fitness, beauty, humor, technology, gaming, food, inspiration, etc. according to the study, the most popular category of micro-celebrities are fashion bloggers followed by food bloggers, inspirational speakers, and musicians.

To find out the most popular micro-celebrities of India, a pilot study was done, based on which a checklist of micro-celebrities was made. This checklist was then given to the respondents. It was seen that the top three popular micro-celebrities in India are Sandeep Maheshwari (motivational speaker), Bhuvan Bham (comedian) and Ashish Chanchalani (comedian). The majority of the respondents of the study said that they follow these three micro-celebs.

The second segment of the study would be beneficial for marketers as it studies the influence of micro-celebrities on customer engagement. By 2020, generation Z will account for 40% of all consumers and will be an influencer for others on spending decisions (Chamberlain, 2018). The new generation uses a wide variety of social media platforms on a day to day basis. The study found that the top three social media platforms used the most by generation Z are Instagram followed by WhatsApp and YouTube. Thus, the marketers can tap these platforms for endorsing their commodities and for a wider customer reach.

A lot of companies are associating with these micro-celebrities for their product endorsement as it gives them better reach and customer engagement. In this research, we tried to find out if people buy commodities endorsed by the micro-celebrities that they follow. It was observed that most of the people feel that the micro-celebrities do not use the brands that they endorse. And thus people do not end up buying all the commodities endorsed by the micro-celebrities. Though association with micro-celebrities gives companies better customer reach. But the influence of these micro-celebrities on the purchase decision is not very effective.

The third segment explored the emergence of micro-celebrity as a career option. It was seen that many youngsters today aspire to become micro-celebrity themselves. And the majority of the respondents of the study find it as a good career option. The main reason for choosing this as a career option is that they get to follow their passion. Some respondents also feel that the earning of micro-celebrities is very lucrative.

At the same time, some youngsters do not consider micro-celebrities as a good career option. Majority of them suggest that it is not a very stable career option, also the efforts required are high. Micro celebs spend huge amount of time to create content and to ensure that whatever they create goes with their overall brand image. Also, the earning is not regular.

Many researchers suggest that, as compared to the previous generation, Generation Z gives a lot of importance to security. Unlike other generations they have easy access to all the news and happenings of the world, they tend to be more cautious and alert. They have been raised to aware of safety risks. The way this generation fulfills this security need is by getting a good education and suitable careers (Wellner, 2000; Jayson, 2009).

Thus, it can be said that generation Z follows various micro-celebrities and have a positive perception of them. Many of them also aspire to become one. When it comes to a career choice, some would prefer to take it as a side hustle.

The study will help the marketers in understanding the perceptions of generation Z towards micro-celebrities and will allow them to make suitable branding strategies.

FUTURE RESEARCH DIRECTIONS

The study focuses on understanding the perception of generation Z towards micro-celebrities. It deals with three areas; perception of generation Z towards micro-celebrities, the influence of micro-celebrities in customer engagement and micro-celebrity as an emerging career option. Further studies can be carried out to study other aspects related to micro-celebs. As the current research only focuses on the new generation, further research can be done considering the impact of gender and age. The study is restricted to generation Z of India thus the results of the study cannot be generalized. Further studies can be done on generation Z from other countries. Inter-country comparative analysis can also be made.

REFERENCES

Barreda, A. A., Bilgihan, A., Nusair, K., & Okumus, F. (2015). Generating brand awareness in online social networks. *Computers in Human Behavior, 50*, 600–609. doi:10.1016/j.chb.2015.03.023

Bhatacharya, A. (2019). *Socail media influencers are the latest obsession among Indian marketers*. Quartz India.

Burgess, J. E., & Green, J. B. (2009). *YouTube: Online video and participatory culture*. Cambridge: Polity Press.

Chamberlain, L. (2018). Gen-Z Will Account for 40 Percent Of All Consumers By 2020. *GeoMarketing from Yext.*

Clarewells, D. (2014). *CLARE@BLOG*. Retrieved February 1, 2016, from https://clarewells.wordpress.com/2014/04/14/micro-celebrities-and-social-media/

Cohen, R. (2007, July 12). Twixt 8 and 12, the Tween. *International Herald Tribune.*

Coogan, K & Kangas, S. (2001). Nuoret ja kommunikaatioakrobatia, 16-18-vuotiaiden nuorten k. annykk. a- ja internetkulttuurit. Nuorisotutkimusverkosto ja Elisa ommunications. *Elisa tutkimuskeskus. Raportti, 158.*

Couldry, N. (2004). Teaching us to fake it: The ritualized norms of television's "reality" games. In S. Murray & L. Ouellette (Eds.), *Reality TV: Remaking television culture* (pp. 57–74). New York, NY: New York University Press.

Cultureshop. (2015). *The rise of the micro-celebrity: Why brands should tap into this cultural phenomenon*. Retrieved February 1, 2016, from https://medium.com/@QuantumSingapore/the-rise-ofthe-micro-celebrity-why-brands-should-tap-into-this-cultural-phenomenon886961d37639#.rg17v8yd5

Elberse, A., & Verleun, J. (2012). The economic value of celebrity endorsements. *Journal of Advertising Research, 52*(2), 149–165. doi:10.2501/JAR-52-2-149-165

Fietkiewicz, K. J., Dorsch, I., Scheibe, K., Zimmer, F., & Stock, W. G. (2018, July). Dreaming of stardom and money: micro-celebrities and influencers on live streaming services. In *International Conference on Social Computing and Social Media* (pp. 240-253). Springer. 10.1007/978-3-319-91521-0_18

Frey, B., & Rudloff, S. (2010). *Social media and the impact on marketing communication*. Academic Press.

Gamson, J. (2011). The unwatched life is not worth living: The elevation of the ordinary in celebrity culture. *PMLA, 126*(4), 1061–1069. doi:10.1632/pmla.2011.126.4.1061

Goh, K. Y., Heng, C. S., & Lin, Z. (2013). Social media brand community and consumer behavior: Quantifying the relative impact of user-and marketer-generated content. *Information Systems Research, 24*(1), 88–107. doi:10.1287/isre.1120.0469

Gorrell, M. (2008, May 13). When Marketing Tourism, Age Matters, Expert Says. *The Salt Lake Tribune.*

Jayson, S. (2009, Feb. 4). It's Cooler than Ever to Be a Tween. *USA Today.*

Jerslev, A. (2016). Media Times| In The Time of the Microcelebrity: Celebrification and the YouTuber Zoella. *International Journal of Communication, 10,* 19.

Jones, B. (2010). Entrepreneurial marketing and the Web 2.0 interface. *Journal of Research in Marketing and Entrepreneurship, 12*(2), 143–152. doi:10.1108/14715201011090602

Kaplan, A. M., & Haenlein, M. (2010). Users of the world, unite! The challenges and opportunities of Social Media. *Business Horizons, 53*(1), 59–68. doi:10.1016/j.bushor.2009.09.003

Khamis, S., Ang, L., & Welling, R. (2017). Self-branding, 'micro-celebrity' and the rise of Social Media Influencers. *Celebrity Studies, 8*(2), 191–208. doi:10.1080/19392397.2016.1218292

Kim, J., & Haridakis, P. M. (2009). The role of Internet user characteristics and motives in explaining three dimensions of Internet addiction. *Journal of Computer-Mediated Communication, 14*(4), 988–1015. doi:10.1111/j.1083-6101.2009.01478.x

Kolarova, M. (2018). *# Influencer marketing: The effects of influencer type, brand familiarity, and sponsorship disclosure on purchase intention and brand trust on Instagram* (Master's thesis). University of Twente.

Korotina, A., & Jargalsaikhan, T. (2016). *Attitude towards Instagram micro-celebrities and their influence on consumers' purchasing decisions.* Academic Press.

Leena, K., Tomi, L., & Arja, R. (2005). Intensity of mobile phone use and health compromising behaviors -how is information and communication technology connected to health-related lifestyle in adolescence? *Journal of Adolescence, 28*(1), 35–47. doi:10.1016/j.adolescence.2004.05.004 PMID:15683633

Marwick, A., & Boyd, D. (2011). To see and be seen: Celebrity practice on Twitter. *Convergence, 17*(2), 139–158. doi:10.1177/1354856510394539

Marwick, A. E. (2010). I tweet honestly, I tweet passionately: Twitter users, context collapse, and the imagined audience. *New Media & Society.*

Marwick, A. E. (2013). *Status update: Celebrity, publicity, and branding in the social media age*. Yale University Press.

Michaelidou, N., Siamagka, N. T., & Christodoulides, G. (2011). Usage, barriers and measurement of social media marketing: An exploratory investigation of small and medium B2B brands. *Industrial Marketing Management*, *40*(7), 1153–1159. doi:10.1016/j.indmarman.2011.09.009

Nikolova, S. N. (2012). *The effectiveness of social media in the formation of positive brand attitude for the different users*(Doctoral dissertation). University of Amsterdam.

Palley, T. I. (2012). *From financial crisis to stagnation: The destruction of shared prosperity and the role of economics*. Cambridge University Press. doi:10.1017/CBO9781139061285

Pradiptarini, C. (2011). Social media marketing: Measuring its effectiveness and identifying the target market. *UW-L Journal of Undergraduate Research*, *14*, 1–11.

Prensky, M. (2001). Digital natives, digital immigrants part 1. *On the Horizon*, *9*(5), 1–6. doi:10.1108/10748120110424816

Rideout, V. J., Foehr, U. G., & Roberts, D. F. (2010). *Generation M 2: Media in the Lives of 8-to 18-Year-Olds*. Henry J. Kaiser Family Foundation.

Rothman, D. (2016). *A Tsunami of learners called Generation Z*. http://www.mdle.net/JoumaFA_Tsunami_of_Learners_Called_Generation_Z.pdf

Senft, T. M. (2008). *Camgirls: celebrity and community in the age of social networks*. New York: Peter Lang.

Smith, T. W. (2000). *Changes in the generation gap, 1972-1998*. National Opinion Research Center.

State of the media: The social media report 2012. (n.d.). Featured Insights, Global, Media + Entertainment. *Nielsen*. Retrieved December 9, 2012 from http://blog.nielson.com/nielsonwire/social/2012

Tanz, J. (2008, July 15). Internet famous: Julia Allison and the secrets of self-promotion. *Wired*. Retrieved from https://www.wired.com/2008/07/howto-allison/

Taylor, P., & Keeter, S. (2010). *Millennials: A portrait of generation next*. Pew Research Center.

Turner, A. (2015). Generation Z: Technology and social interest. *Journal of Individual Psychology*, *71*(2), 103–113. doi:10.1353/jip.2015.0021

Turner, G. (2004). *Understanding celebrity*. London, UK: SAGE Publications. doi:10.4135/9781446279953

Van Norel, N. D., Kommers, P. A., Van Hoof, J. J., & Verhoeven, J. W. (2014). Damaged corporate reputation: Can celebrity Tweets repair it? *Computers in Human Behavior, 36*, 308–315. doi:10.1016/j.chb.2014.03.056

Wellner, A. S. (2000). Generation Z. *American Demographics, 22*(9), 60–65.

Wellner, A. S. (2003). The Next 25 Years. *American Demographics, 25*, D26–D29.

Williams, A. (2015). Move over, millennials, here comes Generation Z. *The New York Times, 18*.

Williams, K. C., Page, R. A., Petrosky, A. R., & Hernandez, E. H. (2010). Multi-generational marketing: Descriptions, characteristics, lifestyles, and attitudes. *The Journal of Applied Business and Economics, 11*(2), 21.

Zheng, S., Shi, P., Xu, H., & Zhang, C. (2012, June). Launching the New Profile on Facebook: Understanding the Triggers and Outcomes of Users' Privacy Concerns. In *International Conference on Trust and Trustworthy Computing* (pp. 325-339). Springer. 10.1007/978-3-642-30921-2_19

Chapter 8
Transmogrifying to Sustain Stimulating Potency

Anant Deogaonkar
Shri Ramdeobaba College of Engineering and Management, India

Sampada Santosh Nanoty
Maharaja Sayajirao University, India

ABSTRACT

This chapter focuses on exploring the practical implications of sustainability initiatives effectively through the efficient utility of technology by strengthening the marketing practices and ensuring the ease of sale. This is inevitable for standardizing the marketing practices that are globally acceptable.

THE RE-COMMERCE

The joy of dressing is an art and hence is the very manifestation of the fashion. The roots of re-commerce are witnessed by everyone in day to day life. Almost all of us had grandparents creatively practicing the re-commerce in the simplest way, that too very economically. It is an inherent idiosyncrasy indeed. The inclination of millennia towards the variety and diversity of panache camouflaging their pledge towards the conservation of environment emphasizes the inevitability of re –commerce. This drives the way towards the exigency of re-commerce thereby ensuring sustainability. The purchasing pattern of the consumers is moving from a clichéd impulsive buyer to a smart money saver. There are around twenty thousand used merchandise stores generating $17.5 billion of annual sales in communities across US (Phipps, 2018). This is further expected to rise rapidly. The noticeable slowdown in the departmental

DOI: 10.4018/978-1-7998-2728-3.ch008

stores due to the recession phase in 2008 created avenues for re-commerce. This trend of re-commerce in fashion industry needs to be percolated to the consumer market to a greater extent so much so that it becomes the zeitgeist. Despite the fact that there exist effective marketing media options that can be deployed in variety of ways to reach to the consumer market, it poses challenges in terms of successful execution. Creative measures ought to be sought for creating the brand ethos of the re-commerce in fashion industry. The vogue of re-commerce aims to carve its niche by 2022.

PEOPLE, FASHION AND RE-COMMERCE

Re-commerce is a re invention / renovation of the pre-owned fashion which is a creatively feasible way of breaking the extensive production chain causing hazardous threats to the environment. Understanding the fact that the users have their feelings attached to the garments they wear carrying a memory of the fine details of the garment. There is an emotional attachment that prevails, peculiar to their dressing. Therefore, sustaining the fashion market, or rather taking it to even higher echelons with intelligent creativity would be best possible by re-commerce. Moreover, the misconceptions about the re-commerce in fashion, with the very conventional scavenging, displayed in outré stores is the lack of clarity of the significance and perks of re-commerce.

The major stratum of the consumer market thinks economically while spending on garments. The buying decision is a result of the analysis of the price and utility proportions. A commonly observed human trait is that of renting garments for certain occasions and festivities. This is a popularly favored option than spending huge for small time use. This ideology integrates with the concept of re-commerce. Re-commerce is a smarter, more efficient and also more appealing version of this renting business. The onus of the fashion industry ultimately lies with the consumer despite of the fact that the extensive production tolls the environment. The practical application of re-commerce in the market will alter the buying pattern of the consumers, thus encouraging the consumers to buy more with increased diversity of options and at the same time counting their contribution to the conservation of environment, also inclining the market sales.

THE RE-COMMERCE TODAY

The world of fashion so glamorous, so lustrous, is turning out to be futuristically disastrous". On an average the maximum life of a garment is measured to be approximately that of four to five years. The scrap generated by a person in his / her lifetime on an average sums up to be 90 to 100 tons. Out of the generated scrap, substantial quantity is not recycled even though 90% to 95% of it is capable of being recycled. This precludes and barricades the cardinal necessity of the efficacy of re-commerce in the fashion industry. Lately, minuscule developments are observed in the thrift stores. People have been somewhat meagerly attracted towards the concept of thrift stores. But re-commerce in the fashion industry is merely limited to these thrift stores (new circular business models specifically by Ellen MacArthur Foundations Make, n.d.).

The expeditiously rising production and environmental threats, simultaneously along with the continuous avant-garde in the fashion trends, the pace of development of re-commerce is uncomprehending. People have been observed to be flexible in the re-commerce of electronics, with trivial to no defects but rather tend to show up rigidity towards re-commerce in the fashion industry. Certain dogmas and stigmas are attached to it. The joy which is experienced by people in buying pre-used books is somehow not experienced in that of clothes. Many conventional questions come up to their minds while considering, "the re-usage of the pre-used clothes". The etched stigma of the fact that they are pre-used makes it harder to accept their re-usage. This sheer lack of complete knowledge about the process becomes the sole reason for the lack of acceptance of re-commerce of the apparels. This calls for the urgent and prompt aggressive marketing of the significance and clarity of re-commerce in the fashion industry. To avail the benefits of the re-commerce to people is what is important for the future.

Vintage with a dent is greatly exquisite than the aroma of a fresh scent

Possessing vintage is the very hype of the era. For the progression of this hype, certain parameters are to be devised and certain techniques need to be revised. The ease in re-commercialization can be sought.

THE FASHION AGENCY MODEL

The big time market holders, being veterans of the industry, with their experience of production and selling in the industry for so many successful years now, makes it imperative for them to establish a new segment under their very own starry labels. This can be done in various parts. These colossal brands can create a new window for entering into re-commerce, by establishing recycle plants (to begin with, at a small scale) taking up the required re-processing. Establishing Fashion Agencies would be a part of their stores. A Fashion Agency would be a platform both virtual and on the map. It will not just be working as a conventional cloth bin but rather will be providing its customers the experience and satisfaction of being associated with an agency a private one or something that can be termed as a feasible fashion hub. It would be accepting the used apparel from its customers and will be simultaneously selling the recycled and re-processed clothes at the customer admired rates. For the ease of operation the virtual agencies will function by providing cloth bins at the customer doorstep and likewise also the very creative buying options for the virtual customers. These fashion agencies would enrich its customer base with the feeling of fulfillment of its social responsibility. This will gradually incline its consumer base by providing an entirely new buying experience.

ADVANTAGES OF RECYCLED APPAREL

The prime most advantage of the re-cycles apparel is its low cost. For both, the buyer and the seller the re-commerce in the fashion industry is smartly economical. The total re-cycling and re-processing costs when compared with the total cost of the new production, the re-commerce option results in the low total cost of production than the costs incurred in the entire new production costs. This is due to the very simple fact that the process of re-commerce just needs to complete approximately on an average the 40% of the remaining process being at the re-process stage, since that the cloth has already been through approximately an average 60% of the production process during its first time production (World Economic Forum Annual Meeting 2018, 2020). The raw material used in the recycling process has been through the basic process when it was produced for the first time. Moreover, the raw material for the re-processing is cheaply available. People readily give up their used garments. The used garments have the scrap value and hence become the source of cheaply available material. Used garments are also given up as donations by many people. This curtails the raw material cost to a great extent as compared to the raw material costs incurred for the first time production of the garments.

Moreover, the pre-processed clothes when re-processed the level of creativity seen in these clothes will have reached its pinnacle. The clothes that had been attractive in the past carry that beauty with them. The re-processing of these clothes will add five stars to the output. Withstanding the fact that this would be creative imitation, it would be the most appealing prêt-a-porter. Re-processed clothes will be the exquisite range of exotic couture. Re-commerce in the fashion industry is the process that fetches the most intricate and conspicuous end results for the customers as well as the sellers.

THE QUALITY

Though low buying cost is one of the most attracting factors for the customers of re-commerce, but the very obvious question about the quality of the clothes re-commercialized, pops up.

The quality concerns can be ruled out by introducing the quality tests at the various stages, throughout the re-process. This will ensure the quality of the re-cycled garments. Therefore the reliability of quality maintenance is a factor taken care of by the re-processing units. The quality sustainability is complementary to the very economical re-commerce ideology. Hence, quality credibility ushered with sustainability.

Notwithstanding the fact that the reprocessed clothes are not as appealing as the fresh ones, the reprocessed clothes are the trendsetters of the fashion industry. Reprocessed clothes have their own vogue. Application of re-commerce in the fashion industry is curbing the fashion industry with a swift shift. Not just at the fashion campaigns or on the ramps but re-commerce even graces the mainstream urban routes and the countryside lanes. Re-commerce trends have enabled the people to flaunt the versatility of their garment with the authenticity of its panache. Possessing an element of sterling vintage in your garment is indeed very stunning.

The circular trend in the market is the biggest booster of the sustainability (World Economic Forum Annual Meeting 2018, 2020). A circular planet surely calls for the circular ways of business. It is very rational to maintain the circularity inside the planet rather than experiencing the earth's wardrobe malfunction. Circularity of the fashion business is thrifty, nifty and also ensures safety.

CORPORATE SOCIAL RESPONSIBILITY

Brands can play a very vital role in generating employment through the application of re-commerce. They can engage certain sections of the people such as the economically backward ones. Even the tribal people, known for their very creative and innovative abilities in the most natural way can be employed in the recycling process. Due to the fact that the tribal people are believed to create things with utmost simplicity and precision, they would be able to make indeed a very successful contribution towards the re-commerce in fashion industry. The brands by indulging in the re-commerce will not just increase their customer base and set new fashion trend globally, but also will be able to generate employment for the needful ones. Therefore, the brands, by engaging in the re-processing can be said to fulfill their corporate social responsibility. Employing these people will also help in spread of the ideology of re-commerce. As a result, it will seek more people's attention towards it thus benefitting each of its side.

The efficacy of re-commerce brings with it the benefits attached to it. It is ushered with the sustainability of the environment and the global fashion market by reducing the environmental concerns up to a great extent by exempting pollution caused by the massive garment production. Moreover, it imparts a feeling of the fulfillment of the social responsibility by the sellers as well as the consumers. Further, re-commerce is the most intelligent tool for the market sustainability in this concurrent era (7 Well-made clothes How fast fashion garments are made to fall apart, n.d.). The digital age in itself is the very evidence of how re-commerce is the breath of the era. The virtual applicability of the re-commerce is the popular version which attracts the tech savvy millennia. Powerful media is the road through which the success of re-commerce travels.

ENVIRONMENTAL BENEFITS

With the rapidly escalating figures of the environmental hazards and each rising day introducing a new environmental concern, it is crucial to ensure the adequacy of measures in time. With the latest raised concern of the increasing forest fires the fashion industry cannot afford to create more environmental concerns. Therefore the inevitability of re-commerce is clearly evidential. Introduction of re-commerce has cure for several environmental ailments. Eluding the utilization of virgin fabrics, instead recycling for environmental and market health. A massive reduction in the extensive exploitation of energy and water. This further declines the rate of pollution. Moreover, because of re-commerce in the fashion industry the lands acquired by the landfills will tumble down (What is a Capsule Wardrobe?, 2020). Also the harmful greenhouse gas emissions due to the decomposition of the natural fibers will fall down to a great extent. Materials like polyester which do not decompose, can be recycled and reprocessed hence reducing the environmental concerns. Re-cycling and reprocessing of the garments will in a way lessen the rate of deforestation. Re-commerce in fashion industry is indeed a very knobby just like re-processed garments which groom their own authentic wardrobes.

REFERENCES

New circular business models specifically by Ellen MacArthur Foundations Make. (n.d.). Retrieved March 16, 2020, from https://www.coursehero.com/file/p3bs4gu7/new-circular-business-models-specifically-by-Ellen-MacArthur-Foundations-Make

Phipps, L. (2018, October 10). *4 companies pioneering the clothing recommerce market.* Retrieved March 16, 2020, from https://www.greenbiz.com/article/4-companies-pioneering-clothing-recommerce-market

Well made clothes How fast fashion garments are made to fall apart 2018. (n.d.). Retrieved March 16, 2020, from https://www.coursehero.com/file/p5m0jpe/7-Well-made-clothes-How-fast-fashion-garments-are-made-to-fall-apart-2018

What is a Capsule Wardrobe? (2019, April 20). Retrieved from https://thefairbazaar.com/blogs/fairblog/capsule-wardrobe

World Economic Forum Annual Meeting 2018. (2018). Retrieved March 16, 2020, from https://www.weforum.org/events/world-economic-forum-annual-meeting-2018

World Economic Forum Annual Meeting 2018. (2020). Retrieved March 16, 2020, from https://www.weforum.org/events/world-economic-forum-annual-meeting-2018

Chapter 9
Thread of Sustainability:
Crafting Fashion for Conscious Community and Conservation

Nagma Sahi Ansari
National Institute of Fashion Technology, India

Anannya Deb Roy
National Institute of Fashion Technology, India

Sharmistha Banerjee
University of Calcutta, India

ABSTRACT

This chapter aims to look into the current practices of fashion production and consumption and argues for a sustainable model. This model advocates the need of conscious creation and consumption, mindful connection with the community, and conservation of the ecology. It opens up conversations about fetishistic attitudes vs. sustainable practices and how production and consumption behaviors are manufactured in postmodern society. With interpretative epistemological stance, this chapter follows qualitative research methodology to develop an alternative model of fashion production and consumption. This alternative model, 'C3 Model of Art of Fashion', is the result of a qualitative study conducted amongst artisans, consumers, and entrepreneurs of Kantha.

INTRODUCTION

The twenty first century neologism, "You are what you buy!" has tethered its hook on the postmodernist society looming large in its fundamentalist capitalism. When Danielle Todd (2011) wrote about postmodern consumption drawing upon how popular culture both manufactures consent for fetishistic attitudes and cries foul for commoditization of culture; we were on the verge of another turn in information age. It paved way for the democratization of media and social networking websites, which in turn recreated a parallel narrative of presence and purchase. Next was the introduction of algorithmic prediction (based on previous viewing/interest) as a booster for marketing in these digital spaces. It is not uncommon to find haunting recommendations for product purchase on social media networking platforms (SNS). What's more? We are caught unawares between a pattern of conspicuous consumption and materialistic fetishism. The result of which is driven by capitalistic forces of production: of commodity and related waste. The fashion industry only comes second to oil industry in being the largest polluter globally (Szokan, 2016). About 5000 gallons of water waste is generated in creating a pair of denims and a T-shirt. Farming of cotton itself creates around 24% of insecticides and 11% of pesticides, despite using only 3% of the world's arable land. China, which is leading the clothing manufacturing market alone, generates 2.5 Billion tons of wastewater annually on an average; one person discards about 70 pounds in clothing waste (Edgexpo, 2019).

Textiles industry is considered as the second most pollutant industry after oil (Szokan, 2016). It is a highly water intensive and water pollutant industry (Quantis and ClimateWorks, 2018). According to the study (Quantis and Climate Works, 2018) based on data of 2016, global consumption of fibred materials was 11.4kg per capita. The per capita emission related to this estimated global consumption was 442kg of CO_2 eq in 2016. This is equivalent to taking about 150 baths. Different phases of the apparel production and supply chain are responsible for the adverse environmental impact. Dyeing and finishing, yarn preparation and fiber production are the first three drivers of global pollution within textile industry followed by distribution and consumption of apparels. Textiles industry also contributes 35% of the total micro plastic in the oceans (Boucher & Friot, 2017). Textiles industry is considered as the second most pollutant industry after oil (Szokan, 2016).The statistics here is only a representation of a smaller section of both process and geography but it raises alarms once one starts to contextualize the unorganized mechanisms associated with the fashion industry.

The trend of fast fashion which encouraged people to consume fashion more and frequently is only in the contradiction of the need of consume more consciously and reduce the adverse environmental impact. Increasing the lifespan of the fashion merchandise is one of the needs of the hour. But if fashion stands for cyclical change of trend then longer usage of same fashion items sounds an impractical dream.

Both the production and generation of waste is tied closely to our fetishistic patterns of consumption and disregard for our environment. The chapter at hand not only introduces readers to various perspectives on conspicuous consumption of fashion but also introduces a more sustainable model of production and consumption with a specific way termed as art of fashion. The chapter deals with how fashion industry needs to build a sustainable base in order to preserve, conserve and march towards a holistic growth.

From the dawn of civilization, human beings have evolved to be the most significant force influencing the world's physical, economic and social environment. Consequently depletion and exhaustion of natural resources grew at a faster rate than the growth in population. However, the world is at the threshold of most resources, with oil reserves remaining only for the next four decades, natural gas for the next five decades and towns going dry. These may be accounted for by increased industrialization, urbanization and, subsequently, mass-production, that create challenges of over-production, product obsolescence and excessive waste. Such modern societies set aside traditional forms of knowledge, and instead adopted a philosophy — or ideology — of materialism.

The "Take-make-use-dispose" model of linear economy, in which products are usually disposed at the end of life, date back to the industrial revolution and had been practiced by the global economy for years. The authors posit that the linear economy, focusing on profits alone gave rise to the exploitation of natural resources which coupled with disposal processes does not encourage a sustainable economy. Literature also indicates that the linear economy model is unsustainable and require an urgent need of an alternative model i.e. the circular economy (CE) that mirrors the natural life cycles (Andrews, 2015). This belief had global support and thus evolved the triple bottom line, as a reporting mechanism. In 1994, John Elkington, a thought leader in the field of sustainability and corporate responsibility, introduced the label "triple bottom line (TBL)". The triple bottom line theory expands the traditional assessment framework to include, besides profits, two other performance areas: the social and environmental impacts of their company. These three bottom lines include people, planet, and profit.

With passage of time, the triple bottom line of sustainability, as proposed by Elkington (1997) was reshaped to incorporate the potential for more substantial change in thinking and global activities. It was criticized that the triple bottom line deals with broad issues — i.e. society (people), environment (planet) and economy (profit), that are far removed from the decision making variables of an ordinary individual. TBL also assigns equal weightage to economic considerations and environmental and social responsibilities. To address these concerns a quadruple bottom line has been proposed (Walker, 2011) that comprises: Practical meaning, which is understanding nature and meeting societal needs without harmful environmental impacts, the extension of 'planet'; Personal meaning which promotes pursuit of wisdom, inner growth and values, core ethics, referring to individual spirituality, questions of ultimate concern, the extension of 'people'; Social meaning propounding justice, moral behavior, and relationship with and responsibility to community and social equity, issues of tolerance, empathy which leads to the sense of 'purpose'. The economic dimension or profits is considered subordinate to the other three and regarded as a means to an end, not an end in itself. For clarity, Quadruple bottom line (QBL) provides mechanism for addressing and assessing integration of culture, spirituality, and faith with responsibility towards environment and relationships with people in reporting. This is often interpreted as people, planet, profit and purpose. QBL reporting focuses on the value generation to the society that is created or destroyed by an organization and it emphasize the importance of creating value for all stakeholders of an organization, not just the financial benefits to the shareholders (Tipping, 2012).

The objective of this study is to explore a feasible alternative model based on the philosophy of the circular economy, for the fashion industry. The proposed model emphasizes community based sustainable enterprises in contrast to market driven profit oriented enterprises of the fashion industry. 'Kantha' has been proposed as a craft which will act as the centre stage of this illustrative model to promote conscious creation and consumption, with an aim to achieve community connection and conservation of the ecology.

Sustainable Lifestyle and Fashion Industry

Fashion is considered as the prevailing trend and style followed by a substantial number of consumers in the market at a given time. Tracing fashion across the linear economy, it may be observed that during 80s, organizations produced fashion items, especially apparels in large scale and have limited variety with cost reduction as their focus. During 90's organizations started producing apparels with varied styles and design. They made attempt to entice consumers with these apparels which are more trendy and fashionable than the standardize apparels of 80's. To promote this consumerism, it was needed to redefine the traditional seasons of autumn/winter and spring/summer by creating new seasons. By increasing the number of seasons, fashion houses started creating more business opportunities for them. Increasing season means increasing business opportunities to replenish the stock more quickly to ensure quick economic growth. These 'return on investment' motive driven corporates started encouraging consumers to refresh their wardrobe frequently with the change in seasons, mostly crated by them. The term 'fast fashion' has started evolving to lure consumers for fast consumption. Proponents of fast fashion like 'Zara' or 'H&M' might conceive as many as 20 micro seasons in a year (Christopher et al., 2004).This emergence of fast fashion has brought about tremendous negative impact on the environment. Scholars have documented that fashion industry has brought about damages to the environment at different stages of supply chain and production cycle. (Brito et al., 2008; Turker & Altuntas, 2014). This leads the authors to argue that materialism philosophy, with least concern for the environment is a predominant outcome of the linear economy. Additionally, contemporary views suggest a systemic shift in the economic activities and bring a focus on the purpose and practice of sustainable design and fashion. The authors argue that for optimal integration of sustainable lifestyle into the fashion industry a designer shall priorities sustainability of fashion through energy efficiency, responsible material usage and product longevity and give due importance to the artisan and the creator. The fashion industry may therefore append the financial objectives (practical) with those of conscious creation and consumption, connection to community and conservation of the ecology.

In the process of integrating sustainable lifestyle with the fashion industry, the measurement mechanism termed QBL may be relevant as in case of the evaluation of enterprises in a circular economy, which minimizes the use of virgin stock resources and the production of unrecoverable waste. It is based on systems thinking where the "waste" of one manufacturer becomes the food for another which is the framework of the Circular economy (CE), as alternative to the linear economic system. Circular economy and QBL concepts are developing in parallel to each other but merging gradually, for the successful application of world sustainability.

Sustainable development was defined as development process that takes care of betterment of the present without compromise the future. As put in the UN Document 2015, "Sustainable development is development that meets the needs of the present without compromising the ability of future generations to meet their own needs." It asks us to explore the question, "Are we creating something from the natural provision for the consumption in the present moment, that can reduce or extinct the possibility to meet the need in future. So, sustainable development is a way of life that reduces or eliminates adverse implication on the ecology we inhabit.

In this paper the authors suggest 'Kantha' as a paradigm for practicing the art of fashion operating in the circular economy, a socially responsible product for design that fosters expressions of conscious creation & consumption, solders community connection, and contributes favourably in conservation of ecology. The authors therefore, prepare the backdrop of this paradigm by exploring the potential of sustainable practice of fashion consumption within a capitalistic system of production. This necessitates developing an understanding of the very idea of commodity and artifact in related disciplines.

Commodity and Artifacts

In the philosophical tradition, an artifact is defined as *objects that are created with an intention of fulfilling some pre-conceived purpose* (Aristotle). Artifact has a utilitarian value as its focal point and not necessarily an economic one. As both their purpose and function is defined by actors (human and non-human) engaged in creating it, it becomes a site for coding socio-cultural values.

On the other hand, commodity (as defined in economics) is any tangible object which has an exchange value. According to Smith (1776), "The value of any commodity, [...] to the person who possesses it, and who means not to use or consume it himself, but to exchange it for other commodities, *is equal to the quantity of labor* which it enables him to purchase or command." Marx provides a counter critic of this value that is tied to labor, by stating how a fetishistic attitude is constructed around commodity, by *placing value in the tangible object itself rather than the labor put to produce it*. Now, this clarifies two things: a) fetishism removes human actor from the site of production, thereby reducing commodity into economic value b) commodity (economic value) plus labor (human actor) posits 'value' away from capital driven account to a more socio-cultural praxis. (Ritzer, 2018)

We shall talk about fetishism and related politics later in the chapter, first we will discuss about a circular conversion cycle that throws light upon how a socio-cultural artifact translates into an economic object (commodity) and vice-versa.

A riveting socio-political process is at the helm of assigning value and transforming an artifact into a commodity. This conversion is processual i.e. it is a series of processes and not a singular event. The process of commodification occurs when an artifact, made for fulfilling some purpose (assigned task) is placed in the process *of exchange*. As pointed out by Kopytoff (1986), an artifact goes through a state of being coded of some (socio-cultural) value (by human actor), once enters a market (and or exchange in barter systems) the social identity of the artifact is modified and an economic value is assigned to convert it into a commodity.

Now, when an exchange happens, this coded commodity is placed in the socio-cultural fabric of its end-user and hence another layer of meaning and value gets added (which may or may not erase/transform the earlier codes/values). As this stage, is usually devoid of exchange (Marxist exchange of commodities), we may consider de-commodification and return of this economic object (commodity) as an artifact. Once again, if this artifact, in its dormant de-commodified space is placed in active space of exchange, re-commodification occurs (Appadurai, 1995).

However, that a capitalistic produce aimed only to bring forth an economic profit and seen (by producers) outside the praxis of socio-cultural meaning making (as propelled by mindless consumption) is not only a site of meaning production but also meaning consumption and thereby inevitably a part of the very fabric it runs from. We shall talk about this fabric of socio-cultural production and consumption in relation to sustainable practice later in the chapter (while discussing kantha as a case in point).

This leads to the idea of consumeristic fetishism which is created as a by-product of capitalistic assembly line production. As capitalistic society is only interested in reaping economic profit and thus a factory belt is introduced to maximize production in a given time. The human actors who were once the creators are reduced to being a laborer and are responsible for production of fractured sections of a single commodity. Temporality takes centre stage in a capital driven economy, thereby breaking a design into pieces which are only con-joined in the last phase of the assembly line. This creates alienation among the actual creators, who now do not associate themselves with the created commodity. This takes away one site of coding value on to the economic object thus created. Although, one may argue over what codes are lost, and if the capitalistic commodity can have a different code, yet an entire episteme is lost in translation.

Modern means of aggressive marketing and reductive advertising leads to a disillusioned consumer. A much needed currency for creating demand of overconsumption and thereby creating consumeristic fetishism. The idea of fetishism is two-folds: (i) production in quantities larger than required for an everyday living practice (ii) forging a market for thus produced economic commodity by simulating a consumeristic practice of mindless consumption. The hyper real space created by this kind of market thus leads to capitalistically induced fetish of accumulating commodities as one (consumer) starts to see their individual value in terms of their capacities of calling upon an 'exchange'(Feuerbach 1956).

Connecting the dots between conspicuous consumption that leads to unsustainable habitat of creation amongst producers and an unsustainable ecology by generating related production waste, this paper uses the craft of kantha. Drawing upon kantha, (a system of creation by reusing old clothes and sewing them with a running stitch to traditionally make a blanket) one can argue over the traditional ways of production, which not only situate the producers within the realm of being owner-creator, thereby removing alienation) but it is a widely popular method of recycling, up-cycling and re-consumption; which can significantly bring down fashion waste. Once alienation is removed, we open up praxis of personal narrative and socio-cultural meaning (the laborer becomes the producer).

In the course of this chapter, we shall argue upon the above mentioned politics by bringing in the arguments of circular economy and our proposed 'Art of Fashion'. The earlier arguments now direct us to the research questions: a) how can traditional knowledge of creation and consumption pave the way for a more sustainable practice b) what can the personal narrative tell us about both: (i) kantha as a craft (ii) the artisans engaged in practicing it c) how can we make a traditional practice more sustainable by adding economic value to the thus produced artifact.

Re-lensing the fashion industry production cycle, one can safely argue over how profit (economic) is integrally connected to people and planet in the larger system. And thus the model proposes that any action taken on the production belt also has equal effects on ecology and community.

Theoretical Model

Fashion is known as a prevailing style followed by a group of people at a particular time. This style is determined by various social, cultural, and political factors which create a pattern of desire, known as fashion trend. Fashion trend keeps on changing and fashion industry, comprises of manufacturers, retailers and marketers try to utilise this trend to ensure their economic growth. Corporations motivated by this continuous economic growth take the help of technological innovation for the production of goods which most often surpasses existing demands. Consequently, producers and marketers take the help of trans-media marketing promotion and create a culture of over consumption to push the output of their production system. This strategy of over production for the profit maximization, and promoted culture of mindless consumption result different unsustainable practices which are devastating for the environment, promote injustice in the society and rise economic inequity.

Unsustainable practices by these manufacturers and marketers encourage an unsustainable lifestyle and create a culture of materialism. Consumers under this materialistic culture relentlessly run after various products and services for deriving satisfaction and pleasure. But soon they find a new offer in the market, powered by some marketing or technological innovation, which announces psychological or technological obsolescence of the existing product. Consumers also discover that the product they are using with pride is no longer in the trend. This unpleasant discovery produces a sense of discontentment and they again get ready for another round of fresh product acquisition madness. Owners and share holders of the corporations look at this maddening scamper and make strategic plan to intensify or control this hyper activity of the consumer.

This drive of the fashion house for the continuous economic growth and profit maximization also encourages them to institutionalize the system of planned obsolescence of their product. This in turn promotes the mantra of hyper consumerism in the name of fast fashion. Consumers were encouraged to come frequently to purchase 'new collection' to catch up a weekly emerging trend. Inevitably to cater to that continuous consumption practice, manufacturers need to get into unsustainable production practice by getting into various types of cost reduction practices like sourcing form country of low cost production based primarily on low wage labor.

The search for low wage labour encourages fast fashion manufacturer to source their product from the developed countries which in turn promotes incidents like the collapse of Rana Pratap factory complex in Dhaka, Bangladesh, killing thousands of garment manufacturing workers in 2013 (BBC, 2013). This incident is not a single incident to showcase the fate of millions of garment manufacturing workers producing garments for the global fashion business houses in a working environment which is operates sometime even without basic work safety and security. This work right violation becomes a norm most often when the manufacturers try hard to get the order of the fashion business houses in most cost effective manner and facilitate the brand in pursuing their economic goal.

To counteract this unsustainable practice of the fashion houses in the name of fast fashion another fashion movement has gaining some ground. This trend has been promoted in the name of slow fashion which is not simply intended to slow down the over production and over consumption trend propagated by fast fashion but also endorsed the idea of reducing or stopping environmental, social and community related externalities (Ertekin & Atik, 2015).

Sustainability, we argue thus can come from our understanding of this maddening behaviour to attain satisfaction out of new product acquisition and instant gratifications. This way of life that goes for impatient instant gratification is running counter to our tradition, ancient wisdom and spirituality. We propose a model of sustainable life with art of fashion at its core and consciousness, community and conservation as its three pillars. We propose this theoretical model based on the review of extant literatures in the domain of sustainability followed by a qualitative exploratory research.

As a part of the qualitative research we have taken interpretative epistemological stance with ethnography as the methodology. We have taken in-depth ethnographic interview of two artisan-entrepreneurs and one entrepreneur doing business with Kantha as a commodity. We have taken the interview of 5 Kantha artisans to interpret the role of Kantha as an artifact or a commodity. To get the mindset of the potential consumers regarding Kantha we have conducted a focus group interview with 10 participants

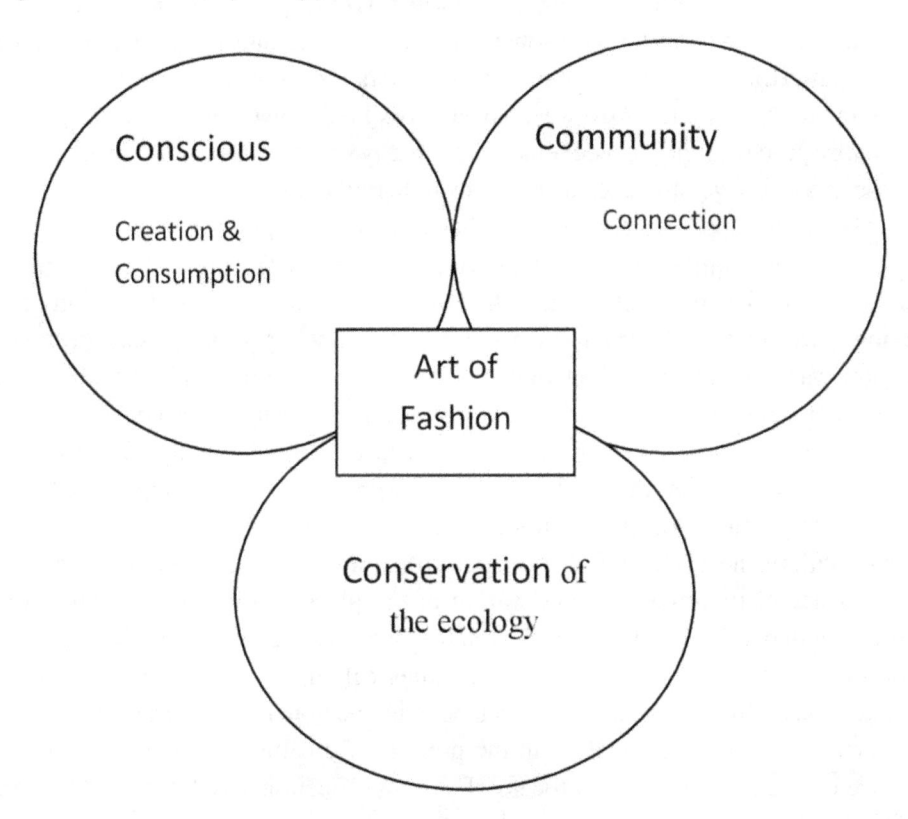

Figure 1. C3 model of art of fashion

```
        Conscious              Community
      Creation &               Connection
      Consumption

              ┌─────────┐
              │  Art of │
              │ Fashion │
              └─────────┘

              Conservation of
                the ecology
```

Three facets of our proposed *C3* model of *Art of Fashion* signify critical role of *a. Conscious creation & consumption, b. Community connection* and *c. Conservation of the ecology*. We first elaborate them as a general model and then illustrate how Kantha as an artifact can fulfil the requirement of this model.

The essence of the *C3* model of *Art of Fashion* is a concept of fashion that promotes sustainable life. This philosophy of sustainable life hinges on three ideological pillars: a conscious approach to creation and consumption, deliberate connection with the community and efforts to conserve the ecology. We assert that both the designers and the consumers need to nurture a level of consciousness while designing the product or consuming it. Built on our exploration of the concept of artifact and commodity, we argue that fashion designers should ask a critical question to themselves "Do my consumers need this?" if the answer is yes then for what? From the conventional designing solutions: do good, look good and feel good options, designers need to pick up first option more often and the last two as additional benefits. In this designing solution, planned technological, material and psychological obsolescence will be considered as cynical and undesirable practice.

A fashion product once conceptualized with this basic premise of utilitarian value, designers need to codify it with some personal meaning and values that transform it into an artifact. Product design with this personal coding will bring personal meaning to the designer. Also we advocate possible involvement of the designer in the entire process of product development directly or indirectly so that development of the product never alienates designer from her creation.

Alienation happens at two levels of the product development process: alienation due to the detachment of the creator at some level of the product development process and alienation due to the detachment of the creator from her family and living space. To meet the requirement of the factory level mass production, designer/creator was compelled to alienate herself from her family, significant others and most often her immediate community. This detachment can only promote a creation which is possibly detached from the true need of the community. Our alternate model stress local community based creation process with the help of materials that can be procured locally. Creator getting the opportunity to express her creative selves with the help of materials procured from the local sources will be able catch the essence of traditional cultural values of the place and the society. Thus, this product will become a cultural artifact rather than a mare commodity. Creation with conscious understanding of the cultural values will also provide a purpose for the creator and a sense of meaning. She can code her personal life experience and deep understanding in to her creation in the process of creating a meaningful artifact. As we have elaborated in the process of commodification and dicommodification of the artifacts, once users procure the artifacts by some exchange value they can again transform it to another artifact by assigning some personal meaning to it. We emphasises this process of personal coding to a product and a consumption practice as a prerequisite for practicing art of fashion. This coding with personal meaning will add a level of emotional and cultural value that will not be susceptible to psychological obsolescence.

Sustainable practice of production here will not only promote recycle, refurbish and reuse philosophy of circular economy but will also facilitate reduction or better elimination of the adverse impact of production and consumption on the environment. But this conscious creation of artifacts needs to be endorsed by a conscious practice of consumption. Conscious consumption can only develop the context for the conscious creation and vice-versa. Now, the question is whether consumers can develop and practice conscious consumption habit where they will value the cultural, social and personal meaning offered by the product.

Second facet of our *C3* model of *Art of Fashion* is *community connection* which emphasises that a creation process based within the immediate community of the creator helps her to live by the values and ideology of the community. Close proximity of the immediate community which comprises of family, relatives, neighbours and users of the products will provide the sense of connection and consciousness about the journey of the artifact, its role in the life of the users and its role in the community. Creator also gets the critical feedback about her creation and the way users value the meaning added by the creator and then add their own meaning in it. Creator, designer and the users of the artifact all become conscious about this meaning creation and possibly will develop the art of appreciating the inherent value of the product instead of succumbing to the marketing propaganda of fashion trend based on the psychological obsolescence.

Our third facet of *C3* model of *Art of fashion* is *conservation* which again hinges on the other two facets, *conscious creation & consumption* and *community connection*. When designer and creator starts creating artifact with consciousness and community starts valuing intrinsic value of the product as artifact, then we can expected that both the creator and consumers will show more responsibility toward the impact of the creation and consumption on their ecology. This very consciousness of both creator and consumers will strengthen the conscience footprint and will encourage sustainable lifestyle of creation and appreciation of purpose rooted in the conservation of the ecosystem.

In this propose *C3* model of *Art of Fashion,* Creator of fashion will not create just to exercise her creative imagination but will be motivated by a more profound purpose, called meaning of life. This may sound a utopian and somehow impractical idea in the world that endorses fetish commoditization and impulsive consumption driven economic model. But if we look at the creation and consumption pattern of the luxury product our idea of creation of artifact with meaning making process will be distinctly visible. The whole industry of luxury product making and consuming is based on the marketing of handcrafted artifact which carry the signature of the creator. Consumers enjoy the sacrifice of a substantial amount of their resources in terms of economic, time, physical and psychological energy to posses this signature items. Passing on these items which bear personal code of the creator (also some meaning added by the users) to other members of the family is a very common practice. Although this business of luxury product is based on their claimed that items have the personal signature of the creator, it is devoid of almost all the facets of our proposed *Art of Fashion*. With the profit making motives this production of luxury items cannot become a creation that has been created with greater consciousness of community connection and conservation of ecology. Recent case of Burberry, one of the luxury brands of this kind validates our argument. It has been reported that Burberry management has destroyed their unsold products by setting them on fire (BBC, 2018). It is said that management has not heisted to resort to this kind of ecologically irresponsible operation form the motive of protecting their brand equity so to ensure future economic growth.

We will now get into the illustration of a craft called *'Kantha'* made based on traditional way of creation and consumption that will show how the *C3* model of *Art of Fashion* with its triadic facets of consciousness, community and conservation has been practiced for long in the traditional socio cultural fabric of rural India.

'Kantha' as the Paradigm of Sustainable Fashion

Kantha is a handicraft product made from used fabric by the women in the state of Bengal in India. Traditionally Kantha is crafted by running stitches and a distinct type of embroidery on the layers of used fabric-worn out sari or dhoti. Kantha is an indigenous craft in Bengal where rural women who reuse and refurbish their worn out sarees to make quilt, comforter, spreads and wraps for their family members, especially for the new born babies. Three or more saris are placed in layers and a running stitch or "Kantha stitch" is used across the length and width to hold the layers together. These 'Kantha', now a product like a wrap, is then embellished with 'kantha' the embroidery to depict different motifs, and themes from the folklore, and culture. So, Kantha is considered as a cultural artifact. The stitching of the discarded saris is made by the threads that are also pulled out from the borders of the used sari. Thus, Kantha is an interesting craft representing the creative refurbishment of the used product.

Traditionally Kantha was sewed for the personal consumption and some time as a gift for the relatives. It was never produced for commercial purposes. However arrival of machine made alternatives of the Kantha, slowly made it a lost art. During late 20th century Indian Government took the initiative to revive the age old handlooms and handicraft products as part of sustainable craft clusters development and rural livelihood mission. Fashion institutes like National Institute of Fashion Technology as an implementing agency has been extending their designing and marketing intervention to make this craft contemporary and marketable to the urban consumers. Establish designers also rediscovered Kantha as a lucrative product for commercialization. As a result new avatar of Kantha started appearing at different fashion boutique and stores in different forms and shapes. The "Kantha embroidery" has started embellished cotton and silk saris, shawls, bed linen, cushions and other items of home furnishing. Although this modern transformation of the Kantha is not catching the essence of Kantha as a recycled, reuse, and refurbished craft, however, we cannot deny the contribution of this transformation to revive the concept of Kantha and marketing it to the fashion conscious millennial and generation Z.

The skill of making Kantha from the used sari has been passed on to generations, from grandmother, to mother to daughter. This craft is popular among the rural women, irrespective of their socioeconomic class, the affluent landlord's wife makes her own rich embroidered quilt and wife of a peasant makes wrap for her child in a frugal manner. Woman in their craftsmanship make different interesting motifs and themes on the Kantha, representing artifacts of a particular culture and everyday life by colourful threads. So, Kantha becomes a medium for self expression for the woman who is making it and carries the essence of a particular culture. Moreover very often Kantha making session becomes a way of socialization and a break from the family chores for the rural women.

Generally the aged woman members of the family like grandmother or aunt start making this Kantha especially when family is blessed with a new born. The new born baby needs soft wrap and Kantha as a soft and colourful piece of fulfil this purpose effectively. People in many of the rural and suburban places in the state of Bengal in India have grown up with the Kantha created by their 'thakuma' or 'didima' (grandmother). 'My thakuma has made this Kantha when I was two years old' is a precious sentiment carried by many people and many of them preserve this Kantha as a childhood memory. It takes several months of patient and diligent work to make one Kantha out of three to four old sari or dhoti. At the end of the family chores senior women members of the family used to sit to make the Kantha with other members of the family. It was a common scene in the family to see other members making Kantha while sharing their life experiences. Kantha was also use to present as a gift to near and dear one who accept them as a proud and valuable possession because of the hard craftsmanship and sentiments that was invested in making this. Kantha has thus become an artifact with symbolic meaning of cultural, social and personal meaning. Kantha promotes the culture of reuse, recycle, and refurbish mantra of modern circular economy. It encourages creation of artifacts with personal and socio cultural meaning. When one senior member put her experience hand work to make a Kantha she transforms some pieces of old wear out clothes into a meaningful artefact carrying her emotions and symbol of care and love. The users of Kantha value this token of love and emotion and carry it as a remembrance of the creator. Kantha thus created with a conscious choice of reuse, recycle old clothes and inevitably sew the socio cultural fabric of the community. It builds connection among the members of the family and nurture the culture of valuing intrinsic meaning of products with sensible understanding. Kantha, a cultural and social artifact made from used materials traditionally also conserve the ecosystem by infusing new life into the product and abandoning the environmentally devastating 'make-use-discard' trend. Kantha thus exemplify how one of the age old Indian tradition to nurture the so called modern concept of sustainable living.

KANTHA AND THE ART OF FASHION

We argue that a community based model which promotes the community oriented production enterprise with Kantha as a product and rural women as its entrepreneur can meet the requirement of sustainable fashion illustrated through Art of Fashion by providing the opportunity for a. Conscious creation and consumption b. Community connection and c. Conservation and can promote a sustainable life style.

Conscious Creation and Consumption

Kantha fulfils utilitarian need by using materials which are generally discarded after use. Thus it promotes the basic premises of circular economy: reduce, reuse, and recycle. It also promotes a philosophy of thrift and frugality in contrast of the mindless consumerism. So it provides a practical meaning by encouraging the fulfilment of the basic need in a ways that are materially more sustainable and indirectly more responsible towards the environment.

Kantha is the outcome of a conscious creation as the materials and meaning are attuned to the particularities of the area, which the creator creates by working with the natural resources to fit the climate of the local area. Kantha represents the distinctive facets of culture of a specific area and its customs, beliefs and traditions. Design of Kantha also provides practical meaning in terms of fulfilling utilitarian need through reuse, reduce, recycle, reproduce and refurbish. It requires minimal processing and no wastage.

Kantha is a medium which offers the opportunity to experiment with the creative self expression. Artisans work on different motifs and themes on the Kantha with the aim to satisfy the need and test of somebody near and dear to her heart. Getting and avenue of self expression and the sense of creating something without any self interest can provide a sense of purpose.

Community Connection

Kantha typically brings the nostalgic feeling of the grandmother, mother and some other elderly person. Motherly figures in the family start searching for the used sari to start the craft of Kantha as soon as they hear the news of a new born. "My Grandmother spent months to make this Kantha for me" is a very common dialogue that one can find in the family of the rural peasant, and industrial workers. So Kantha promotes relationship. Affluent ladies of the villages use Kantha. Thus bring some social equity by sharing the same consumption pattern of the economically deprived class. Moreover, crafting Kantha is a household work that provides the opportunity to spend time with the family members while get some economic benefits. This concept endorses the idea of the community oriented production enterprise in contrast to the traditional corporate model which separates an individual from her family and community to make her a labour.

Conservation of Ecology

Kantha promotes the creation process based on reuse and recycle of material. The core purpose of kantha is to ensure that old clothing is upcycled with a meaningful purpose. The wastage of old clothing is not only prevented but also purchase of new one delayed. The clothes being woven out of cotton ensures that these have recyclable value and are a direct impact on the ecological cycle. This is one of the critical aspects of conservation of ecology.

The authors posit Kantha as a paradigm for circular fashion because it promotes the three facets of our *C3* model of *Art of Fashion*. Traditionally Kantha was never considered as a means of earning money for the rural women and thus in the proposed community oriented production enterprise we can suggest Kantha puts culture, social fabrics in one layer after another and then sewed them with the colourful threads of the creative self expression.

This community based social enterprise model is in contrast of the prevailing "Product, Promote, and Progress" model and promote more of social innovation than technological innovation thus brings meaning to life.

Our qualitative exploration of existing and potential consumers endorsed the basic facets of our theoretical model. Participants of the focus group reiterated their emotional attachment with Kantha. One of the participants in her late 40's was remembering how she has preserved Kantha used for her daughter, "I have retained most of the Kantha that I have used for my daughter. They are of different sizes, showing the journey of her life from childhood to adolescence to youth. All these Kantha were made in the family from used sari in traditional manner." Interestingly she now-a-days goes to organised store to buy wrap made from brand new fabric with Kantha stitch to give as a gift to new born. Another participant in the same age group said that she buys Kantha stitch sari and Kantha connotes an image of expensive and premium things in her mind. She says that "marketing and promotion of Kantha for a considerable time has transformed this rural economic artifact to a luxury urban lifestyle commodity." Participants in their mid twenties also share their fond memories of using Kantha.

One of the participants of focus group in her 20's was recalling the fond memories of having a Kantha with some beautiful images of birds and flowers. She said that even the touch of the motifs on the surface of the Kantha used to give her good feelings. Kantha according to her offers a bed time story to the kids who can dream about the motifs of different animated and in-animated objects. Kantha is still a much used items in her family. Her aunt still finds time to sew Kantha for the new born babies in their family and family of relatives. Another interesting fact that came out from our focus group interview is diversification of Kantha in different product categories which made it popular among the youth. One participant in her 20's said that she uses Kantha bag, a hand bag made of fabric with Kantha stitch. This opinion is corroborated by other FGD participants also. To them kantha is now a name of an embroidery which has high aesthetic and economic value.

The authors look into the future of the C3 Art of fashion model and feel confident to suggest that kantha will continue to live in the world of fashion not only as a wrap but also as traditional embroidery with multi dimensional applications. In this paper kantha as a wrap is used as an example of a conscious consumption and creation, ecologically responsible product that also has personal, social and cultural meaning. Therefore such an example of an age old craft having such contemporary usage and applicability will show that there are various traditional crafts which may have pride of position in global fashion industry and can show the way to achieve the Art of Fashion with conscious creation & consumption, mindful connection to community and conservation of ecology.

REFERENCES

Andrews, D. (2015). The circular economy, design thinking and education for sustainability. Local Economy. *The Journal of the Local Economy Policy Unit, 30*(3), 305–315. doi:10.1177/0269094215578226

Appadurai, A. (1995). *The social life of the things: Commodities in cultural perspective*. Cambridge: Cambridge University Press.

Aristotle, & Hope, R. (1968). *Metaphysics*. Ann Arbor: University of Michigan Press.

Bangladesh factory collapse toll passes 1,000. (2013, May 10). Retrieved from https://www.bbc.com/news/world-asia-22476774

Boucher, J., & Friot, D. (2017). *Primary Microplastics in the Oceans: A Global Evaluation of Sources*. doi:10.2305/IUCN.CH.2017.01.en

Brito, M. P. D., Carbone, V., & Blanquart, C. M. (2008). Towards a sustainable fashion retail supply chain in Europe: Organisation and performance. *International Journal of Production Economics, 114*(2), 534–553. doi:10.1016/j.ijpe.2007.06.012

Burberry burns bags, clothes and perfume worth millions. (2018, July 19). Retrieved from https://www.bbc.com/news/business-44885983

Christopher, M., Lowson, R., & Peck, H. (2004). Creating agile supply chains in the fashion industry. *International Journal of Retail & Distribution Management*, *32*(8), 367–376. doi:10.1108/09590550410546188

Elkington, J. (1994). Towards the Sustainable Corporation: Win-Win-Win Business Strategies for Sustainable Development. *California Management Review*, *36*(2), 90–100. doi:10.2307/41165746

Elkington, J. (1998). *Cannibals with forks: the triple bottom line of 21st century business*. New Society Publishers.

Ertekin, Z. O., & Atik, D. (2014). Sustainable Markets. *Journal of Macromarketing*, *35*(1), 53–69. doi:10.1177/0276146714535932

Fashion Industry Waste Statistics. (2020, January 8). Retrieved from https://edgexpo.com/fashion-industry-waste-statistics/

Kopytoff, I. (1986). The cultural biography of things: Commoditization as process. In A. Appadurai (Ed.), *The Social Life of Things: Commodities in Cultural Perspective* (pp. 64–92). Cambridge: Cambridge University Press. doi:10.1017/CBO9780511819582.004

Marx, K. (1986). *Capital a critique of political economy*. London: Penguin Books.

Quantis, and Climate Works Foundation. (2018). *Measuring Fashion: Insights from the Environmental Impact of the Apparel and Footwear Industries Study*. Author.

Ritzer, G., & Stepnisky, J. (2018). Sociological theory (8th ed.). Academic Press.

Smith, A. (1776). *An Inquiry into the Nature and Causes of the Wealth of Nations Book 1*. London: W. Strahan and T. Cadell.

Szokan, N. (2016, June 30). The fashion industry tries to take responsibility for its pollution. *Washington Post*. Retrieved from https://www.washingtonpost.com/national/health-science/the-fashion-industry-tries-to-take-responsibility-for-its-pollution/2016/06/30/11706fa6-3e15-11e6-80bc-d06711fd2125_story.html?noredirect=on

Taylor, C. (1978). Feuerbach and Roots of Materialism. *Political Studies*, *26*(3), 417–421. doi:10.1111/j.1467-9248.1978.tb01307.x

Tipping, M. A. (2012). *Quadruple Bottom Line Reporting – Would You Adopt It For Your organisation*. https://thetippingpoint.me/2012/05/09/quadruple-bottom-line-reporting-would-you-adopt-it-for-your-organisation

Todd, D. (2011). *You Are What You Buy: Postmodern Consumerism and the Construction of Self.* Retrieved: https://hilo.hawaii.edu/campuscenter/hohonu/volumes/documents/Vol10x12YouAreWhatYouBuy-PostmodernConsumerismandtheConstructionofSelf.pdf

Turker, D., & Altuntas, C. (2014). Sustainable supply chain management in the fast fashion industry: An analysis of corporate reports. *European Management Journal, 32*(5), 837–849. doi:10.1016/j.emj.2014.02.001

United Nations Sustainable Development Summit. (2015). New York: UN.

Walker, S. (2014). *Wasteland: Sustainability and Designing with Dignity.* Academic Press.

Chapter 10
Self-Construals Theory Applications for an Effective Communication of Sustainable Luxury

Ludovica Gallo
https://orcid.org/0000-0001-8534-0458
LUISS Guido Carli, Italy

Matteo De Angelis
LUISS Guido Carli, Italy

Cesare Amatulli
University of Bari, Italy

ABSTRACT

The next generations of luxury buyers will be increasingly involved in social and environmental issues, gradually asking for more CSR accountability. Luxury maisons, despite recognizing sustainability as a business imperative, seldom communicate their initiatives due to the apparent incompatibility of the two worlds. Past research has demonstrated how the concurrent elicitation of conflicting concepts of self-enhancement and self-transcendence typical of sustainable luxury communication negatively impact brand evaluation. This study investigates how self-construal manipulation plays a role in mitigating the cognitive disfluency phenomenon arising from CSR communication by luxury brands. On a sample of Americans and Italians, three different priming conditions are tested: an independent prime, an interdependent (collective) prime, and a neutral prime. The results of the experiment reveal that eliciting the interdependent self-construal by emphasizing collective concepts prior to the CSR message exposure positively affects brand evaluation via an increase in information fluency.

DOI: 10.4018/978-1-7998-2728-3.ch010

INTRODUCTION

In their seminal work on stakeholder marketing and CSR communication, Smith, Palazzo and Bhattacharya (2010) argue on how brands, understanding their power to satisfy consumers' self-definitional needs, have started to see in CSR and cause related marketing a strong tool to build positive and strong links with the consumers. A related study from Curras-Perez et al. (2009), builds on the notion of consumer-company (C-C) identification to bring empirical evidence on the positive effect of CSR based C-C identification on brand attractiveness. Brand attractiveness is hence defined by the authors as "the positive evaluation of its identity, examined and assessed in relation to how it helps consumers satisfy their self-definitional needs" (p. 550); in the same paper, it is demonstrated that brand attractiveness has a positive relationship with CSR image via two intermediate variables: brand prestige and brand distinctiveness. Specifically, it is assessed by the authors that socially responsible companies are perceived as more prestigious and as more unique and distinct from other corporations, arguing that a brand with such characteristics will be evaluated by consumers as a valuable element through which achieving an enhanced and distinctive self-concept.

Bhattacharya and Sen (2003) add that if C-C identification wants to be achieved, companies shall pursue a coherent, effective and clear brand identity communication strategy. Such element is assessed as fundamental to foster brand bonding through the communication of the identity traits that consumers are likely to perceive as distinctive and close to their own. Notably, industry reports such as McKinsey's "The State of Fashion 2019", have indeed pointed out some important consumer shifts towards a more value oriented consumption:

Over the past three years a third of consumers worldwide have expanded the scope of their purchasing decisions to incorporate principled values and views. A new global ethos is emerging, and billions of people are using consumption as a means to express their deeply-held beliefs. (The State of Fashion 2019, p. 45)

The report identifies radical transparency, purpose-driven brand image and sustainability to be some of the key drivers that will be attracting consumers and talents to luxury and fashion companies in the upcoming years, prospecting the next generations of luxury buyers to be increasingly involved in social and environmental issues, gradually asking for more CSR accountability on companies' side. Supporting this view, the 2017 Cone Gen Z CSRstudy, reports that out of the 1000 Americans belonging to Gen Zinterviewed, 94% believes that companies should address social and environmental issues; the report identifies "Poverty and Hunger", "Environment" and "Human Rights" as the top three issues Gen Z would like companies to address. Nearly nine-in-ten of them state that they would rather buy from a socially or/and environmentally active brand over one that is not, expressing their willingness to switch to a brand associated with a good cause having similar price and quality of a non-CSR-oriented company. It can then be argued that it is no coincidence that lately the fashion and luxury industry have observed the rise of brands characterized by strong values and identity, brands that have not been afraid to speak up for what they stand for. Worthy of note is the example of the direct-to-consumer label Reformation that has made sustainability commitment the main pillar of its brand DNA. The brand, famous for its distinctive values and green philosophy, has experienced a steady growth of an average of 60 percent y-o-y since 2014 and an estimated revenue of $100 Million in 2017 according to Business of Fashion (2017)."Being naked is #1 most sustainable option. We are #2" is how Reformation narrates itself to consumers, this motto being just one example of how the company has been communicating its effort and commitment to environmental causes to its audience. On the other hand, also leading luxury conglomerates have recently started to take a stance on environmental and social causes: LVMH has declared its commitment to having equal gender representation in executive ranks by 2020, while Kering has implemented the "Environmental P&L"with the aim of "making the various environmental impacts of the Group's activities visible, quantifiable, and comparable". Still, the luxury industry has been relatively quiet about such initiatives, making them public only in annual reports having stakeholders as their ultimate audience or in dedicated sections of the corporate website. Thus while the benefits from CSR have been recognized by high-end maisons, as well as the demand from their consumers for a more sustainable corporate conduct, CSR communication is still weak if not inexistent for many players in the market.

In the light of the relevant literature on the subject, this paper aims at proposing a novel solution for sustainable luxury communication. The theoretical framework will be articulated in three sections: (1) the state of art, in which findings and opinions of scholars on sustainable luxury (SL) will be analysed, (2) the identification of an informational issue around SL based on the relevant literature and (3) the identification of a processing disfluency issue around SL communication.

THEORETICAL FOUNDATIONS

The State of Art: Conflicting Views on Sustainability

The existence of a possible overlap between luxury and sustainability worlds is a controversial subject in the literature. Kapferer (2013) and Godart and Seong (2014) see luxury and sustainability as compatible universes as they share the notions of beauty, rarity and durability. In his paper, Kapferer encourages the luxury industry to lead the way by redefining the concept of luxury dream no more as a selfish and individual one, but as deeply bonded to ethical issues, envisioning the rich of the future choosing a high-end product to signal not only his taste, but also his altruism. Additionally, Godart and Seong (2014), suggest possible ways to achieve sustainable fashion: a "degrowth" strategy featuring slower fashion cycles or an "innovative" strategy that sees the introduction of more sustainable materials in the production process and the recycling of the discarder clothes. This view chimes with the work of Joy et al. (2010) which opens up to the possibility of having luxury brands that are both "green and gold", envisioning sustainable luxury as the perfect connubium between fashion ideals and environmental sustainability values. Indeed, stressing on the long-standing concern of luxury brands for supporting local craftmanship, high ethical standards in sourcing and efficient use of raw materials and opposing them to the planned obsolescence practices of fast fashion, the authors see in luxury a more congruent business model to match with the values of ethical consumption. Supporting this "green and gold" stream of research, an important contribution to cross-cultural literature comes from Cervellon and Carey (2011) who investigated individual and social consumers' motives behind sustainable luxury consumption across four culturally diverse samples. Interestingly, the authors identify several ego-centred values satisfied through the consumption of green luxury, one of them being the ability of sustainable luxury to grant to the consumer a "guilt free pleasure", a value particularly relevant for French and Italian samples where the feeling of guilt related to expensive purchases was more prominent. Durable quality was another ego-centred value deemed relevant by all samples; durability was seen as the strongest link between luxury and sustainability as the participants could clearly point out how durable products have a lower impact on the environment. This piece of research looks at sustainable luxury under a new light, focusing on how this kind of consumption would not only satisfy society's welfare but also individual, ego-centred motives. On the companies' side, Lichenstein et al. (2014) provide support on the notion that involving in CSR behaviour can result in corporate benefits such as more favourable brand evaluations and increased purchase behaviour. Others like Ducrot-Lochard and Murat (2011), believe that the luxury industry will eventually head towards sustainability as its customers have now redefined their high quality expectations to include environmental factors. Supporting the compatibility of luxury and sustainability, an experiment conducted by Steinherd et al. (2013) shows the positive effect of eco-labelling on consumers perception of luxury products. Respondents were asked to imagine scenarios in a supermarket in which they had to choose between toilet paper (a 'utilitarian' product) or 'fancy napkins' (their example of a luxury) that were either marked with an eco-label or not. It is claimed in the results that for both the utilitarian and the luxury product, the environmental label positively affected consumers perception. Yet, the generalization of such finding to the whole luxury industry might be debatable as luxury cannot exclusively be defined as merely unnecessary or non-utilitarian, but should also include the dimensions of beauty, dream and aspiration (Kapferer, 1996; Kapferer & Michaut-Denizeau, 2014; Kapferer & Michaut, 2015). Still, extensive literature has highlighted the difficulties and even the risks arising from the merge of these two worlds, that are luxury and sustainability. An empirical study from Acabou and Dekhili (2013) reports an example of one of the possible backfire effects coming from the introduction of a green luxury product: even though convinced of the benefits of recycling, the experiment participants reported a strong negative attitude towards the presence of recycled material in a luxury product, due to a perceived quality trade-off. Likewise, a study from De Angelis et al. (2017) has also investigated the possible expression of sustainability through design features, however results show that for durable products targeted to consumers that are knowledgeable about the brand, the design should not differ from the label signature one. Along the same lines, Voyer and Beckham (2014) observed in their experiment that participants ranked luxury bags labelled as sustainable as less luxurious; additionally, in contrast with the view of Kapferer (2013), Godart and Seong (2014) and Joy et al. (2010), the authors stress how inherent luxury values such as hedonism, expense, and 'inessentiality' are in strong opposition to the values of responsibility such as altruism and moderation. Going through the relevant literature on the subject, it seems clear how academic research on consumers' sensitivity on ethics in the luxury industry have brought up contrasting findings and opinions, making the linkages between luxury and sustainability even more complex. On the basis of this scenario, starting the talk about CSR with luxury buyers seems a tough challenge.

The Informational Problem: When Speaking Up Becomes Necessary

Sproles et al. (1978) argues that efficient decision making requires consumers to be fully informed. In their study, Kapferer and Michaut-Denizeau (2014) reported that 33.8 percent of their sample, after reading a definition of luxury, declared luxury and sustainability to be contradicting concepts. To investigate the drivers of this perceived disconnect between the two concepts, the authors performed a regression analysis with nine predictors. The results unveil two main variables causing perceived incompatibility: the consumers' perception of luxury as superficial (i.e. failure of brand true values communication to the customer) and the belief that luxury causes social unrest (i.e. enhances social disparity). Based on these findings the authors stress that "luxury brands need to promote their true values credibly to consumers. If consumers cannot perceive how the true values of luxury are in line with sustainable development principles, they continue to perceive only superficiality in the industry" (p. 15). A problem of incomplete information has also been highlighted by related literature: Carrigan and Attalla (2001) findings suggest that most consumers are confused or have limited knowledge about luxury companies that are engaged in CSR and those who aren't, most of them being skeptical about companies actually differing on an ethical ground. If there was more information available, consumers would at least be able to discriminate more in their purchasing decisions. The authors stress the need for luxury companies to spread information about their ethical initiatives more widely. Similarly, Davies et al. (2012) reports that 70% of the respondents in his study appeared disinformed about ethical luxury, while being quite aware about sustainable commodity goods instead. Participants of the study reported that information on green luxury is hard to find, highlighting an overall lack of publicity and promotion of such offers and the consequent failure in making consumers aware of their existence. Another widespread misbelief has been identified by scholars in the so called "fallacy of clean luxury" (Davies et al., 2012; Achabou et al., 2013; Kapferer & Michaut-Denizeau, 2014) where luxury products are seen by the consumers as completely dissociated from any form of ethical issues, trusting the brand name and seeing in the higher price tag a sort of "ethical guarantee". On the basis of these findings, the need for luxury maisons to be more vocal about their sustainable initiatives has been brought up by the consumers themselves.

Individualism, Conflicting Motives and Processing Disfluency

In his "The structure of hip consumerism" Joseph Heath (2001) argues on how the modern consumer is now driven by the urge to avoid conformity and by the desire to stand out from the mass, in an attempt to affirm and express his identity, bringing to light a new and more individualized form of consumption. This phenomenon becomes even more accentuated in the case of luxury consumption whose underlying motives rely on status signaling, self-expression and self-affirmation. Culture also plays a crucial role in shaping consumption motivations and attitudes, with the most evident differences arising between individualist and collectivist cultures (Amatulli et al., 2016; Cervellon & Shammas, 2013; Triandis et al., 1989; Miller et al., 1990). Citing Triandis (1996) "in collectivist cultures people are interdependent within their in-groups (family, tribe, nation, etc.), give priority to the goals of their in-groups, shape their behaviour primarily on the basis of in-group norms, and behave in a communal way" while "in individualist societies people are autonomous and independent from their in-groups; they give priority to their personal goals over the goals of their in-groups" (p. 909). These cultural characteristics have several implications on luxury consumption motivations. For instance, a study from Amatulli and Guido (2009) identifies self-fulfilment and self-confidence to be among the main values behind high-end consumption in the Italian market. According to Chiao (2009) and Shukla and Purani (2012), people in the United States and Western Europe generally value uniqueness and self-expression, constantly finding ways to to define themselves as different from the group. Additionally, Han et al. 2010, explain how luxury buying is instrumental for self-expression and self-representation purposes. These self-centred inner motives behind high-end consumption have been identified to be in contrast with the self-transcendence values of caring for society and environment related to CSR initiatives. Based on the theory of basic human values by Shwartz (1987), a study from Torelli et al. (2012) has pointed out how the simultaneous activation of self-enhancement and self-transcendence concepts arising from communication of CSR information during a luxury product purchase, negatively affects brand evaluation and attitude. Indeed, as hypothesized by Schwartz, the concurrent pursuit of values coming from conflicting sets (universalism and benevolence versus power and achievement) gives raise to processing disfluency. It is argued by the authors that the cause of the disfluency has also to be found in the fact that people's attitudes toward a persuasive message are less favourable when the frame of the message conflicts with their higher-order self-regulatory goal than when the frame matches this goal (Torelli et al., 2012, Lee & Aaker 2004). Torelli et al. 2012 suggest that the raise of this perceived disconnect between luxury and sustainability motivations might especially hurt brands that build an image strongly linked to self enhancement concepts, which is the case of many high-end companies in the market (Janssen et al., 2017). This view is further explained by Cervellon and Shammas (2013) in the fact that brands that are perceived as more conspicuous due to the prominence of their logo or particular attributes of their product do not fit with the concept of sustainability at the eye of the consumer, thus creating skepticism and lack of credibility around CSR initiatives undergone by such firms. Harmful consequences of such perceived disconnect are highlighted by Palazzo et al. (2010) who state that when communicated values appear contradictory with brand behaviour, the resulting brand incoherence will undermine consumer-company identification, thus lowering brand attractiveness. The next step of this paper will be to propose a solution to the processing disfluency issue emerging from sustainable luxury communication and highlighted by academics, leveraging on the notions of self-construal theory.

Self-Construal Theory

Cross et al. (2009) give a definition of self-construal as "how individuals define and make meaning of the self in relation to others" (p. 512). Crediting the work of Markus and Kitayama (1991), Cross et al. (2009) further identify two self-construals: *independent* and *interdependent*. The independent self-construal sees the individual as separate from others, having the aim to confirm his uniqueness, internal traits and self-coherence across different contexts. In contrast, the interdependent self-construal pictures the individual as striving to subordinate his personal goals in favour of in-group goals and regulating his behaviour in order to maintain in-group harmony. While authors agree that all individuals possess both self-construals, they also assert that cultural context will promote the development of either one or the other in a more prominent way, resulting in variability in the elaboration and retrieval of such dimensions across cultures. Specifically, it is argued that the independent self-construal is more prominent in Western countries, while the interdependent self-construal is more accentuated in non-Western countries.

Framing research brings some important insights on the relationship between self-construals and attitudes towards sustainability. A study from Brewer and Kramer (1986) on social dilemmas demonstrates how people prosocial response depends on the extent to which they "think of themselves as single and autonomous individuals or whether, in contrast, they regard themselves as sharing membership in and identification with a larger aggregate or social unit" (p. 545). Cooley (1902) defines the empirical self as all the statements made by an individual, including the words "I", "me", "mine" and "myself".

On the basis of this elaboration, Triandis (1989) argues that such statements that people make, that define the self, influence the way they retrieve information in several ways:

1. Individuals will sample self-relevant information more frequently than information that is not self-relevant. Individuals will sample self-relevant information more quickly than information that is not self-relevant.
2. Individuals will assess information supporting their self-structure more positively than information that is in contrast with their self-structure.

Further, Triandis (1989) defines the self as "an active agent that promotes differential sampling, processing, and evaluation of information from the environment, and thus leads to differences in social behavior" (p. 506). In the same paper, the author shows how different aspects of the self (private, public and collective self) are sampled differentially depending on how individualist and complex the culture of belonging is: subjects belonging to highly individualist and complex cultures will be more likely to retrieve private-self construals and less likely to retrieve collective self-construals. It is then concluded from the author that people in individualist cultures such as those from North and Western Europe and North America, sample with high probability elements of the private self, while people from collectivistic cultures, like those from Africa, South America and Asia, sample with high probability elements of the collective self. Indeed, by definition, individualist subjects identify and describe their self-image more in terms of "I" than in terms of "We"

(Hofstede cultural dimensions, 1980); such self-construals have proven to have a strong influence on personal values formation and their willingness in engaging in prosocial behaviours (e.g. Brewer et. al, 1986; Gardner et al., 1999; Miller et al., 1990). Similarly, the two baskets theory elaborated by Trafimow et al. (1991) states that cultural background determines the accessibility of private and collective self-concepts; specifically if private and collective self-concepts were to be organized in two separate baskets, people from individualist cultures would be more likely to retrieve information from the private self-concepts basket as opposed to the collective self-concepts basket. In his paper, Trafimow demonstrates how priming Chinese and North American subjects with a collective (private) self-prime made them retrieve collective (individualistic) cognitions.

Self-Construal Manipulation: Research Questions and Hypothesis Formulation

On the basis of the above findings it could be speculated that in order to activate an individual's prosocial response, aspects from the collective-self need to be recalled and retrieved. This task might come across as particularly challenging in individualist subjects. However, research on self-representation offers relevant insights investigating on the possibility to shift from social to collective self. Brewer and Gardner (1996) illustrate how the proportion of interdependent self-construals can be increased through a word search task in which participants are instructed to circle either plural (collective) pronouns (i.e. we, us etc.) or singular (individualistic) pronouns. Trafimow et al. (1991) also demonstrated another successful method of self-construal manipulation: in their study participants were exposed to the story of a ruler who has to choose a general to send to war based on either individualistic motives (increasing the ruler's status) or collectivistic concerns (the general was part of the ruler's family). In a later study, Gardner et al. (1999) proved the effectiveness of both methods by using them in their experiments, showing how in the interdependent priming condition the embracement of collectivistic social values was fostered.

Extending the above-mentioned findings to the subject of interest, that is luxury sustainability communication, priming could play a decisive role in green luxury communication coping with the processing disfluency raising from conflicting motives, namely self-enhancement vs self-transcendence. This piece of research aims at addressing the following research questions:

When communicating sustainable luxury initiatives:

1. Does interdependent priming help mitigating cognitive disfluency in individualist subjects?

2. And, if so, does interdependent priming affect final (i.e. post CSR information communication) luxury brand evaluation?

Specifically, it is hypothesized that the use of interdependent (vs independent) priming helps in mitigating or neutralizing the cognitive disfluency rising from sustainable luxury communication by helping individuals retrieve congruent values from the collective self.

H1: Interdependent vs independent priming moderates the effect of cognitive disfluency on luxury brand evaluation in a CRS communication context such that (a) consumers primed with an interdependent self-construal will have a more favourable brand evaluation post CSR information exposure and (b) consumers primed with an independent self-construal will have a less favourable brand evaluation post CSR information exposure.

The hereby proposed conceptual framework was developed to illustrate the hypothesized moderating role of interdependent versus independent priming on the effect of cognitive disfluency on brand evaluation in a luxury sustainability communication context. The model bases its foundations on the theoretical framework developed by Torelli et al. (2012) and integrates it with priming theory, especially referring to Gardner and Brewer priming methods.

Figure 1. Conceptual framework
As a re-adaptation of the model from Torelli et al. (2012)

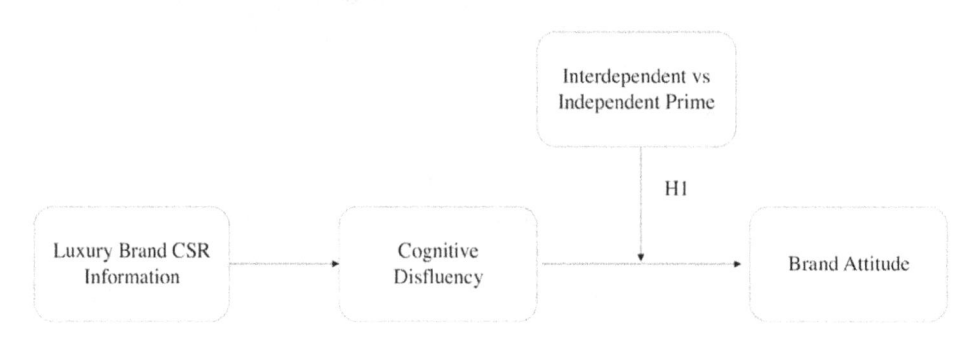

EXPERIMENT

The Moderating Effect of Self-Construal Prime

The experiment had the aim to assess whether self-construal plays a cognitive moderator role in the relationship between information fluency and brand attitude. Rolex has been chosen for this experiment as, in line with the findings of Torelli et al. (2012), its label strongly elicits self-enhancement concepts. Most importantly, this year, the brand has launched its "Perpetual Planet" initiative which is featured on the separate section of the company website "about rolex.org". This serves as the perfect example of a brand with a highly conspicuous profile, which is also active in CSR initiatives but has chosen a subtle communication strategy. The experiment is premised on the idea that eliciting either collective or individual self-construals makes different aspects of the self more accessible which, in turn, influence information processing and attitude formation (Brewer et al., 1986; Gardner et al., 1999; Miller et al., 1990, Triandis, 1989; Gardner et al., 1999).

Participants

An online survey was run. Two hundred and two American and Italian respondents (105 males and 97 females, $M_{age} = 34.63$, $SD_{age} = 14.15$, 60% workers, 27% students, 13% professionals or retired) completed the questionnaire.

Procedure and Measures

Before being randomly assigned to one of three priming conditions, all participants completed a 10-item version of the Singelis self-construal scale (á= .61; D'Amico & Scirma, 2015; a= 0.63) to assess their predominant self-construal before the experiment. The experimental design consisted in three different priming conditions; the priming paradigm employed has been varied and readapted from Brewer and Gardner (1996). In the first condition the individual self-construal was elicited through a word search task in which the respondent were instructed to highlight the pronouns "*I*", "*mine*" and "*me*" in a paragraph about a man about to present his own book in Paris. The narrative was purposely about a man fulfilling his dream of becoming a writer to further emphasize aspects of the individual self such as self-fulfilment and self-enhancement. In the second condition the collective pronouns "*we*", "*us*" and "*our*" were highlighted in a story about a young couple about to marry; also in this case the story was instrumental in emphasizing aspects of the interdependent self such as seeing the self in relationship to others. Lastly, a neutral priming condition was added in which participants searched and highlighted the article *"the"* in a descriptive text. Roughly 33% of the sample was assigned to each of the three experimental conditions and each paragraph contained between 15 and 19 target words. In the second part of the experiment, participants in all conditions saw an ad of the Rolex "Sky-Dweller" watch. The ad featured the Rolex logo as headline, the advertisement message, the image of the watch and the image of an explorer climbing a mountain. The last image carried the headline "Perpetual Planet". After telling how the "Sky Dweller" watch has always been a reliable and precious tool for explorers in their adventures, the copy continued:

Exploration is in the DNA of Rolex. Today Rolex has invested in bold people and transformative ideas, pushing the boundaries of exploration to increase understanding of our world and generate solutions for a healthy, more sustainable future for the generations to come.

After reading the ad, participants were asked to rate their information processing experience on a 7-point Likert scale with four items (1 = very difficult to understand / imagine / process / required a lot of effort, 7 = very easy to understand / imagine/ process/ required very little effort; a= .91; Torelli et al., 2012). Next, respondents also their attitude towards Rolex on a 7-point, three items Likert scale (1 = poor / unfavourable / bad, 7 = excellent / favourable / good; a = .95; Torelli et al., 2012). The last part of the survey consisted in demographic questions.

Results

Sample Predominant Self-Construal

In line with literature findings (Triandis, 1998; Trafimow et al., 1991; Gardner et al., 1996) which categorize Italy and US as individualist cultures, the sample scored with a mean of 4.67 (Min = 2, Max = 7; SD = 1.05) on Singelis independent self-construal items and a mean of 3.73 (Min = 1, Max = 6.6; SD= 1.05) on interdependent items, revealing a prevalently individualist orientation of the sample participants.

Brand Attitude

A factorial MANOVA was run on the three subscales measuring brand attitude; the independent variables were: information fluency (as the mean of its scale items), prime type (coded as 0 = neutral prime, 1 = individual prime, 2 = interdependent prime) and the interaction between such two variables. As predicted, the results yield a significant interaction effect "Fluency*PrimeType" ($F_{(138, 88)} = 11.55$, $p < .001$) and a significant main effect of information fluency on brand attitude

($F(20,88) = 12.60$, $p < .001$); the direct effect of prime type alone on brand attitude resulted non-significant instead ($F(4,88) = 1$, n.s.). The analysis also reports a higher fluency mean score for the interdependent prime group ($M_{Fluency} = 5.21$) versus the mean score of the independent condition ($M_{Fluency} = 5.05$). Furthermore, the post hoc test of multiple comparisons highlights significant mean differences between the interdependent and independent prime groups on all the three subscales of brand attitude (Brand_attitude_1: $M_{diff} = 0.24$, $p < .001$; Brand_attitude_2: $M_{diff} = 0.15$, $p < 0.05$; Brand_attitude_3: $M_{diff} = .37$, $p < .001$). The sample brand attitude means by prime type are reported as follows: Prime Type (0): $M = 5.19$, Prime Type (1): $M = 5.06$; Prime Type (2) = 5.31. As predicted in H1, the individuals assigned to the interdependent priming condition reported a higher brand attitude mean compared to individuals in the independent priming scenario.

Discussion

Results from this experiment grant empirical evidence to the predicted moderating role of self-construal between experienced processing disfluency and brand attitude. As theorized and demonstrated by Torelli et al. 2012, the information disfluency caused by the concurrent elicitation of self enhancement and self-transcendence values taking place in luxury CSR communication negatively impacts brand evaluation.

Building on such finding, the present paper leveraged on priming and self-construal theory to mitigate such cognitive discrepancy and attenuate its backfire effects.

Indeed, even if the sample resulted to be predominantly independent and self-focused in nature and the chosen brand had a very conspicuous profile, the collective self-construal manipulation resulted effective in facilitating the CSR message processing by increasing information fluency and eventually leading to a positive brand evaluation.

GENERAL DISCUSSION

Theoretical Contributions

This study contributes to two main streams of research.

First it brings novel insights in the field of sustainable luxury communication identified by Amatulli et al. (2017) as one of the key research topics in luxury sustainability.

Past research has highlighted possible backfire effects arising from CSR communication in luxury (Acabou & Dekhili 2013; De Angelis, 2017; Voyer & Beckham, 2014) and tried to understand the causes behind such issues (Kapferer et al., 2017). The current study is complementary to such stream of research by proposing a novel solution to possible negative outcomes stemming from luxury sustainability communication and recognized by the literature.

Secondly, by applying findings from priming theory (Torelli et al., 2012; Trafimow et al., 1991; Triandis, 1989) and cross-national studies (Brewer et al., 1986; Gardner et al., 1999; Miller et al., 1990) the present investigation brings a new contribution to the field of consumer behaviour and international marketing applied to the field of luxury. Most importantly, following the pioneer study of Gardener et al. (1996) of self-construal manipulation, the present paper is, at our best knowledge, the first to incorporate self-construals theory in sustainable luxury research with the aim to foster CSR communication in such industry.

Managerial Implications

In light of the recent awakening of a more conscious, ethical and value-oriented consumer, the present research offers valuable findings on sustainable branding and communication. As the CSR talk has been timid and weak on the luxury maisons side, this paper offers some guidance in conveying sustainable initiatives to customers, so to allow brands to better leverage on their sustainable efforts. Particularly it addresses the widespread concern that making sustainability an integral part of the marketing and communication process might negatively impact the brand and spoil the aura of the luxury dream; on the contrary, the findings of our study prove that, when communicated with correct framing practices, CSR marketing does improve consumers' evaluations of the brand.

Particularly, this piece of research gives insights on two of the most influential and profitable luxury consumers' countries, namely Italy and US. Marketing managers, communication managers, brand managers and corporate sustainability teams might leverage on these empirical findings to better build an effective CSR communication strategy. For instance, professionals of the field could integrate collective concepts, narratives and evocative images in their green marketing campaigns and advertisement, aiding the consumer to connect the brand's core values with CSR values.

REFERENCES

Achabou, M. A., & Dekhili, S. (2013). Luxury and sustainable development: Is there a match? *Journal of Business Research*, *66*(10), 1896–1903. doi:10.1016/j.jbusres.2013.02.011

Amatulli, C., De Angelis, M., Costabile, M., & Guido, G. (2017). *Sustainable Luxury Brands: Evidence from Research and Implications for Managers*. Palgrave Advances in Luxury. doi:10.1057/978-1-137-60159-9

Amatulli, C., De Angelis, M., Pino, G., Mileti, A., & Guido, G. (2016). *Shame and negative word-of-mouth: The differential effect in individualistic vs. collectivistic culture*. Academic Press.

Amatulli, C., & Guido, G. (2011). Determinants of purchasing intention for fashion luxury goods in the Italian market: A laddering approach. *Journal of Fashion Marketing and Management, 15*(1), 123–136. doi:10.1108/13612021111112386

Anido Freire, N., & Loussaïef, L. (2018). *When Advertising Highlights the Binomial Identity Values of Luxury and CSR Principles: The Examples of Louis Vuitton and Hermès*. Corp. Soc. Responsib. Environ.

Bhattacharya, C., & Sen, S. (2003). Consumer-Company Identification: A Framework for Understanding Consumers' Relationships with Companies. *Journal of Marketing*, ▪▪▪, 67.

Brewer, M. B., & Gardner, W. L. (1996). Who is this 'we'? Levels of collective identity and self representations. *Journal of Personality and Social Psychology, 71*(1), 83–93. doi:10.1037/0022-3514.71.1.83

Brewer, M. B., & Kramer, R. M. (1986). Choice behavior in social dilemmas: Effects of social identity, group size, and decision framing. *Journal of Personality and Social Psychology, 50*(3), 543–549.

Carrigan, M., & Attalla, A. (2001). The myth of the ethical consumer - do ethics matter in purchase behaviour? *Journal of Consumer Marketing, 18*(7), 560–578. doi:10.1108/07363760110410263

Cervellon, M.-C. (2013). Conspicuous Conservation: Using semiotics to understand sustain- able luxury. *International Journal of Market Research, 55*(5), 695–717. doi:10.2501/IJMR-2013-030

Cervellon, M.-C., & Carey, L. (2011). Consumers' perceptions of 'green': Why and how consumers use eco-fashion and green beauty products. *Critical Studies in Fashion and Beauty, 2*(1-2), 117–138. doi:10.1386/csfb.2.1-2.117_1

Cone. (2017). *Cone Generation Z Study*. Retrieved at: https://www.conecomm.com/2017-cone-gen-z-csr-study-pdf

Cooley, C. H. (1902). *Human nature and the social order*. New York: Seribner.

Cross, S. E., Hardin, E. E., & Swing, B. G. (2009). Independent, relational, and collective-interdependent self-construals. In M. R. Leary & R. H. Hoyle (Eds.), *Handbook of individual differences in social behavior* (pp. 512–526). New York: Guilford.

Currás-Pérez, R., Bigné-Alcañiz, E., & Alvarado-Herrera, A. (2009). The Role of Self-Definitional Principles in Consumer Identification with a Socially Responsible Company. *Journal of Business Ethics, 89*(4), 547–564. doi:10.100710551-008-0016-6

D'Amico, A., & Scrima, F. (2015). The Italian Validation of Singelis's Self-Construal Scale (SCS): A Short 10-Item Version Shows Improved Psychometric Properties. *Current Psychology (New Brunswick, N.J.), 35*(1), 159–168. doi:10.100712144-015-9378-y

Davies, I., Lee, Z., & Ine, A. (2012). Do consumers care about ethical luxury? *Journal of Business Ethics, 106*(1), 37–51. doi:10.100710551-011-1071-y

De Angelis, M., Adıgüzel, F., & Amatulli, C. (2017). The role of design similarity in consumers' evaluation of new green products: An investigation of luxury fashion brands. *Journal of Cleaner Production, 141*(January), 1515–1527. doi:10.1016/j.jclepro.2016.09.230

Ducrot-Lochard, C., & Murat, A. (2011). *Luxe et développement durable: La nouvelle alliance*. Paris: Eyrolles.

Fernandez, C. (2017, December 14). Reformation Raises $25 Million to Fuel Brick-and-Mortar Growth. *Business of Fashion*. Retrieved from: https://bit.ly/2CFA9Fe

Gardner, W. L., Gabriel, S., & Lee, A. Y. (1999). "I" value freedom, but "we" value relationships: Self-construal priming mirrors cultural differences in judgment. *Psychological Science, 10*(4), 321–326. doi:10.1111/1467-9280.00162

Han, Y. J., Nunes, J. C., & Drèze, X. (2010). Signaling status with luxury goods: The role of brand prominence. *Journal of Marketing, 74*(4), 15–30. doi:10.1509/jmkg.74.4.015

Heath, J. (2001). The structure of hip consumerism. *Philosophy and Social Criticism, 27*(6), 1–17. doi:10.1177/019145370102700601

Hofstede, G. (1980). *Culture's consequences*. Beverly Hills, CA: Sage.

Janssen, C., Vanhamme, J., & Leblanc, S. (2017). Should luxury brands say it out loud? Brand conspicuousness and consumer perceptions of responsible luxury. *Journal of Business Research, 77*, 167–174. doi:10.1016/j.jbusres.2016.12.009

Joy, A., Sherry, J. F. Jr, Venkatesh, A., Wang, J., & Chan, R. (2010). Fast fashion, sustainability and the ethical appeal of luxury brands. *Fashion Theory*, *16*(3), 273–296. doi:10.2752/175174112X13340749707123

Kapferer, J. N. (2010). All that glitters is not green: The challenge of sustainable luxury. *European Business Review*, 40–45.

Kapferer, J. N., & Michaut-Denizeau, A. (2014). Is luxury compatible with sustainability? Luxury consumers' viewpoint. *Journal of Brand Management*, *21*(1), 1–22. doi:10.1057/bm.2013.19

Kapferer, J.N., & Michaut-Denizeau, A. (2015). *Luxury and sustainability: a common future? The match depends on how consumers define luxury*. Academic Press.

Lee, A. Y., & Aaker, J. L. (2004). Bringing the Frame into Focus: The Influence of Regulatory Fit on Processing Fluency and Persuasion. *Journal of Personality and Social Psychology*, *86*(2), 205–218. doi:10.1037/0022-3514.86.2.205 PMID:14769079

Lichtenstein, D., Drumwright, M., & Braig, B. (2004). The Effect of Corporate Social Responsibility on customer Donations to Corporate-Supported Nonprofits. *Journal of Marketing*, *68*(4), 6. doi:10.1509/jmkg.68.4.16.42726

McKinsey. (2019). *The State of Fashion 2019*. Retrieved at: https://mck.co/2twu77j

Miller, J. G., Bersoff, D. M., & Harwood, R. L. (1990). Perceptions of social responsibilities in India and the United States: Moral imperatives or personal decisions? *Journal of Personality and Social Psychology*, *58*(1), 33–47. doi:10.1037/0022-3514.58.1.33 PMID:2308074

Schwartz, S., & Bilsky, W. (1987). Toward a psychological structure of human values. *Journal of Personality and Social Psychology*, *53*(3), 550–562. doi:10.1037/0022-3514.53.3.550

Shukla, P., & Purani, K. (2012). Comparing the importance of luxury value perceptions in cross-national contexts. *Journal of Business Research*, *65*(10), 1417–1424. doi:10.1016/j.jbusres.2011.10.007

Singelis, T. (1994). The measurement of independent and interdependent self-construals. *Personality and Social Psychology Bulletin*, *20*(5), 580–591. doi:10.1177/0146167294205014

Smith, N., Palazzo, G., & Bhattacharya, C. (2010). Marketing's Consequences: Stakeholder Marketing and Supply Chain Corporate Social Responsibility Issues. *Business Ethics Quarterly*, *20*(4), 617–641. doi:10.5840/beq201020440

Sproles, G. B., Geistfeld, L. V., & Badenhop, S. B. (1978). Informational inputs as influences on efficient consumer decision-making. *The Journal of Consumer Affairs, 12*(Summer), 88–103. doi:10.1111/j.1745-6606.1978.tb00635.x

Steinhart, Y., Ayalon, O., & Puterman, H. (2013). The effect of an environmental claim on consumers' perceptions about luxury and utilitarian products. *Journal of Cleaner Production, 53*, 277–286. doi:10.1016/j.jclepro.2013.04.024

Torelli, C. J., Basu-Monga, S., & Kaikati, A. (2012). Doing poorly by doing good: Corporate social responsibility and brand concepts. *The Journal of Consumer Research, 38*(5), 948–963. doi:10.1086/660851

Triandis, H. C. (1989). The self and social behavior in differing cultural contexts. *Psychological Review, 96*.

Triandis, H. C. (1995). *Individualism and collectivism*. Boulder, CO: Westview.

Chapter 11
Recommercing Luxury Goods:
A Market in Booming That Needs New Sustainability-Oriented Collaborative Strategies

Floriana Iannone
https://orcid.org/0000-0001-5659-2461
Università degli Studi di Napoli "L'Orientale", Italy

ABSTRACT

The aim of the work is to show that, in the luxury segment, retail operators are called to greater challenges imposed by the expansion of new competitive pressures especially driven by the dynamics of the demand trends increasingly oriented towards sustainability. The work provides a picture of the omnichannel strategies and of the practices adopted by the most important re-commerce players worldwide currently influencing the luxury brand choices in reassessing the opportunity offered by the re-commerce of the so-called 'gently-used' personal goods. The ultimate goal is to underline the need for new collaborative strategies for luxury brands in order to better organize the retailing activities in an omnichannel perspective, especially considering the opportunities opened by the theme of sustainability.

INTRODUCTION

Sustainability goals cannot be achieved by the work of a single company: in order to become a prerogative of consumers too, it requires common rules and regulations for sustainable consumption. This perspective implies a new point of view and suggests collaboration and innovation practices for many companies involved in the

DOI: 10.4018/978-1-7998-2728-3.ch011

engagement of consumers in order to redefine their own value proposition. In other words, competitors in the fashion business should have the common futuristic goal of changing the consumption patterns of buyers, only possible by maintaining the innovative mindset within the organizations: that's why the concept of shopping for second-hand goods has been redefined.

Exploring and proposing solutions and best practices to sustainable development goals (SDGs) in the fashion industry means also rethinking on the design, on the production and, on the distribution moving towards shared business and social objectives.

For example, looking at the distribution strategies the wholesale (the largest channel for personal luxury) grew only 1%, in 2018 hampered by department store performance and a slowdown among specialty stores facing tough competition from the online channel (Bain & Co., 2019). In addiction, if the retail channel continued growing during 2017 (gaining 8%) in 2018, it grew by only 3%, as the strong performance of specialty stores was partially offset by the disappointing performance of department stores globally.

The relentless march toward e-commerce continued, with online sales jumping by 24% in 2017, reaching an overall market share of 9%. The retail channel grew 4% in 2018, with three-quarters of that increase coming from same-store sales growth. A stable growth is expected in 2019 even if the future of luxury is taking shape with several key characteristics, including new kind of consumers (f.e.: Chinese Generation Z), access, ownership, sustainability and social responsibility, the impact of digital across the entire value chain, preference for luxury experiences over products, and consumer networks as a new measure of value.

Luxury resale is a contentious business (expected to grow under the pressure of an accelerated second-hand market favored by digital players with global scale) and the relationship between luxury brands, department stores and companies involved in re-commerce is not exempt from legal problems and disputes. This relationship is still largely unsettled. In fact, if on one hand, the fear among fashion's well-established houses seems to be that luxury resellers are cannibalizing their business, or some of the significant arrays of second-hand good being peddled are fake, allegedly piggybacking on the reputation and appeal of luxury brand; on the other hand, that resale can represent a point of entry-level access for young customers who can't yet shop full-price luxury.

In today's retail marketplace, a mix of thrift stores, high-end stores, and online retailers are recognizing the value of second-hand hosting flea markets or launching their own vintage product collections. Amazon itself, the most customer-obsessed company in the world, acknowledging that consumer behavior is evolving across the world (and that millennials, in particular, are interested in the second-hand product) acquired Shopbop enabling it to expand its services and to enhance the customer experience.

Furthermore, if the major luxury companies, such as Richemont and Farfetch, have entered the market by acquiring resale platforms of their own (Watchfinder and Stadium Goods, respectively), the popularity of online businesses such as TheRealReal, Vestiaire Collective and Rebag has paved the way for more retailers and brands to enter the resale market.

Based on these premises, the paper deals with the managerial approaches that characterize the luxury fashion goods reselling strategies, and analyzes the contributions of the scientific and sectorial debate regarding the themes of the second-hand goods and the luxury goods, together with the second-hand fashion consumption motivations.

The aim is to explain that, unlike the rest of the resale apparel market which has thrived off the uncertainty of the "treasure hunt", luxury retailers have to deal with bigger challenges, imposed by the sustainability issue, too.

In fact, it is becoming increasingly obvious that the present linear (take-make-dispose) model of economy has slim chances of effectively adopting sustainable development principles. The limits of the present linear economy model (take-make-waste) are well illustrated by the textile and clothing sector, an essential consumer goods industry and also concerns the luxury segments. The necessity to move towards the circular model of the economy is also indicated by the industry experts and practitioners: a new circular economic model is necessary and has to be addressed to the digitization of products, distribution and retail processes, consumer/end-user interaction, too.

The work also presents a picture of the actual market trends, its value, its potential and future development prospects realized using qualitative empirical tools (descriptive and explanatory) of the phenomenon investigated through a desk analysis, with regard to the luxury fashion system. In the second section, the contribution proposes some paradigmatic cases of strategies, practices and, performances in recommencing luxury goods.

Finally, given the relevance of the issue of the re-commercing strategies to gain sustainability in the fashion luxury industry, the work provides some managerial implication regarding the behaviors necessary for the development of strategies and practices based on sustainability, hi-lighting the need of a collaborative approach among firms and within the supply chains of the fashion system.

SECOND-HAND GOODS AND LUXURY GOODS

The concepts of luxury retailing and re-commerce don't traditionally go hand in hand. Luxury is often defined by a sense of exclusivity and brand equity that attracts a more affluent crowd, while resale has been seen as "the masses" seeking out random merchandise at a low price.

A cross-cultural study among six different countries located in Asia, Europe and, USA revealed that millennials worldwide perceived luxury to be closely associated with the word "prestige" (Godey et al., 2013) in contrast to the word "recycle", which is associated with disposal (Ha-Brookshire & Hodges, 2009).

The second-hand goods offer, often perceived as a philanthropic activity related to the poorer social levels (Williams, 2003) requires a new elaboration of the meanings associated with commodity and consumption. This kind of goods bring hybrid ways of exchange that often are classified within the schemes of the "item" of "gifts" (Miller, 2000), and that can be distinguished from new goods because they are pre-used and pre-owned (Luchs et al., 2011).

On the opposite side, luxury goods evoke perceptions of rarity, privilege and an exceptional life (Kapferer, 2015) on the point that Janssen et al. (2014) associated luxury with self-enhancement. Luxury goods, previously been reserved to the privileged classes, have become increasingly accessible (Danziger, 2004) now becoming more accessible for young consumers and for a wider audience in general.

This is partly due to the new role of the social media and to the opportunity they provide to "like", instead of having to "buy" a small part of the luxury dream.

SECONDHAND FASHION GOODS CONSUMPTION

According to Kapferer (2015), the issue of sustainability - which entails the concept of promoting the conservation of the natural resources - is closely associated with the concept of "durability", which is a core component to luxury brands.

Thus, it may be important for luxury brands to consider a significant shift toward sustainability efforts. In doing so, luxury brand have to consider that the millennials' brand perceptions may improve based on sustainability and have become identified with characteristics of altruism, sobriety and, moderation (Achabou & Dekhili, 2013).

Considering these these attributes of the concept of sustainability, a privileged link would seem to be expected looking to the millennials, a generational cohort born between the early 1980s and early 2000s (Lu et al., 2013), increasingly consuming luxury goods and the most sustainability-conscious consumer segment (Giovannini et al., 2015; Pasricha & Kadolph, 2009).

As underlined by Choi & Cheng (2015) the promotion of second-hand fashion plays a critical role in altering customers' purchase behaviors and disposal habits, and second-hand fashion businesses have a significant contribution to sustainable consumption.

Second-hand consumption has been quietly undergoing a makeover in recent years showing, in the last 40, a significant change since «second-hand shops of all forms are increasingly attempting to copy traditional retail practices» (Gregson & Crewe, 2003, p.75).

To be brief, second-hand consumption can be conceived as a niche form of consumption and therefore does not correspond to the norm (Crewe & Gregson, 2003; Williams & Paddock, 2003).

Some studies have tried to clarify the motivation of second-hand fashion consumption, indicating that it is motivated not only by money-saving. Consumers are oriented in looking for distinction by buying products that are currently not available on the market.

In the attempt to explain the reasons guiding second-hand consumption Williams & Windebank (2002) suggest that consumers turn to this choice because they cannot afford new goods and have been excluded from traditional retail channels as 'excluded consumers'.

On the contrary, it has been suggested that many second-hand shoppers are not necessarily poor but want to shop clever (Gregson & Crewe, 2003) by not putting a strain on their wallet and the ecosystem. Consequently, they practice a form of minimalism or anti-consumption, whereby they place more emphasis on personal growth than on social status (Lee & Ahn, 2016).

Some Authors indicated that compared to cheap fashion, which represents disposable fashion, luxury fashion brands represent a more sustainable conscientious type of fashion (Carrigan et al., 2013). Others find that the motivations of vintage fashion consumption are quite different from those of second-hand fashion consumption (Cervellon et al., 2013). One of the primary two motivations that drive vintage fashion consumption is "nostalgia" together with "fashion involvement", both of which influence vintage fashion consumption directly and indirectly through treasure hunting. However, the main motivation of second-hand fashion consumption is frugality, which affects second-hand fashion consumption through bargain hunting.

Even if second-hand fashion consumption is motivated by rarity and nostalgia (Guiot & Roux, 2010), it seems possible to affirm that environmental concerns could motivate customers to resell and donate fashion products, but economic benefits are the main consideration on reusing and purchasing (Joung & Park-Poaps, 2013).

Anyway, it seems possible to affirm that consumers have realized the role they play and are becoming more responsible about their excessive lifestyles (Balderjahn, 2013).

Consumers engage in second-hand luxury consumption because it is a sustainable choice, they want to find a real deal or a unique find, they are hunting for pre-loved treasures, or they are making a risky investment (Turunen & Leipämaa-Leskinen, 2015).

That's probably why second-hand retailers are breaking away their label of luxury goods sellers reserved to 'excluded consumers' (Windebank, 2002): they are gaining popularity also among consumers fascinated by the luxury fashion goods (Guiot & Roux, 2010) sensitive to the issue of sustainability and/or inspired by the passion for vintage, since becoming 'cool' and 'stylish' (Franklin, 2011, p. 156).

METHODOLOGICAL CHOICES

The methodological choices of the research refer to different tools related to the qualitative research method and collected data from a range of sources (Yin, 1994).

Since the main aim of the study was to better understand fashion luxury re-selling practices, as strategic choices aimed at promoting sustainability, the research adopted a multiple case-study research (Eisenhardt, 1989) conceiving case studies as a way to enable theory building and development even more than quantitative research methods. Table 1 in Appendix summarizes the collected 31 case studies presenting a brief description.

The research data have been collected through desk analysis and from various sources: from magazine articles, reports, contextual data, quantitative data, and online consumer surveys.

- **Desk Analysis**

In order to identify the case studies to be developed, a preliminary desk analysis was conducted on documentation (e.g.: forward plans, policy documents, communication tools) relating to the luxury fashion brand, the international luxury group, and the second hand-luxury retailers.

- **Magazine Articles**

In the attempt to overcome potential retrospective bias, articles related to luxury fashion brands and re-sellers published in the last 3 years were examined to understand and confirm the luxury brand strategic choices related to sustainability in the fashion industry.

- **Contextual Data**

A period of observation was conducted during which it was possible to participate in various events organized by operators in the sector, such as conventions, exhibitions, workshops, and sustainable fashion shows.

- **Quantitative Data**

The research supplemented the findings of the desk analysis with quantitative data regarding the value of the entire market for gently used second-hand luxury fashion.

Furthermore, in order to identify the case studies to be developed, several aspects were considered trying to guarantee a certain variability among case-studies, in terms of size; operating sectors; territorial areas.

The collected data were analyzed in accordance with accepted methods (Glaser & Strauss, 1967; Locke, 2001). Initially, key concepts, terms, actions, and events were identified on the basis of their relevance, then key issues were grouped into categories that were related to the process of field emergence and cognition.

The literature on second-hand goods, luxury goods, and sustainability-conscious demand together with the one on sustainability and retailing of second-hand fashion luxury goods provided the theoretical and conceptual references to relate the terms and the events to more general theoretical concepts.

Triangulation of data sources (interviews, books, magazine articles, and event observation) helped refine and strengthen the categories (Glaser & Strauss, 1967).

RESULTS

In general, it seems possible to affirm that the market for second-hand luxury personal goods continues to grow for the benefit of many parties involved.

In particular, on the supply side, even the traditional resellers are starting to move in this direction and for several reasons:

- Compared to the overall clothing market, the growth of re-commerce has been surprising.
- The number of second-hand product buyers is growing.
- The impact of innovation and technology are also revolutionizing sales strategies and policies.
- The number of consumers sustainability-oriented continues to grow.

The market for gently used second-hand luxury fashion, or what is more accurately called "authenticated luxury consignment" is estimated at $18b, with e-commerce resale reportedly the fastest-growing segment in the fashion resale market, at 35% as compared with 4% overall (TredUp, 2019).

According to fashion resale service ThredUp, the second-hand market generated 360 billion US dollars worldwide in 2017 with online sales of second-hand items growing 35 percent against just 8 percent for brick and mortar stores. By 2022, the market is expected to generate some 400 billion US dollars, with fashion (apparel, footwear and, accessories) leading the way to an estimated growth of about 51 billion US in 2023 (see Figure 1).

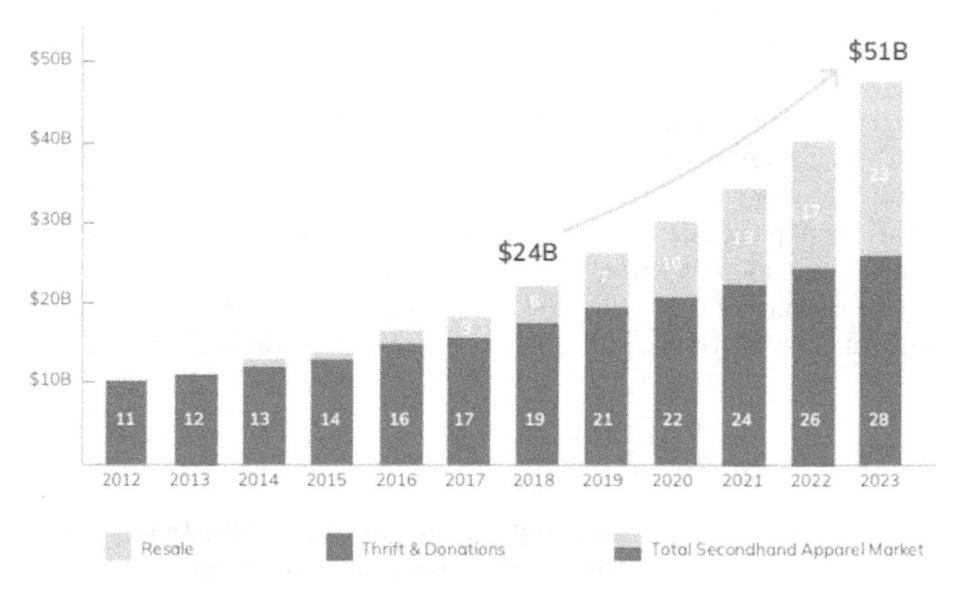

Figure 1. Total secondhand apparel market
source: ThredUp Report (2019)

On the demand side, re-commercing luxury personal goods seem to satisfy two major needs, manifested above all by the younger generations and millennials: "to be always fashionable" and "proving to be a sustainable consumer". The process of purchasing second-hand products may represent an entry-level for young customers who cannot yet buy full-price luxury products using traditional sales channels.

Buying second-hand clothes is nothing new, but the sector has been growing considerably thanks to the Internet. According to (thredup Report, 2019) it seems important to note that second-hand attracts all ages, but 'Millennials' e Boomers' thrift the most (see Figure 2), while 18-37 year olds are adopting secondhand apparel faster than other age groups (see Figure 3)

Figure 2. Secondhand apparel shoppers by age
data source: ThredUp Report (2019)

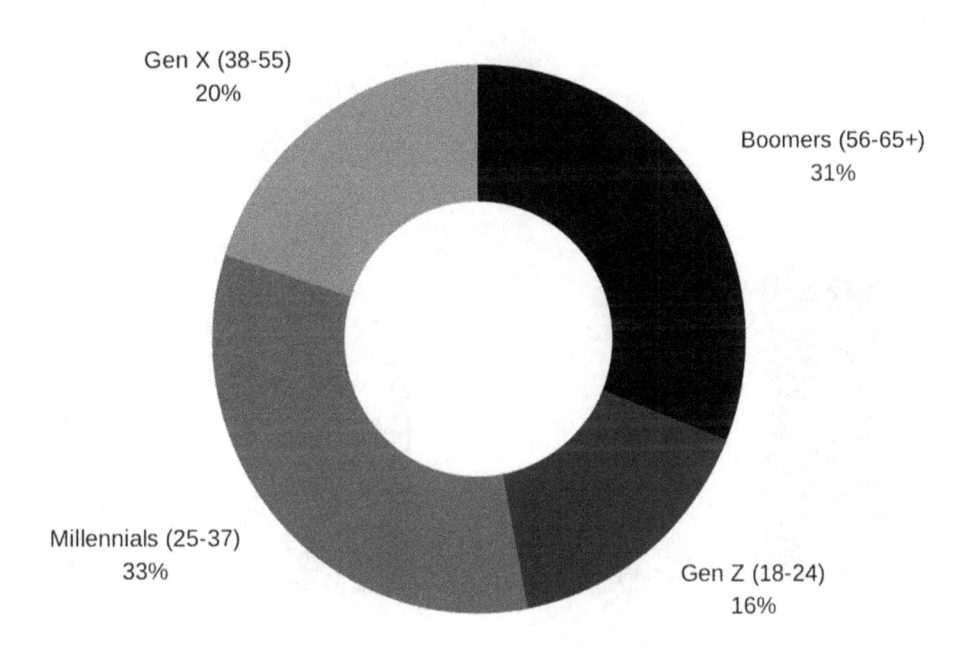

- Gen X (38-55) 20%
- Boomers (56-65+) 31%
- Millennials (25-37) 33%
- Gen Z (18-24) 16%

According to Bain & Co. (2019), worldwide, the personal luxury goods market experienced growth across all regions with positive trends set to result in a currency-neutral uplift of between 6% and 8% (see Figure 4).

China was a clear top performer and with consumers continuing to stand out as a growth driver for the industry, and are more fashion-savvy and digitally advanced than ever before, accelerating the shift of the industry to the millennial state of mind.

While in the Americas, the US luxury market benefitted from a weaker dollar during the crucial Holiday season.

Canada is growing too, although performance in Latin America is mixed. Europe will not achieve similar growth rates. It has been hurt by a stronger euro, which has dented purchases by tourists, but some countries have seen stronger consumption (Russia, France, Switzerland).

However, the UK and Germany have both experienced a slowdown, although in the case of the UK that's not a surprise, given the surge seen in 2016 after the Brexit vote and how much the pound has strengthened in recent months. Bain is expecting growth of between 2% and 4% for Europe.

Figure 3. Percentage of each age group that bought second-hand apparel, footwear and accessorize
data source: ThredUp Report (2019)

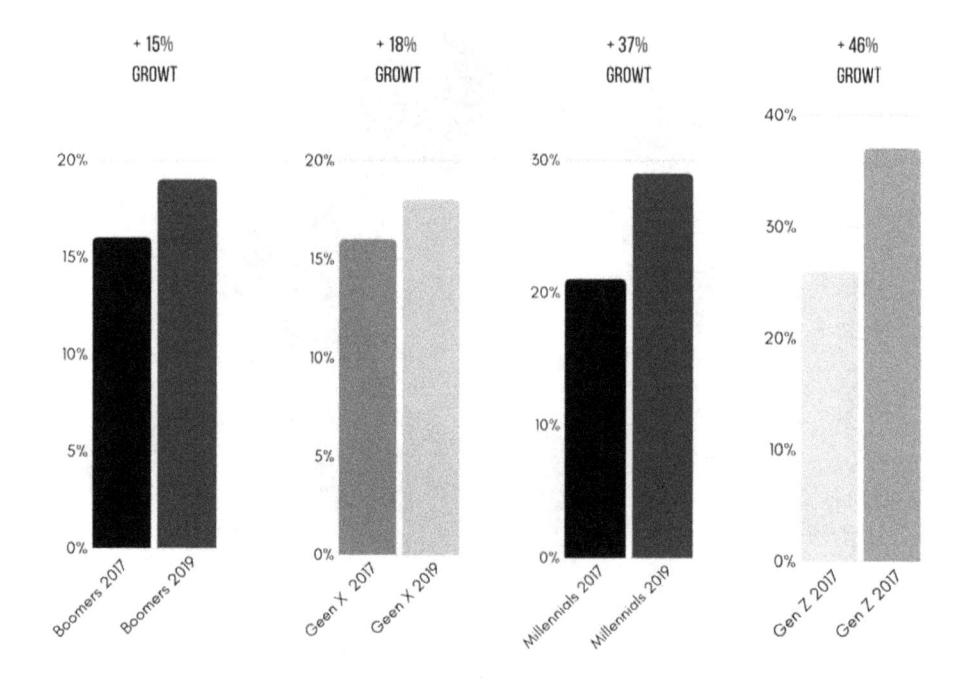

Figure 4. The contribution of the different geographical areas to the growth of the industry
source: Bain & Co. (2019)

Looking at the re-sale market, the results of the work allow affirming that it is a market is booming in term of new players, and that a new resale for the retail model is emerging. This phenomenon, shared across many countries, also becomes manifest in the proliferation of garage sales, second-order out-lets, specialist second-hand retail chains, and the rise of Internet auctions. Among the leading resale sector players, it is possible to mention: thredUp, TheRealReal and, Poshmark (see Appendix for a more detailed description).

In fact, while second-hand luxury goods stores like Milan Station have always existed, several new businesses have been launched online giving shoppers the option to buy must-have clothing and accessories at a fraction of the price, while sellers get to offload their unused items. Additionally, the popularity of online businesses such as The RealReal, Vestiaire Collective and Rebag has led the way for more retailers and brands to enter the resale market. Those websites are earning major space in the luxury resale business and more and more shoppers are looking to this sustainable and affordable option to purchase designer clothing, shoes and handbags at prices below retail value.

Online marketplaces have made it easier for consumers to buy and sell used clothing, footwear and, accessories, especially luxury goods. According to Bain & Co. (2017) since 2009, re-commerce companies all over the world, such as Poshmark, Swap.com, The RealReal, ThredUp and Vestiaire Collective have seen more than a half-billion US dollars in venture capital investment.

One of the more prominent strategic choices implemented by those companies includes peer-to-peer marketplace services, where the reseller completes transactions directly with the buyer on a hosted platform, such as Poshmark and Tradesy. Peer-to-peer options are great when done right: the user interface is easy to navigate, sellers can list for any price they deem fit, and commission can range from 10% to 20%. However, the level of required consumer participation is high. Photographing, posting, and shipping products, not to mention pricing research and customer servicing require a level of commitment that is too much for some resellers.

On the next level, those marketplaces offer the option of consignment, an activity requiring a lot less of a time investment if compared to peer-to-peer selling. The sellers have only to bring in the item, whether by shipping, dropping off in-store, or requesting a concierge service, and receiving a listing price upfront. That's why little research activity is required by the seller as the consignment service will provide pricing, photographing, and customer servicing, but the trouble begins when it comes to actually sell the item and receiving payment. In this case, commission fees vary depending on the item's value (Vestiaire Collective's commission begins at 25% while The RealReal may take up to 45%) and the seller will not be paid until the item actually sells. This leads to frustration over the uncertainty of the transaction, the volatility of prices, and the extensive duration of the process. All consumers love instant gratification, but most consignment shops miss the mark in this category.

Although there are services that provide upfront payment for lower-end items, such as thredUp and brick-and-mortar retailers like Buffalo Exchange, there are few services that provide the same for high-valued luxury items. One of these services is Rebag a platform exclusively for selling and buying pre-owned designer handbags. The platform offers a resale experience with a seller-first mindset that is all about immediacy and transparency. Rebag purchases the bags outright at fair market prices, which are calculated by the service's highly-trained buying team, and the process itself is designed to be as easy and straightforward as possible; no consignment, no commission, no tricks. Sellers simply upload a few pictures to get a free quote and receive a payment within 2-3 days of Rebag evaluating and approving the items.

With the growth of second-hand luxury marketplaces, luxury companies are being forced to reconsider the resale channel. Berenberg projections estimate that the second-hand market could represent 9% of the total luxury goods market by 2020.

Beginning in the 1960s, second-hand fashion retailing became a formal business model with multimillion-dollar revenues through retail stores, consignment stores, and charity shops. One of the core operation parts of the business is recycling. Fashion product recycling could be categorized into three types: "up-cycling", "down-cycling", and "reusing". Second-hand fashion retailing relates most to "reusing", which represents collecting, selling, and exchanging used fashion products.

That's probably why, given those tendencies, the major luxury retail platform such as Richemont and Farfetch have entered the market by acquiring resale platforms of their own. In particular, Richemont acquired Watchfinder, an online retailer of second-hand watches based in Maidstone, United Kingdom. It is the UK's largest seller of second-hand watches. Farfetch acquired Stadium Goods, a streetwear and sneaker resale store and e-commerce site which has grown quickly over the past two years. The company sells the most sought after footwear, apparel, and accessories from Nike, Supreme, Jordan, Adidas, and more. LVMH too acquired a minority stake in Stadium Goods while Neiman Marcus adopted the same strategic choice with Fashionphile a pre-owned luxury handbag and accessory retailer. Fashionphile is an online fashion resale website where consumers can buy and sell women's luxury designer used handbags, accessories and jewelry. As part of the investment, Neiman Marcus will create space for Fashionphile at some of its stores, where shoppers can drop off items, get an immediate quote on their value and get paid.

According to McKinsey for Business of Fashion (2019), while established brands have traditionally turned a blind or scorning eye towards secondhand retail, they are now wading into the pre-owned and rental markets. For this reason, the number of brands getting into the rental, resale, and refurbishment businesses can be expected to grow, markedly increasing.

The research conducted also allows to affirm that there is a still-largely-unsettled relationship between luxury brands retailers and resale companies. Luxury fashion's well-established houses have often expressed concerns that the main one is that ceiling companies are cannibalizing their business.

Chanel, for example, has filed a lawsuit against What Goes Around Comes Around in March and another against The RealReal in November 2019, claiming that a significant array of second-hand Chanel good peddled is fake. Chanel's suits, which argues that What Goes Around Comes Around and The RealReal are actively attempting to "deceive or mislead consumers," this is still an area of the market that is widely contentious and only set to grow more so.

On the other hand, even disliking luxury resale, many brands are engaging in this practice. As Julie Wainwright - the founder and CEO of The RealReal - told during an interview to TechCrunch, at least one brand whose name «begins with a "C" is particularly unhappy with the likes of The RealReal, which stocks ready-to-wear from Gucci, Givenchy, Chloe, Louis Vuitton, and Celine; jewelry and watches from Chanel, Lanvin and Valentino; Cartier and Bulgari, and Rolex and Patek Philippe, among others, and recently began offering menswear». Wainwright claims that the status quo is changing, whether brands like it or not. Luxury and the brands that are most closely tied to it, she says, are «going through an evolution. Our first year, I heard [the brands] hated us. Now, they're keen to find a way to work together. They've realized they can maybe learn something from our data».

The luxury brand have understood that is possible to anger in partnership with a re-commence big player in a few different ways, from the simple sharing of resale data to consignment partnerships and promotional relationships with like-minded brands around a shared mission. For example, 'The RealReal' claiming to be a valuable member of the luxury goods community, "the gateway drug to their brands", proposes itself an asset to them, rather than a threat. For instance, the data the company collects gives them the ability to track brands by age and over time. In this regard, Kering - the Paris-based parent company of Gucci, Balenciaga, Saint Laurent, and Bottega Veneta, among other brands - affirmed to actively collaborate with The RealReal on merchandising.

The notion that luxury and resale are not mutually exclusive but instead, are more aptly described as allies has been echoed by Sébastien Fabre, CEO of Vestiaire Collective, who said that resale is «a point of entry-level access for young customers who can't yet shop full-price luxury».

Similarly, Tracy DiNunzio, CEO of Tradesy, has noticed a similar pattern: «The resale market leads to customers making more purchases at retail. When a customer knows she can resell her item, she's going to be willing to pay a little more for it».

As Julie Wainwright argued, «It's proven pretty clearly now that by us reselling brands, we establish a resale value for that brand, and it actually reinforces the primary sale, and if you buy something of value, it should circle back into the economy».

On the point, Allison Sommer, Director of Strategic Initiatives at The RealReal, states: «We're seeing resale shift people's shopping habits in the primary market. As shoppers get savvier about how they invest and the impact what they're buying has on the planet, they're turning to luxury resale as both a replacement for fast fashion and a barometer of value».

Julie Wainwright to insists that new and resale purchases are not mutually exclusive. «We find people are buying both new and previously owned. Americans are value shoppers more than anything. So, we find they buy from our site and buy new and then consign things they may have kept for a couple of months. Then they use the money from consignments to buy new or buy from us again».

Looking at the sustainability objectives of the sector, it seems clear that such ambitious goals cannot be achieved by the work of a single company. In fact, more than 80 billion pieces of clothing are produced worldwide each year, 75 percent of which will end up in landfills. Consigning obviously lengthens the lifecycle of clothing, reducing the amount that gets discarded.

In this attempt one best practice case is represented by Stella McCartney, who considers sustainability and social responsibility an integral part of the business. That's why, of all luxury brands, it can be considered the first to come out as an official proponent of "re-commerce" with The RealReal. In fact, the luxury consignment site has signed on 'Stella McCartney' as its first official brand partner. The partnership will involve programming, the details of which are still being ironed out, in Stella McCartney's U.S. stores, as well as The RealReal's NYC concept store and website. In a recent statement, Stella McCartney affirmed: «We believe that consignment and re-commerce can play a significant part in reducing the amount of raw materials that are required each year from our planet. This is key in our commitment to becoming part of a more circular economy. By ensuring that our products are used for the entirety of their lifecycle, it is possible to begin to slow down the amount of natural resources currently being cultivated and extracted from the planet for the sake of fashion».

The list of the "Circular Fashion Pioneers" can be enriched. Thanks to a partnership between Eileen Fisher and Renew customers can bring their old Eileen Fisher clothes back and receive a $5 Rewards Card for each item; Stella McCartney customers who consign with The RealReal receive an immediate $100 credit to shop at Stella stores. The partnership between thredUP and Reformation drives brand loyalty and has helped Reformation meet apparel recycling goals; similarly, the collaboration between thredUP and Cuyana provides that customers can clean out with thredUP and earn Cuyan a credit, replacing cluttered wardrobes with fewer, better things.

DISCUSSIONS

Results allow identifying two main trajectories for the discussion:

1. The unsettled relationship between luxury brands and resale companies.
2. The need for a collaborative approach to achieve sustainability goals and maintain the resale value.

In particular, on the first point, for-profit stores have increased competitive pressure in the industry. Given the potential to profit from these high-end goods, more for-profit companies entered the space and have successfully expanded. This creates competitive pressure between second-hand retailers, enlarging the competition to the luxury brands and to the department stores, these last now realizing the benefits of a liquid secondary market for luxury goods. Moreover, many buyers of preowned luxury goods are also first time buyers who get to experience a new brand for the first time. From that perspective, these resale services are a customer acquisition channel for luxury brands and a veritable gateway for younger consumers to enter their brand experience.

Finally, by encouraging re-selling, a brand can inspire more consumer confidence because it's also saying its wares will hold up long enough to resell. It seems possible to affirm that in a best-case scenario, a brand customer will take what they make from selling a product and use it to buy a new one.

On the second point, the world of luxury resale is creating a new paradigm, a high-end product ecosystem that is a win-win for the entire industry: brands, department stores and of course the customers themselves. The best part of it all is that it makes fashion more sustainable and can represent an important force behind the growing sustainability movement guiding the entire fashion industry along with new strategies.

That's why fashion luxury brands are now called to face the challenge to gain sustainability leadership. That's just one of the reasons why the sustainability challenge requires new points of view suggesting collaboration and innovation practices for many companies engaging consumers in a redefinition of value. In other words, competitors (luxury brand and re-commerce operators) should have the common futuristic goal of changing the consumption patterns of buyers, which can be possible by maintaining the innovative mindset within the corporations.

CONCLUSION

The research conducted allows affirming that the luxury resale market is continuously growing to the benefit of all parties involved. Even traditional retailers are starting to embrace second-hand for different reasons:

1. Compared to the overall apparel market, resale's growth has been phenomenal.
2. There are more second-hand shoppers than ever before.
3. "Millennials" and "Gen Z" are driving the growth of second-hand.
4. Innovation & Technology created a resale revolution.
5. Consumer trends drive second-hand growth.
6. Conscious consumers are rising in number.
7. Resale satisfies two biggest demands of the Instagram generation: be seen in new styles constantly and be a sustainably conscious consumer.
8. Resale can represent a point of entry-level access for young customers who can't yet shop full-price luxury.

As the market continues to grow, luxury brands are now called to decide whether they should scale up their own resale strategy, especially given that second-hand sales can support demand for first-hand products in the long term; entry into luxury resale can be challenging and require careful planning, especially if retailers aren't prepared for the random nature of merchandising required by the model or handle its product authenticity concerns; second-hand sales can represent a strategy for luxury brand involved in sustainability practices.

Like any sector of the fashion industry, the business of reselling is dictated by changing trends, but there are a few brands that are managing to hold onto their value and proving the most bang for their buck. As millennials lead the charge towards a more sustainable future, expect to see the resale market and sharing economy continue to thrive.

LIMITATIONS AND FUTURE RESEARCH DIRECTIONS

The results stimulate several further research questions guiding future directions focused on e-commerce and digital marketing as a critical component of second-hand retail sustainability driven.

In fact, most successful second-hand retailers have an online presence and offer goods for sale through, at least, one online channel. Of the two trajectories, the omnichannel one has been active for the longest time since the 2000s, while the sustainability one is more recent. But, in any case, the two challenges have common characteristics: they are both transversal, connected, and continuously evolving under the pressure of global consumers.

That's probably why, as demonstrated by the presented cases, a greater attention to the two joint themes could represent an essential trajectory for those organizations engaged in the challenge of growing the competitive advantage.

Despite the non generalizability of the results related to the nature of the research, qualitative in the conceiving and in the method, the work provides more detailed information to explain the complexity of the second-hand luxury recommercing politisc and strategies in the perspective of sustainability linked to the omichannel opportunities.

At this stage of the research, whose emphasis is on explaining a phenomenon rather than counting numbers of firms who think or behave in certain ways, the used tools seemed to be appropriate.

Subsequent research should explore - for axample - the behavior of the consumers, highlighting a key feature for both sustainability and omnichannel challenges: the generational shift of the market. The "millennials", but also the "Z generation" (which can be reshaped into an "hashtag" generation) are in fact leading the trends and influencing the distribution strategies continually raising the technological bar.

Furthermore, the perspective could be shifted on the consumers that seems to be open to the 'secondary behavior' in general for a variety of reasons: the recession, the better access to online resources, highly education level in the retail and resale space, the knowledge about the "value" of luxury goods, and last, but not least, the sustainability consciousness and orientation.

REFERENCES

Achabou, M. A., & Dekhili, S. (2013). Luxury and sustainable development: Is there a match? *Journal of Business Research*, *66*(10), 1896–1903. doi:10.1016/j.jbusres.2013.02.011

Bain and Company. (2017). *Luxury Goods Worldwide Market Study. The New Luxury Consumer. Why Responding to the Millennial Mindset Will Be Key*. Available on line at: https://www.bain.com/insights/luxury-goods-worldwide-market-study-fall-winter-2017/

Bain and Company. (2019). *Bain Luxury Goods Worldwide Market Study*. Available on line at https://altagamma.it/media/source/Altagamma%20Bain%20Worldwide%20Market%20Monitor_update%202019.pdf

Balderjahn, I. (2013). *Nachhaltiges Management und Konsumentenverhalten* [Sustainable management and consumer behaviour]. Konstanz: UVK.

Beh, L. S., Ghobadian, A., He, Q., Gallear, D., & O'Regan, N. (2016). Second-life retailing: A reverse supply chain perspective. *Supply Chain Management, 21*(2), 259–272. doi:10.1108/SCM-07-2015-0296

Bly, S., Gwozdz, W., & Reisch, L. A. (2015). Exit from the high street: An exploratory study of sustainable fashion consumption pioneers. *International Journal of Consumer Studies, 39*(2), 125–135. doi:10.1111/ijcs.12159

Carrigan, M., Moraes, C., & McEachern, M. (2013). From conspicuous to considered fashion: A harm-chain approach to the responsibilities of luxury-fashion businesses. *Journal of Marketing Management, 29*(11-12), 1277–1307. doi:10.1080/0267257X.2013.798675

Cervellon, M. C., Carey, L., & Harms, T. (2012). Something old, something used: Determinants of women's purchase of vintage fashion vs. second-hand fashion. *International Journal of Retail & Distribution Management, 40*(12), 956–974. doi:10.1108/09590551211274946

Choi, T. M., & Cheng, T. C. E. (2015). *Sustainable Fashion Supply Chain Management from Sourcing to Retailing*. Cham, Switzerland: Springer International Publishing.

Cowen and Company (2018). *Thrift & Retail Resale Is Major: Understanding thredUP*. Author.

Danziger, P. (2004). *Why people buy things they don't need: Understanding and predicting consumer behavior*. Kaplan Publishing.

Delai, I., & Takahashi, S. (2013). Corporate sustainability in emerging markets: Insights from the practices reported by the Brazilian retailers. *Journal of Cleaner Production, 47*, 211–221. doi:10.1016/j.jclepro.2012.12.029

Eisenhardt, K. M. (1989). Building Theories from Case Study Research. *Academy of Management Review, 14*(4), 532–550. doi:10.5465/amr.1989.4308385

Franklin, A. (2011). The ethics of second-hand consumption. In T. Lewis & E. Potter (Eds.), *Ethical Consumption – A Critical Introduction*. New York: Routledge.

Fuentes, C., & Fredriksson, C. (2016). Sustainability service in-store: Service work and the promotion of sustainable consumption. *International Journal of Retail & Distribution Management, 44*(5), 492–507. doi:10.1108/IJRDM-06-2015-0092

Giovannini, S., Xu, Y., & Thomas, J. (2015). Luxury fashion consumption and generation Y consumers: Self, brand consciousness, and consumption motivations. *Journal of Fashion Marketing and Management, 19*(1), 22–40. doi:10.1108/JFMM-08-2013-0096

Godey, B., Pederzoli, D., Aiello, G., Donvito, R., Wiedmann, K., & Hennigs, N. (2013). A cross-cultural exploratory content analysis of the perception of luxury from six countries. *Journal of Product and Brand Management, 22*(3), 229–237. doi:10.1108/JPBM-02-2013-0254

Gregson, N., & Crewe, L. (2003). *Second-hand cultures*. Oxford: Berg. doi:10.2752/9781847888853

Guiot, D., & Roux, D. A. (2010). Second-hand shoppers' motivation scale: Antecedents, consequences and implications for retailers. *Journal of Retailing, 86*(4), 355–371. doi:10.1016/j.jretai.2010.08.002

Ha-Brookshire, J. E., & Hodges, N. N. (2009). Socially responsible consumer behavior? Exploring used clothing donation behavior. *Clothing & Textiles Research Journal, 27*(3), 179–196. doi:10.1177/0887302X08327199

Hvass, K. K. (2014). Post-retail responsibility of garments - A fashion industry perspective. *Journal of Fashion Marketing and Management, 18*(4), 413–430. doi:10.1108/JFMM-01-2013-0005

Janssen, C., Vanhamme, J., Lindgreen, A., & Lefebvre, C. (2014). The catch-22 of responsible luxury: Effects of luxury product characteristics on consumers' perception of fit with corporate social responsibility. *Journal of Business Ethics, 119*(1), 45–57. doi:10.100710551-013-1621-6

Joung, H.-M. (2014). Fast-fashion consumers' post-purchase behaviours. *International Journal of Retail & Distribution Management, 42*(8), 688–697. doi:10.1108/IJRDM-03-2013-0055

Joung, H.-M., & Park-Poaps, H. (2013). Factors motivating and influencing clothing disposal behaviours. *International Journal of Consumer Studies, 37*(1), 105–111. doi:10.1111/j.1470-6431.2011.01048.x

Kapferer, J. N. (2015). *Kapferer on Luxury: how Luxury Brands Can Grow yet Remain Rare*. London: Kogan Page Publishers.

Kumar, P. (2014). Greening retail: An Indian experience. *International Journal of Retail & Distribution Management, 42*(7), 613–625. doi:10.1108/IJRDM-02-2013-0042

Lee, M. S. W., & Ahn, C. S. Y. (2016). Anti-consumption, materialism, and consumer well-being. *The Journal of Consumer Affairs, 50*(1), 18–47. doi:10.1111/joca.12089

Lu, L., Bock, D., & Joseph, M. (2013). Green marketing: What the millennials buy. *The Journal of Business Strategy, 34*(6), 3–10. doi:10.1108/JBS-05-2013-0036

Luchs, M., Naylor, R.W., Randall, L. R., Jesse, R. C., Roland, G., Sommer, K., & … Weaver, T. (2011). Toward a sustainable marketplace: Expanding options and benefits for consumers. *Journal of Research for Consumers, 19*, 1–12.

McKinsey-BoF. (2019). *The State of Fashion 2019 Survey*. The Business of Fashion and McKinsey & Company. https://www.mckinsey.com/industries/retail/our-insights/the-state-of-fashion-2019-a-year-of-awakening

Pasricha, A., & Kadolph, S. J. (2009). Millennial generation and fashion education: A discussion on agents of change. *International Journal of Fashion Design, Technology, & Education, 2*(2/3), 119–126.

Shen, B. (2014). Sustainable fashion supply chain: Lessons from H&M. *Sustainability, 6*(9), 6236–6249. doi:10.3390u6096236

The Worn, the Torn, the Wearable: Textile Recycling in Union Square. (n.d.). Available online at: http://bada.hb.se/bitstream 2320/12345/1NJ2012_Nr2_DG_1209_redigerad%20upp.pdf

TredUp. (2019). *Resale Report*. Available on line at: https://www.thredup.com/resale

Turunen, L. L. M., & Leipämaa-Leskinen, H. (2015). Pre-loved luxury: Identifying the meaning of second hand luxury possessions. *Journal of Product and Brand Management, 24*(1), 57–65. doi:10.1108/JPBM-05-2014-0603

Williams, C. (2003). Explaining Informal and second-hand goods acquisition. *The International Journal of Sociology and Social Policy, 23*(12), 95–110. doi:10.1108/01443330310790426

Williams, C., & Paddock, C. (2003). The meaning of alternative consumption practices. *Cities (London, England), 20*(5), 311–319. doi:10.1016/S0264-2751(03)00048-9

Williams, C., & Windebank, J. (2002). The "excluded consumer": A neglected aspect of social exclusion? *Policy and Politics, 30*(4), 501–513. doi:10.1332/030557302760590422

Wilson, J. P. (2015). The triple bottom line: Undertaking an economic, social, and environmental retail sustainability strategy. *International Journal of Retail & Distribution Management, 43*(4/5), 432–447. doi:10.1108/IJRDM-11-2013-0210

Yin, R. K. (1994). *Case Study Research, Design and Methods*. Londres: Sage Publications.

ADDITIONAL READING

Dall'Olmo Riley, F., & Lacroix, C. (2003). Luxury branding on the Internet: Lost opportunity or impossibility? *Marketing Intelligence & Planning, 21*(2), 96–104. doi:10.1108/02634500310465407

Okonkwo, U. (2009). Sustaining Luxury Brands on the Internet. *Journal of Brand Management, 16*(5/6), 302–310. doi:10.1057/bm.2009.2

Seringhaus, F. H. R. (2005). Selling Luxury Brands Online. *Journal of Internet Commerce, 4*(1), 1–25. doi:10.1300/J179v04n01_01

Wiedmann, K. P., & Hennigs, N. (2013). Placing Luxury Marketing on the Research Agenda Not Only for the Sake of Luxury–An Introduction. *Luxury Marketing,* 3-17.

KEY TERMS AND DEFINITIONS

Fashion Industry: Fashion industry consists of enterprises from textile, clothing and accessories, and tanning sectors.

Fashion Product: Product for which demand changes frequently because of changes in consumer tastes or product attributes. Where consumer tastes are fickle and consumers seek to be fashionable, suppliers can take advantage of this by frequent restyling of products.

Luxury Goods: Products which are not necessary, but which tend to make life more pleasant for the consumer. In contrast with necessity goods, luxury goods are typically more costly and are often bought by individuals that have a higher disposable income or greater accumulated wealth than the average.

Omichannel Retail Strategies: Approach to sales and marketing that provides customers with a fully-integrated shopping experience by uniting user experiences from brick-and-mortar to mobile-browsing and everything in between.

Re-Commerce: Process of selling previously owned, new or used products through physical or online distribution channels to companies or consumers willing to repair, if necessary, and reuse, recycle or resell them afterwards.

Second-Hand Good: Pre-used or pre-owned good that is being purchased by or otherwise transferred to a second or later end user.

Sustainability: Originated with the Brundtland Report in 1987, this concept describes sustainable development as one that satisfies the needs of the present without adversely affecting the conditions for future generations.

APPENDIX

Table 1. Brief description of the selected cases

Case	Brief Description
Vestiaire Collective	Vestiaire Collective offers one of the largest selections of pre-owned goods, posting thousands of new listings each week - and is a favorite with the *Bazaar* fashion team. Boasting an online fashion community of more than 3.5 million shoppers, items you buy on Vestiaire Collective are guaranteed to come from a respectable closet. A nifty feature is the ability to set email alerts, letting you know when a particular item you are hunting for is listed.
Milan Station	Milan Station is principally engaged in the retail of unused and second-hand luxury branded handbags and apparel products in Hong Kong, the PRC and Macau. It is a market leader and ranked number one in terms of both sales value and sales volume amongst the top five luxury branded handbag independent retailers in Hong Kong in 2009. Milan Station possesses nearly ten years of operation history. Since the opening of its first Milan Station retail shop in 2001 in Tsim Sha Tsui, Hong Kong, Milan Station has established a retail network in Hong Kong and expanded its operation to Macau in 2007 and the PRC in 2008. Milan Station has been listed on Stock Exchange of Hong Kong in 2011 (stock code #1150). It operates retail shops under the brand names of Milan Station and France Station. Milan Station carries over 20 brands of handbag products and over 30 brands of other products from international luxury fashion houses. A pioneer in capitalizing changes in urban lifestyles, such as less storage space, an increase in the frequency of changing brands and styles through trade-ins and growing environmental consciousness, Milan Station makes luxury branded handbags more accessible and available. Focusing on retail sales of second-hand luxury branded handbags since its establishment, Milan Station expanded its product range to include other luxury branded products. The products offered by Milan Station include unused and second-hand handbags, clothing, shoes, watches and other accessories.
Swap.com	Swap. com is an online consignment store offering used baby, kid's, maternity, men's and women's apparel and accessories. Swap. com enables a community of thrifters to find affordable, quality secondhand apparel for the whole family. Being an online thrift store, Swap. com makes it easier than ever to filter through like-new, pre-owned clothing. Together we keep millions of items out of landfills which is something everyone can feel good about.
The RealReal	The RealReal is the leader in authenticated luxury consignment. With an expert behind every item, we ensure everything we sell is 100% real. As a sustainable company, The RealReal give new life to pieces by brands from Chanel to Cartier and hundreds more. The RealReal was founded in 2011 by Julie Wainwright, an e-commerce entrepreneur. By July 2018, the company had raised $288 million in venture capital funding. In 2017 The RealReal opened its first permanent retail store in New York City. It also opened pop-ups in San Francisco and Las Vegas. In 2018, it opened its second retail location in Los Angeles. In early 2019 the company announced it would be adding a half-million square foot e-commerce space in Perth Amboy, New Jersey to its existing e-commerce centers in Secaucus, New Jersey and Brisbane, California. On May 31, 2019, The RealReal submitted a preliminary filing (S-1) to the SEC to go public. On June 28, 2019, The RealReal went public on Nasdaq under the symbol REAL. In 2017, The RealReal announced a sustainability partnership with luxury fashion brand Stella McCartney. The partnership launched in 2018 and was extended through 2019. It also established the first Monday in October as National Consignment Day, an annual holiday. The following year, to mark National Consignment day, The RealReal launched a custom sustainability calculator. Developed with environmental consulting firm Shift Advantage, it measures the environmental impact of consignments processed by the company.
ThredUp	ThredUP is a fashion resale website for consumers to buy and sell secondhand clothing online. ThredUP is part of a larger Collaborative Consumption movement, which encourages consumers to live in a more collective, sharing economy. In early 2009, James Reinhart, Chris Homer, and Oliver Lubin co-founded thredUP in Cambridge, Massachusetts, testing a stealth pilot for peer-to-peer online sharing of men's dress shirts, and in September 2009, they launched their first official product focused on swapping men's and women's clothes. Due to underperformance in the men & women demographics, thredUP pivoted towards children's clothing in April 2010. This pivot resulted in greater growth, which attracted the attention of the venture capital community.
The Luxury Closet	The Luxury Closet is a fast-growing online market platform that buys, sells, and consigns luxury items, mostly pre-owned, at a discounted price maintaining brand and item integrity and the assurance of authenticity. The Luxury Closet is the first of its kind in the GCC region in terms of size, market reach and, scalability.
Bagista	Bagista offers pre-loved designer bags a second home; customers can buy, sell or swap their luxury handbags. The company is great at keeping its followers in the loop, regularly posting to Instagram Stories about new arrivals, so you can keep on top of the latest product drops. Before a bag makes it onto the site, it's been checked by experts to ensure authenticity, whether it's a one-off piece or everyone's favorite must-have.
High Society	From Max Mara to Manolo Blahnik, High Society houses authentic pre-owned luxury items from all premium brands. If you have pieces to sell, complete an online form and the team will get back to you within 48 hours with a selling price estimation. Like HEWI and Vestiaire Collective they also offer a VIP service, making selling your designer pieces as easy as possible.
Guiltless	Guiltless isn't officially trading yet although its blog section hints at the types of treasures you will be able to find when the site is up and running, ranging from Alexander McQueen's shoes to Dolce dresses. Aide from clothing and accessories, there will also be a lifestyle section. Unlike other marketplaces, Guiltless will hold stock for sellers, which will be available to buy for up to 80 percent off retail. They take up to 30 percent commission from sellers but also offer dry cleaning, restoration as well as very chic packaging.
Rebag	Rebag purchases high-end designer handbags for cash, offering guaranteed pricing and a prepaid shipping box anywhere within the US.
Poshmark	Poshmark is a social commerce marketplace where people in the United States can buy and sell new or used clothing, shoes, and accessories. The company is headquartered in Redwood City, California
Tradesy	Tradesy is an online peer-to-peer resale marketplace for buying and selling women's luxury and designer contemporary fashion. The company is headquartered in Santa Monica, California.

continued on following page

Table 1. Continued

Case	Brief Description
Luxify	Luxify has probably been around the longest and as such has over 9,000 users and over HK$3.5 million worth of merchandise. It can be considered as a high-end eBay – basically the site is a marketplace connecting dealers and sellers with buyers, the majority of whom are based in Hong Kong. Items can be vintage, new or used, and range from anything from bags and shoes to art, wine and, property. Most items have a set price although users can try their luck and "make an offer." Concierge service helps sellers with everything from photos to pricing.
Rewind Vintage	Rewind Vintage specializes in unique luxury vintage fashion, stocking pre-loved items from top labels including Chanel, Saint Laurent and, Celine (or Céline, as the case may be), as well as rare vintage pieces. Rewind has also launched its own project, Emotional Baggage, which customizes classic designer bags and provides customers with a personalization service. To sell with Rewind, contact an authorized representative via phone or email to arrange a consultation.
Watchfinder	Watchfinder & Co. is an online retailer of second-hand watches based in Maidstone, United Kingdom. It is the UK's largest seller of second-hand watches
Fashionphile	Fashionphile is an online fashion resale website where consumers can buy and sell women's luxury designer used handbags, accessories and, jewelry.
Buffalo Exchange	Buffalo Exchange is a privately owned, family-operated fashion resale retailer that buys and resells used clothing. In the 45 years since that 450 square foot store near the University of Arizona has blossomed into 50 stores in 19 states.
What Goes Around Comes Around	The go-to online retail destination for modern style, Shopbop offers a comprehensive, hand-picked collection of apparel and accessories from the industry's foremost contemporary and designer labels. Since its launch in 2000 as a denim-focused e-commerce platform, Shopbop has grown into one of the world's leading fashion authorities. Along with renowned customer service, Shopbop delivers unparalleled wardrobe advice, cutting-edge editorial look books, innovative features, and exclusive collaborations with forward-minded brands. The result is a highly personalized, satisfying, and—above all—fun shopping experience that caters to style-minded women around the globe. In 2006, BOP LLC was acquired by Amazon.com, Inc., the world's largest internet retailer, enabling Shopbop to expand its services to enhance the customer experience. A trusted, globally recognized fashion merchant, Shopbop sells only quality, authentic designer merchandise. Shopbop'is part of the Amazon.com Inc. group of companies.
Vide Dressing	Vide Dressing is a go-to site for buying and selling luxury, with 30,000 items selling per month. It acts as a third party between buyers and, sellers, ensuring sales, payment, delivery and returns run smoothly. The company's legal experts and authentication system mean that your money is in safe hands, which is reassuring for both you and your bank account when you buy high-end.
Edit second-hand	The team carefully selects the highest-quality designer pieces, offering shoppers authentic designer labels at up to 70 percent off retail price. Listing pieces on the site is easy: simply email a round-up of items you want to sell and Edit will respond with an estimate price of what it will pay for them. Our favorite thing about it is the speed of the service; you will receive payment for your items within two days of them arriving at Edit's HQ.
HEWI London	HEWI (Hardly Ever Worn It) is like eBay, but exclusively for new or barely worn pre-owned designer goods. Shoppers can watch items, follow sellers and choose to either "buy it now" or make offers on future purchases. Sellers can list items themselves without fees or alternatively opt for the VIP service, whereby HEWI London will handle everything on your behalf - from collecting items to handling all buyer inquiries. This allows people to sell anonymously; all they need to do is choose how they want to be paid.
Designer Exchange	Established in 2013, Designer Exchange was the first company to offer instant cash payment and exchange on designer items. It's the right place to head if somone is thinking about swapping a Chanel for an upgrade. Every one of their items is checked in-house by a team of experts to make sure everything is authentic and top quality. As well as being available online, Designer Exchange also has stores in Knightsbridge, Kensington, Manchester, Birmingham and, Madrid.
Stadium Goods	Stadium Goods is the world's premier sneaker and streetwear marketplace. We sell the most sought after footwear, apparel, and accessories from Nike, Supreme, Jordan, Adidas, and more.
Collector Square	Collector Square launched in Asia in November although it was founded in Europe in 2013. Thanks to its connections with leading French auction house ArtCurial, each of the 5,000 items available have been selected by a team of experts who have extensive experience working for international auction houses. The emphasis here is on accessories – watches, jewelery and, handbags – from major brands like Dior, Hermes and Louis Vuitton. Many of the pieces are classics such as Cartier's Trinity rings or styles that are no longer available making the site great for collectors. In terms of pricing, most of the items are listed as 30 to 40 percent lower than retail.
Shopbop	Shopbop was founded by Bob Lamey, Martha Graettinger, and venture investor Ray Zemon in November 1999 in Madison, Wisconsin. It was originally the internet presence of brick and mortar clothing dealer Bop in downtown Madison (the shop was closed in 2014). Graettinger and Lamey chose Madison because it was a college town with a strong fashion-conscious student base. Shopbop was acquired by Amazon.com in February 2006. At the time of the deal, it was selling 103 different lines of high-end clothing. Since the acquisition Shopbop ran almost completely independently from Amazon, which also sells clothes and accessories and even competed with it. In September 2013 Shopbop opened the East Dane contemporary menswear website. The website went through several redesigns, particularly in 2012 and 2017 (among the redesigns, a loyalty program was added to the website).
Farfetch	Farfetch is an online luxury fashion retail platform that sells products from over 700 boutiques and brands from around the world. The company was founded in 2007 by the Portuguese entrepreneur José Neves with its headquarters in London and main branches in Porto, Guimarães, Braga, Lisbon, New York, Los Angeles, Tokyo, Shanghai, Hong Kong, São Paulo and, Dubai. The e-commerce company operates local-language websites and mobile apps for international markets in English, French, Japanese, Chinese, Arabic, Portuguese, Korean, German, Russian and Spanish. Farfetch has offices in 11 cities and employs over 3,000 staff
Richemont	Richemont is a Switzerland-based luxury goods holding company founded in 1988 by South African businessman Johann Rupert. Through its various subsidiaries, Richemont produces and sells jewelry, watches, leather goods, pens, firearms, clothing, and accessories. Richemont is publicly traded as CFR on the SIX Swiss Exchange and the JSE Securities Exchange. The brands it owns include A. Lange & Söhne, Azzedine Alaïa, Baume & Mercier, Cartier, Chloé, Dunhill, IWC Schaffhausen, Giampiero Bodino, Jaeger-LeCoultre, Lancel, Montblanc, Officine Panerai, Piaget, Peter Millar, Purdey, Roger Dubuis, Vacheron Constantin, and Van Cleef & Arpels. As of November 2012, Compagnie Financière Richemont SA is the sixth largest corporation by market capitalization in the Swiss Market Index. As of 2014, Richemont is the second-largest luxury goods company in the world after LVMH.

continued on following page

Recommercing Luxury Goods

Table 1. Continued

Case	Brief Description
LVMH	LVMH is a French multinational luxury goods conglomerate headquartered in Paris. The company was formed in 1987 under the merger of fashion house Louis Vuitton with Moët Hennessy, a company formed after the 1971 merger between the champagne producer Moët & Chandon and Hennessy, the cognac manufacturer. It controls around 60 subsidiaries that each manage a small number of prestigious brands. The subsidiaries are often managed independently. The oldest of the LVMH brands is wine producer Château d'Yquem, which dates its origins back to 1593. Christian Dior SE is the main holding company of LVMH, owning 40.9% of its shares, and 59.01% of its voting rights. Bernard Arnault, the majority shareholder of Dior, is Chairman and CEO of both companies. In 2017, Arnault purchased all the remaining Christian Dior shares in a reported $13.1 billion buy out. The Dapifer reports that LVMH will gain ownership of Christian Dior haute couture, leather, both men's and women's ready-to-wear, and footwear lines. Arnault's successful integration of various famous aspirational brands into a single group has inspired other luxury companies to do the same. Thus, the French conglomerate Kering and the Swiss-based Richemont have also created extended portfolios of luxury brands. The company is a component of the Euro Stoxx 50 stock market index.
Neiman Marcus	Neiman-Marcus is an American chain of luxury department stores owned by the Neiman Marcus Group, headquartered in Dallas, Texas. The company also owns the Bergdorf Goodman department stores and operates a direct marketing division, Neiman Marcus Direct, which operates catalog and online operations under the Horchow, Neiman Marcus, and Bergdorf Goodman names. Neiman Marcus is currently owned by the Toronto-based Canada Pension Plan Investment Board and Los Angeles-based Ares Management.
Kering	Kering is an international luxury group based in Paris, France. It owns luxury goods brands, including Gucci, Yves Saint Laurent, Balenciaga, Alexander McQueen, Bottega Veneta, Boucheron, Brioni and Pomellato. The company was founded in 1963. It was known as Pinault S.A. until 1994, as Pinault-Printemps-Redoute from 1994 to 2005, as PPR from 2005 to 2013, and as Kering since 2013. It has been quoted on Euronext Paris since 1988 and has been a constituent of the CAC 40 index since 1995. The company has been headed by François-Henri Pinault since 1985
Amazon	Amazon is an American multinational technology company based in Seattle, Washington that focuses on e-commerce, cloud computing, digital streaming, and artificial intelligence. It is considered one of the Big Four technology companies along with Google, Apple, and Facebook. Amazon is known for its disruption of well-established industries through technological innovation and mass scale. It is the world's largest e-commerce marketplace, an assistant provider, and cloud computing platform as measured by revenue and market capitalization. Amazon is the largest Internet company by revenue in the world, the second largest private employer in the United States, and one of the world's most valuable companies. Amazon is also econd largest technology company by revenue. In 2015, Amazon surpassed Walmart as the most valuable retailer in the United States by market capitalization. In 2017, Amazon acquired Whole Foods Market for $13.4 billion, which vastly increased Amazon's presence as a brick-and-mortar retailer. In 2018, Bezos announced that its two-day delivery service, Amazon Prime, had surpassed 100 million subscribers worldwide.

Chapter 12

The Impact of Circular Economy on the Fashion Industry:
A Research on Clothing Share Services

Tugce Aslan
https://orcid.org/0000-0002-5556-225X
Duzce University, Turkey

Adem Akbiyik
https://orcid.org/0000-0001-7634-4545
Sakarya University, Turkey

ABSTRACT

The fundamental changes in technology and globalization have changed consumer preferences along with the way people buy and consume. This change has profoundly affected new business models and consumption systems in all commercial markets, including the fashion industry in particular. Moreover, fashion businesses have begun to shift from traditional proprietary access business models to the sharing economy. The effect of the sharing economy or circular economy on the fashion industry is increasing day by day. Clothing sharing services, recycling, and re-use of used garments contribute to environmental sustainability and contribute to economic and social sustainability through sales revenue and employment. However, there is limited academic research on clothing sharing models. This research focuses on Dolap application, a clothing sharing service. It examines the role of trust in clothing sharing services from a consumer perspective. As a result of the analysis, it was found that trust in the platform positively and significantly affected the trust given to the service provider.

DOI: 10.4018/978-1-7998-2728-3.ch012

INTRODUCTION

Although the amount of sharing varies from generation to generation, sharing has always been a part of society. However, Sharing Economy(SE) or the Circular Economy(CE) is the phenomena of the internet age. The sharing economy is expressed in many different ways as circular economy, collaborative consumption, and access-oriented consumption. The sharing services sector has had a direct and indirect impact on individuals' consumption habits and traditional business models, leading to drastic changes in consumption patterns. The change in consumer behaviors and habits of individuals starting with eBay, which is called the pioneer of this sector, has caused global impact and spread to all segments. With the rapidly developing information and communication technologies, the sharing economy sector, which arises against the asset-weighted lifestyle, is getting more and more attention in the world.

In essence, sharing economy is an essential part of a circular economy(Korhonen, Nuur, Feldmann, & Birkie, 2018). Sharing and collaborative models can only form part of the big picture of the circular economy(Egerton-Read, 2016). The circular economy (CE) is a process in which resources are used for as long as possible and reused with recycling after reaching maximum value from them(Brussels, 2015). CE is an approach that promotes effective and re-use of resources. CE is an economic model aimed at minimizing the sustainable use of natural resources, the use of raw materials, and the production of waste(Lahti, Wincent, & Parida, 2018). The sharing economy is the activity of donating or sharing goods and services coordinated among peers through online services. In this context, more efficient use of resources provides a more sustainable and innovative use of natural resources(Botsman & Rogers, 2010). In this respect, it can be considered as a kind of circular economy because it serves the same purpose as the circular economy.

Renting and redistribution of unused or underused goods in the hands of consumers ensures an effective reduction of environmental footprints. For example, several people offer the opportunity to meet new people, as well as traveling together, reducing driving costs and adverse environmental consequences. Besides, vehicle sharing can reduce the congestion of roads and parking lots and reduce energy consumption. This is an indication that the sharing economy can be a solution to ecological damage. In another example, instead of buying a new dress for a day's activity, renting a dress enables a person to reach their goal without increasing their closet or maintenance expenses. Also, it reduces storage or maintenance costs for individuals that are only temporary and less necessary and eliminates the numerous items that they rarely use as household waste(Mun, 2013).

The reflections of the new economic system on society have been an increasingly important research area for scientists and practitioners. At this point, it is crucial to clarify the trust factors that affect consumers' decision to adopt and participate in clothing sharing services. This study aims to investigate the role of trust in clothing sharing services in the sharing economy from the point of view of consumers. In this article, we focus on Dolap, one of the most prominent examples of clothing sharing services in the sharing economy. Dolap app is a collaborative clothing consumption application. Here, rare or never used clothing products are sold. A research model was proposed based on the literature review. The research model was tested using questionnaire data collected from 180 samples.

The findings show that the most important determinant for consumers' trust in the clothing sharing service platform is the platform reputation. Also, increasing consumer trust in the platform that offers clothing sharing services positively affects consumers' trust in clothing on the platform. This study reveals that the companies that will make clothing sharing services should do different studies in order to gain trust to service providers. Moreover, this study may reveal that firms providing sharing services should focus on consumer groups with high trust tendencies in order to capture the right markets. This study will contribute to the current literature about the relationship between sharing economy and the fashion industry in terms of the trust. Besides, the study is expected to fill the scientific deficiencies in collaborative clothing consumption.

LITERATURE REVIEW

Circular Economy

From the past to the present, our industrial economy has been governed by a one-way linear production and consumption model where products are produced, sold, used, and then burned or disposed of as raw materials. Nowadays, an increasing global population and consequently increasing consumption cause adverse environmental effects such as climate changes and depletion of non-renewable energy sources. Therefore, the need for sustainable development has increased. The circular economy was born in response to these problems. The circular economy promises hope for a sustainable future. The transition from the current linear economic model to the circular economy has recently attracted the attention of large global companies and researchers(Macarthur, 2013).

CE, has many definitions derived from various scientific disciplines and semi-scientific concepts(Korhonen et al., 2018). In general, CE is defined according to the "3Rs" principle(Naustdalslid, 2014). Reduction, Reusing, and Recycling.

- **Reduction**: In the production or consumption process, the amount of material input should be reduced as much as possible and kept as low as possible.
- **Reusing**: Reuse of less used or not worn items. The aim is to extend the service life of the products.
- **Recycling**: Waste from one type of production should be used as raw material for the manufacture of other products.

The aim of the circular economy is to achieve production and economic growth without being dependent on natural resources. The circular economy enables the companies to continue to reuse resources by means of recovery and strengthening by producing in a closed loop(World Economic Forum, 2014). The circular economy has focused on converting the remaining unusable parts of a product after consumption into a new source for a purpose(Esposito, Tse, & Soufani, 2017). It is also not only related to production but also aims to develop sustainable consumption together with sustainable production(Korhonen et al., 2018; Naustdalslid, 2014).

The linear economy that emerged as a result of the industrial revolution has negatively changed the ecology of the world and our relationship with the environment. However, the circular economy and the sharing economy can change this relationship positively(Esposito et al., 2017). It requires us to apply new paradigms to today's systems on a collaborative scale to achieve a real impact.

For example, one study found that in Europe, 92% of the time cars were parked. Therefore, switching to a circular economy can eliminate 100 million tons of material waste worldwide in the next five years. Besides, a circular economy offers a meaningful solution to address the problems of low employment and economic stagnation(Esposito et al., 2017).

Despite all technological innovations, our natural capital is rapidly depleted, and our world ecology is rapidly affected. For example, despite technological advances in fertilization and irrigation, productivity growth in cereal products has fallen by 66% since the 1970s(Esposito et al., 2017). CE, which focuses on conservation of natural resources, is described as an effort to develop a new economy based on ecological principles. Therefore, CE is seen as a strategy for harmonizing the relations between nature and economy(Naustdalslid, 2014).

The circular economy has benefits from 3 different aspects. The first creates environmental benefits in terms of reduced resource use, the second creates cost savings from reduced resource requirements, and the third creates benefits in terms of the creation of new markets (in terms of job creation or wealth creation) by circular economic practices(Taranic, Behrens, & Topi, 2016). Decision-makers should be able to strike a balance between the two in order to pave the way for the sharing economy to play a meaningful role in the circular economy(Esposito et al., 2017).

Sharing Economy

The sharing economy is an integral part of the circular economy. Both the sharing economy and the circular economy focus on efficient and sustainable resource use(World Economic Forum, 2013). The sharing economy and the cyclic economy were born in response to many problems such as global warming, increased resource use, and increased environmental pollution. The new way of sharing, known as the Sharing economy, has led to numerous new non-traditional business and business models with the spread of technology and the use of the Internet. Technological developments have been central to the development of the sharing economy(The Economist, 2013).

Today, as a rapidly growing and intensely debated phenomenon, Sharing Economy is a globally spreading economy, but it does not have a standard definition(Hou, 2018; Schor, 2014). According to Hamari et al., (2015), the sharing economy is the activity of donating or sharing goods and services coordinated among peers through community-oriented online services. According to Mair & Reischauer (2017), the sharing economy is a market network where various forms of payment are used to ensure the redistribution and access to resources mediated by a digital platform operated by an organization.

The sharing economy is an environmental business model that enables the optimization of resources through redistribution and utilizes information technologies through the sharing and reuse of excess capacity and unused portions of goods and services(Hamari, Sjöklint, & Ukkonen, 2016; Hook, 2016; Prieto, Baltas, & Stan, 2017). SE provides the same benefits as the circular economy, such as minimizing waste, recycling, redistribution of unused or underused goods. SE, provides several benefits such as the more efficient use of financial resources in the economic sense, the more sustainable and innovative use of natural resources in the environmental sense, and the more social relations between peers become social(Botsman & Rogers, 2010; Martin et al., 2015).

Excessive consumption, which started with the industrial revolution, causes serious environmental problems such as the depletion of natural resources and excessive waste generation. In addition to over-consumption, the ever-increasing human population threatens natural resources and increases competition on natural resources. Natural resources, including soil, potable water, and oil, are rapidly depleted. Simultaneously increasing young population and developing health technologies and prolonging human life have led to an increase in world population and urbanization(Rinne et al., 2013). Today, the global population exceeding 7.5 billion is estimated to exceed 9 billion by the middle of the century(Finley, 2012; Worldometers, 2018). In order to prevent unnecessary use of resources and excessive losses in our world whose population is increasing day by day, it is necessary to limit new purchases and encourage the reuse of old products(Tukker & Tischner, 2006). This may create an impulse to change our consumption behavior. According to Gansky (2010), in order to have a more peaceful, prosperous, and sustainable world, there is an obligation to do more efficient sharing of our existing resources.

SE, renting and redistribution of unused or underused goods in the hands of consumers, effectively reduces environmental footprints. For example, traveling with several people offers the opportunity to meet new people as well as reduce driving costs and adverse environmental consequences. Also, vehicle sharing can reduce the congestion of roads and parking lots and reduce energy consumption. This is an indication that the sharing economy can be a solution to ecological damage. In another example, instead of buying a new dress for a day's activity, renting a dress enables a person to reach their goal without increasing their closet or maintenance expenses. Besides, it reduces storage or maintenance costs for individuals that are only temporary and less necessary and eliminates the occasional use of household waste(Mun, 2013).

The ownership-based lifestyle of consumers has changed renting, exchanging, and sharing. Thus, goods and service owners and buyers interact with each other. Moreover, this facilitates the social interaction between people and cultures of different sexes, different ages(Perlacia & Duml, 2018). Also, cooperative consumption can provide significant environmental benefits by increasing productivity, reducing waste of resources, and removing old or unwanted materials from the environment. Also, it can create new areas of employment, promote social innovation, and contribute to building stronger and closer communities(Botsman & Rogers, 2010; Gheitasy, 2017; Tukker & Tischner, 2006).

Clothing Sharing Services

In the last decade, the fashion industry has become one of the most critical sectors in the world. The fashion market is continuously growing and changing rapidly(Perlacia & Duml, 2018). The reason behind this is that with the second industrial revolution, new technologies have brought a new production system. This has led to the proliferation of retail stores. As a result, fashion products are produced in more series and sold at fixed prices. In this context, due to innovations in technology, economy, and environmental factors, the fashion industry has developed more rapidly and has become one of the international and globalized industries(Steele & Major, 2019).

There are three forces that contribute to the development of the fashion industry: technology, economy, and society(Perlacia & Duml, 2018). Especially the technological revolution has had a significant impact on the fashion industry. Technology has made all kinds of fashion more accessible to a broader group of entrepreneurs. Moreover, there has been a drastic change in buying and calling habits due to the increase in internet and smartphone usage(Slyce, 2015). Technology has also changed the way suppliers, and retailers do business. Inventory management, sales, and trend research are now becoming much faster. With technology, processing costs have been reduced, producing a product is easier, cheaper, and on a larger scale. Before the Internet, it was possible to rent an asset from another person, but it was quite challenging to do. However, technology has allowed it to overcome such obstacles(The Economist, 2013a).

Smartphone technology and the Internet have accelerated the spread of clothing sharing applications. However, not only technology, but also other economic and environmental factors cannot be overlooked as a major contribution to the growth of the collaborative economy in fashion(Owyang, Samuel, & Grenville, 2014). Collaborative consumption has had a significant impact on the fashion industry. Encouraging people to share, reuse, and recycle fashion products increase environmental sustainability by minimizing the number of materials and amount of waste(Perlacia & Duml, 2018). However, there is limited academic research on different clothing sharing patterns. Not much is known about how companies create and capture value through the sharing of fashion products, as well as the benefits and challenges for these companies(Perlacia & Duml, 2018). Therefore, this article explores the factors that influence the intention to accept and use clothing sharing services.

RESEARCH METHODOLOGY

It has been scientifically proven and widely accepted that excess greenhouse gases resulting from the burning of fossil fuels and consumption patterns exceeding basic needs accelerate climate change and environmental damage(Nasa, 2018). In addition to its environmental effects, overconsumption can create debt, disorder, and complexity in individuals' lives. Researchers have also documented that a consumption-based lifestyle is detrimental to human welfare. Consumption is often associated with overwork, leading to increased stress levels(Schor, 2014). It can also lead to stagnation and unhappiness(Binswanger, 2006). Also, excessive consumption causes financial stress as it stimulates the increase in consumer debt(Mun, 2013). These negative impacts have made the modern consumer more sensitive to environmental issues, and this has made today's consumer more inclined to buy products produced in a more conscious and sustainable way. Many companies have adopted more environmentally and more sustainable practices to develop good relationships with consumers(Nadler, 2014). One of these sustainable business models is the sharing economy.

When the sharing economy first emerged, it was only considered a temporary enthusiasm, but it is now becoming a robust phenomenon(Gansky, 2010). According to a study, the shared economy sector is expected to be worth 335 billion dollars by 2025(Statista, 2019). Therefore, the sharing economy sector is the center of attention of investors and developers. At this point, companies and practitioners have to develop effective strategies by accurately analyzing the needs and needs of potential users in order to be successful in the sector and to gain competitive advantage. However, limited studies have been conducted on this subject. This study is expected to fill the existing deficiency in the literature.

The research question of this study is, "How does trust in online or mobile clothing sharing services affect participation in the sharing economy?"

In this context, the following questions are sought:

1) What are the trust factors that affect consumers' participation in online or mobile clothing sharing services?
2) How does increasing consumer trust in digital environments affect the intention of using clothing sharing services provided through digital platforms?

In the study, firstly, the research aims were determined, and the variables were determined according to these aims. In the second stage, a research model was created, and hypotheses were determined. In the third stage, the determination of data collection techniques, and then a literature review was performed, and the measurement tool to be used in the study was developed. By taking the opinions of the experts, necessary arrangements and improvements were made, and the measurement tool was finalized. The developed scale was distributed online and manually, and the data were collected. The collected data were transferred to SPSS 18 (Statistical Packages for Social Sciences). Afterward, the analysis was carried out according to the research problem by uploading to Smart PLS program. The findings were reported.

Research Model And Hypotheses

Figure 1. Research model

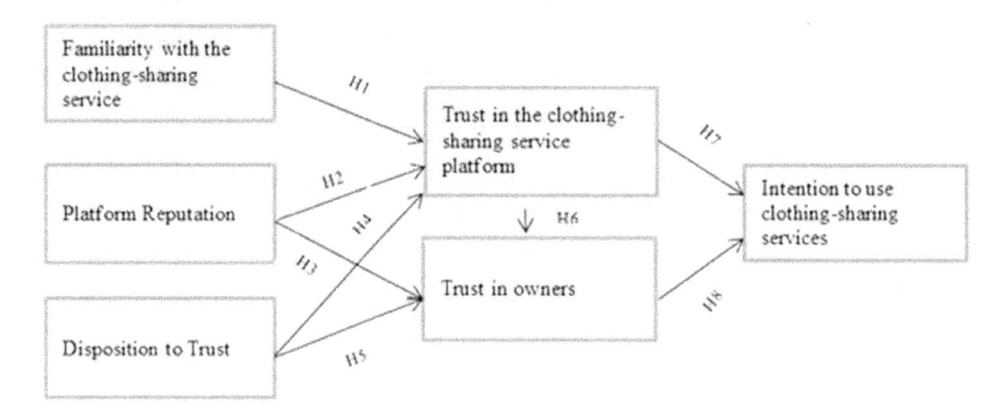

H1: the *Increasing degree of consumer's familiarity with the clothing sharing service platform positively has a positive impact on the consumers' trust in the clothing sharing service platform.*

The fact that the consumers have information about the sharing service and the information about the functions of the sharing service, that is, the increase in the degree of familiarity with the platform, will have a positive effect on the trust of the consumer(Gefen, 2002; Kim, Ferrin, & Rao, 2008; Schoorman, Mayer, & Davis, 2007) Previous research has discovered that the degree of familiarity with the sharing service will increase consumer trust in the sharing service(Gao, Jing, & Guo, 2017; Mittendorf, 2016).

H2: The perceived clothing sharing service platform reputation has a positive impact on the consumers' trust in clothing sharing service platform.

H3: The perceived clothing sharing service platform reputation has a positive impact on the consumers' trust in owners on the platform.

A good reputation is a symbol of the company's talent, honesty, and goodwill. Previous research on online shopping found that perceived reputation has a significant impact on the trust of online companies and their products(Koufaris & Hampton-Sosa, 2004). It is considered that the reputation of both the service platform and the service provider on the platform is crucial for the consumer to decide using sharing services. According to these hypotheses, if the sharing platform is well known, individuals' trust in both the service platform and the service provider will increase.

H4: The stronger the consumers' disposition to trust is, the more they will trust in the clothing sharing service platform.

H5: The stronger the consumers' disposition to trust is, the more they will trust in owners on the clothing sharing service platform.

Some studies have shown that the general trust trend directly affects the formation of e-commerce trust(Kim et al., 2008). According to these hypotheses, the trust tendency is directly related to both to trust the sharing platform and to trust the service provider on the platform.

H6: the *Increased degree of the consumers' trust in the clothing sharing service platform has a positive impact on the consumers' trust in owners.*

According to this hypothesis, it is assumed that the perceived reliability of the service provider on the sharing platform depends on the perceived reliability of the sharing platform. Previous research has found that increased trust in the sharing service increases potential users' trust in the service provider(Gao et al., 2017; Mittendorf, 2016).

H7: the Increased degree of trust in the clothing sharing service platforms will increase the consumers' intentions to use clothing sharing services.

H8: the Increased degree of trust in owners on the clothing sharing service platforms will increase the consumers' intentions to use clothing sharing services.

Earlier research on e-commerce has shown that the higher the consumer's trust in online retailers' websites, the stronger their intention to purchase goods and services from their websites(Gefen, 2000; Jarvenpaa, Tractinsky, & Saarinen, 2000). Consumers' trust in the sharing platform and the service provider on the platform can reduce their uncertainties in the online environment and make them feel comfortable about interacting with the platform and the service provider on the platform. As a result, they are more likely to intend to use sharing services.

An Empirical Study With Dolap

In order to understand the role of trust with clothing sharing services in the sharing economy, the proposed research model was empirically tested with Dolap in Turkey.

Clothing Sharing Service: Dolap

Dolap established in Turkey in April 2016, showed a rapid rise in second-hand clothes market itself. Thousands of used second-hand luxury brand products are sold in the Dolap application. Dolap has announced that it has exceeded 400 thousand members in the first five months of its establishment. Collaborating with Morhipo, Dolap also offers the opportunity to shop first hand with the points accumulated by second-hand sellers(Kara, 2017).

Samples

Research data was collected from Google forms January 5, 2019, between April 10, 2019. The research model was tested using questionnaire data collected from 180 samples.

Structural Model and Hypotheses Testing

The structural model was tested using Smart PLS 3.0. The eight research hypotheses were supported. Smart PLS 3.0 is used to test the structural model in this study. The R^2 (R squared) in Figure 1 denotes to the coefficient of determination. According to the results, the amount of variance in the consumers' intention to use fashion-sharing services explained by the model was 0.41.

In general, this model describes the intention to use the Dolap sharing service by 41%(R^2=0.41). This result indicates that Dolap awareness, trust in the Dolap platform, the reputation of the Dolap platform, the general trust trend and the trust in the clothing owner have a statistically significant effect on the intention to use the Dolap.

In general, all factor loads above 0.50 are considered sufficient for scale validity(Hair, Barry, Babin, & Anderson, 2013). When Table 1 is examined, it is seen that factor loads are 0.851 and above. This value confirms the validity of the scale. The reliability of the scale can be mentioned when Cronbach's Alpha value is above 0.70, CR value is above 0.70, and AVE value is above 0.50(Öngel, 2018). When Table 1 is examined, it is seen that the reliability values of latent (implicit) variables are above 0.70. Accordingly, we can say that all latent variables used in the model are reliable, and therefore, the model created for this research is statistically significant and reliable.

The results of the hypothesis for the Dolap model are shown in table 2 with all the details. When the results are examined, it is seen that all the hypotheses tested are validated.

Table 1. Factor loadings, composite reliability, and AVE for each construct

Construct	Item	Factor Loading	Cronbach's Alpha	CR	AVE
Familiarity	DA1	0.945	0.958	0.973	0.922
	DA2	0.972			
	DA3	0.964			
Disposition to Trust	GG1	0.851	0.815	0.889	0.728
	GG2	0.871			
	GG3	0.837			
Platform Reputation	DU1	0.919	0.940	0.957	0.848
	DU2	0.938			
	DU3	0.917			
	DU4	0.909			
Trust in Dolap	DG1	0.939	0.951	0.968	0.910
	DG2	0.970			
	DG3	0.953			
Trust İn Owners	KFS1	0.893	0.932	0.951	0.831
	KFS2	0.908			
	KFS3	0.924			
	KFS4	0.921			
Intention to Use	DKN1	0.946	0.946	0.965	0.903
	DKN2	0.963			
	DKN3	0.941			

Table 2. Test of hypotheses

Hypotheses	Path Coefficient	Hypothesis Result
H1	0.116	Supported
H2	0.705	Supported
H3	0.146	Supported
H4	0.116	Supported
H5	0.149	Supported
H6	0.515	Supported
H7	0.376	Supported
H8	0.325	Supported

H1 hypothesis suggests that familiarity with the platform positively affects trust in the platform. Accordingly, there is a relatively weak but statistically significant relationship between platform familiarity and platform trust. In other words, familiarity with the sharing platform affects the consumer's trust in the sharing platform positively.

H2 hypothesis suggests that platform reputation positively affects trust in the platform. Accordingly, it was found that there is a statistically significant and significant relationship between platform reputation and platform trust. In other words, the perceived reputation of the sharing platform positively affects the consumer's trust in the sharing service.

H3 hypothesis suggests that platform reputation positively affects trust in service providers. Accordingly, it is seen that there is a relatively weak but significant relationship between platform reputation and trust in service providers. In other words, the perceived reputation of the sharing platform positively affects the consumer's trust in service providers.

H4 hypothesis suggests that trust tendency positively affects trust in the platform. Accordingly, there is a weak but statistically significant relationship between trust tendency and platform trust. In other words, the general trust tendency has a positive effect on the trust of the consumer to the platform providing the sharing service.

H5 hypothesis suggests that trust tendency positively affects trust in service providers. Accordingly, it has been found that there is a relatively weak but significant relationship between trust tendency and service providers trust. In other words, the general tendency of trust has a positive effect on the consumer's trust in service providers.

H6 hypothesis suggests that trust in the platform positively affects trust in service providers. Accordingly, it was found that there is a statistically significant and significant relationship between platform trust and service providers trust. In summary, increasing consumer trust in the sharing platform positively affects the trust in the service provider.

H7 hypothesis suggests that trust in the platform positively affects the intention to use sharing services. Accordingly, it was found that there is a statistically weak but significant relationship between the trust to the platform and the intention to use the sharing services. In other words, increasing consumer trust in the sharing platform positively affects the intention to use sharing services.

H8 hypothesis suggests that trust in the service provider positively affects the intention to use the sharing service. Accordingly, it has been found that there is a statistically weak but significant relationship between trust in service provider and intention to use sharing service. That is, increasing consumer trust in the service provider on the sharing platform will increase the intention of using sharing services.

CONCLUSION

Nowadays, with the increasing consumption, the approach to the depletion of natural resources and the spread of the internet, online social networks and mobile technologies, the most significant change can be seen in the consumption habits of individuals. These factors triggered the participation of individuals in sharing activities, and the sharing economy spread rapidly. At this point, companies and practitioners have to develop effective strategies by accurately analyzing the needs and needs of potential users in order to be successful in the sector and to gain competitive advantage. However, limited studies have been conducted on this subject. This study aims to investigate how trust in online or mobile clothing sharing services affects participation in sharing economies. To do so, a research model was formed, and hypotheses were determined. After the literature review, the measurement tool to be used in the study was developed. The developed scale was distributed online and manually, and the data were collected. The collected data were transferred to SPSS 18 (Statistical Packages for Social Sciences). Then the research model was tested by uploading to Smart PLS program.

According to the findings, it was observed that all changes in the research model had a positive and significant effect on the intention to use the sharing service for Dolap, which is a clothing sharing application. The research model and research hypotheses put forward in the conceptual/theoretical framework were accepted. The most important result of the study, Although it is high trust that the platform is branded or international reputation in Turkey, it has been observed that relatively low trust in the service provider to the brand. In this case, Turkey will do these activities on behalf of the company to win the trust of service providers reveals he had to do different work. Moreover, this study may reveal that firms providing sharing services should focus on consumer groups with high trust tendencies in order to capture the right markets.

The contribution of this study is two-fold. First, based on previous research in different fields, a research model is proposed to examine the role of trust in sharing economics platforms, which may seem a significant contribution to the literature in the sharing economy. Second, the results of this empirical study reveal some practical results for actors involved in fashion sharing services in the sharing economy.

FUTURE RESEARCH DIRECTIONS

While people have shared their existing resources for thousands of years, the sharing economy is a new concept that has emerged in recent years. Although there is no definite opinion as to why the sharing economy has emerged and how it has developed, various researchers have shed light on its emergence. It is argued that the concepts of collaborative consumption and sharing economy emerged with the internet(Belk, 2014). Developing technology has led to the emergence of many innovations, affecting all industry sectors. Especially in the fashion industry, there have been significant changes. The idea of sharing fashion products in a virtual environment through digital networks has gained momentum.

Turkey, with different sampling for the determination of other factors affecting participation in online or mobile platform on behalf of the widespread participation in the services offered through sharing service, is considered that more work needs to be done. It is considered that testing the model in other sharing services within the scope of the research will be beneficial in terms of comparing the results. Besides, this study considers the role of trust in participating in sharing services offered through online or mobile platforms from a consumer perspective. The role of trust in participating in sharing services offered online or on mobile platforms for service providers is left to future studies. Finally, cross-cultural comparisons are recommended for future studies.

REFERENCES

Belk, R. (2014). You are what you can access: Sharing and collaborative consumption online. *Journal of Business Research*, *67*(8), 1595–1600. doi:10.1016/j.jbusres.2013.10.001

Binswanger, M. (2006). Why does income growth fail to make us happier?: Searching for the treadmills behind the paradox of happiness. *Journal of Socio-Economics*, *35*(2), 366–381. doi:10.1016/j.socec.2005.11.040

Botsman, R., & Rogers, R. (2010). *What's mine is yours : the rise of collaborative consumption*. Harper Business.

Brussels. (2015). *Press release - Circular Economy Package: Questions & Answers*. Retrieved July 29, 2019, from https://europa.eu/rapid/press-release_MEMO-15-6204_en.htm

Egerton-Read, S. (2016). What does the sharing economy mean for a circular economy? *Circulate*. Retrieved July 29, 2019, from https://circulatenews.org/2016/08/what-does-the-sharing-economy-mean-for-a-circular-economy/

Esposito, M., Tse, T., & Soufani, K. (2017). Is the Circular Economy a New Fast-Expanding Market? *Thunderbird International Business Review*, *59*(1), 9–14. doi:10.1002/tie.21764

Finley, K. (2012). *Trust in the Sharing Economy: An Exploratory Study.* Academic Press.

Gansky, L. (2010). The mesh - why the future of business is sharing. In Igarss 2010. doi:10.100713398-014-0173-7.2

Gao, S., Jing, J., & Guo, H. (2017). *The Role of Trust with Car-Sharing Services in the Sharing Economy in China : From the Consumers' Perspective.* Academic Press.

Gefen, D. (2000). *E-commerce : the role of familiarity and trust.* doi:10.1016/S0305-0483(00)00021-9

Gefen, D. (2002). *Reflections on the dimensions of trust and trustworthiness among online consumers.* doi:10.1145/569905.569910

Gheitasy, A. (2017). *Socio-technical gaps and social capital formation in Online Collaborative Consumption communities by.* Academic Press.

Hair, J. F., Barry, W., Babin, B. R., & Anderson, E. (2013). Multivariate Data Analysis. In Exploratory Data Analysis in Business and Economics. doi:10.1007/978-3-319-01517-0_3

Hamari. (2015). The Sharing Economy: Why People Participate in Collaborative Consumption. *Communications in Information Literacy*, 1–13. doi:10.1002/asi

Hamari, J., Sjöklint, M., & Ukkonen, A. (2016). The sharing economy: Why people participate in collaborative consumption. *Journal of the Association for Information Science and Technology.* Retrieved from https://www.researchgate.net/publication/255698095

Hook, L. (2016). Review – "The Sharing Economy." *Financial Times.* Retrieved from http://www.ft.com/cms/s/0/f560e5ee-36e8-11e6-a780-b48ed7b6126f

Hou, L. (2018). Destructive sharing economy: A passage from status to contract. *Computer Law & Security Review*, *34*(4), 965–976. doi:10.1016/j.clsr.2018.05.009

Jarvenpaa, S. L., Tractinsky, N., & Saarinen, L. (2000). Consumer Trust in an Internet Store: A Cross-Cultural Validation. *Journal of Computer-Mediated Communication*, *5*(2). doi:10.1111/j.1083-6101.1999.tb00337.x

Kara, M. (2017). *400 bin üyeyi geçen ikinci el moda uygulaması Dolap, Morhipo ile iş birliğini duyurdu.* Retrieved October 30, 2018, from https://webrazzi.com/2017/03/10/400-bin-uyeyi-gecen-ikinci-el-moda-uygulamasi-dolap-morhipo-ile-is-birligini-duyurdu/

Kim, D. J., Ferrin, D. L., & Rao, H. R. (2008). A trust-based consumer decision-making model in electronic commerce: The role of trust, perceived risk, and their antecedents. *Decision Support Systems, 44*(2), 544–564. doi:10.1016/j.dss.2007.07.001

Korhonen, J., Nuur, C., Feldmann, A., & Birkie, S. E. (2018). Circular economy as an essentially contested concept. *Journal of Cleaner Production, 175*, 544–552. doi:10.1016/j.jclepro.2017.12.111

Koufaris, M., & Hampton-Sosa, W. (2004). The development of initial trust in an online company by new customers. *Information & Management, 41*(3), 377–397. doi:10.1016/j.im.2003.08.004

Lahti, T., Wincent, J., & Parida, V. (2018). A definition and theoretical review of the circular economy, value creation, and sustainable business models: Where are we now and where should research move in the future? *Sustainability (Switzerland), 10*(8), 2799. doi:10.3390u10082799

Macarthur, E. (2013). Towards the Circular Economy. *Journal of Industrial Ecology, 1*(1), 4–8. doi:10.1162/108819806775545321

Mair, J., & Reischauer, G. (2017). Capturing the dynamics of the sharing economy: Institutional research on the plural forms and practices of sharing economy organizations. *Technological Forecasting and Social Change, 125*, 11–20. doi:10.1016/j.techfore.2017.05.023

Martin, Upham, P., & Budd, L. (2015). Commercial orientation in grassroots social innovation: Insights from the sharing economy. *Ecological Economics, 118*, 240–251. doi:10.1016/j.ecolecon.2015.08.001

McKnight, D. H., & Chervany, N. L. (2001). *Trust and Distrust Definitions: One Bite at a Time.* doi:10.1177/0734242X05051045

Mittendorf, C. (2016). *What Trust means in the Sharing Economy : A provider perspective on Airbnb . com.* Academic Press.

Mun, J. M. (2013). *Online Collaborative Consumption: Exploring Meanings. Motivations, Costs, and Benefits.* Academic Press.

Nadler, S. (2014). *The Sharing Economy: What is it and where is it going?* Academic Press.

NASA. (2018). *NASA: Climate Change and Global Warming.* Retrieved December 12, 2018, from https://climate.nasa.gov/

Naustdalslid, J. (2014). Circular economy in China - The environmental dimension of the harmonious society. *International Journal of Sustainable Development and World Ecology, 21*(4), 303–313. doi:10.1080/13504509.2014.914599

Öngel, G. (2018). *Sağlık Çalışanlarının Yaşamış Oldukları İş-Aile Yaşamı Çatışmasının Örgütsel Bağlılık, İş Doyumu Ve İşten Ayrılma Niyetine Etkisi.* Academic Press.

Owyang, J., Samuel, A., & Grenville, A. (2014). Sharing Is The New Buying: How To Win In The Collaborative Economy. *Vision Critical; Crowd Companies,* 1–31. Retrieved from http://info.mkto.visioncritical.com/rs/visioncritical/images/sharing-new-buying-collaborative-economy.pdf

Perlacia, A., & Duml, V. (2018). *Collaborative Consumption: Live Fashion, Don't Own It - Developing New Business Models for the Fashion Industry.* SSRN Electronic Journal. doi:10.2139srn.2860021

Prieto, M., Baltas, G., & Stan, V. (2017). Car sharing adoption intention in urban areas: What are the key sociodemographic drivers? *Transportation Research Part A, Policy and Practice, 101,* 218–227. doi:10.1016/j.tra.2017.05.012

Rinne. (2013). Circular Economy Innovation & New Business Models Initiative. *World Economic Forum Young Global Leaders Taskforce Circular, 1,* 16.

Schoorman, F. D., Mayer, R. C., & Davis, J. H. (2007). An integrative model of organizational trust: past, present, and future. In *Academy of Management Review* (Vol. 32). Retrieved from https://pdfs.semanticscholar.org/7aed/d30a40b70ccbadc7c290973d02e8e19b739c.pdf

Schor, J. (2014, Oct.). Debating the Sharing Economy. *A Great Transition Initiative Essay,* 1–19. doi:10.7903/cmr.11116

Statista. (2019). *Value of the global sharing economy 2014-2025.* Retrieved June 25, 2019, from https://www.statista.com/statistics/830986/value-of-the-global-sharing-economy/

Steele, V., & Major, J. S. (2019). *Fashion industry | Design, Fashion Shows, Marketing, & Facts.* Retrieved July 31, 2019, from https://www.britannica.com/art/fashion-industry

Taranic, I., Behrens, A., & Topi, C. (2016). *Understanding the Circular Economy in Europe, from Resource Efficiency to Sharing Platforms: The CEPS Framework.* Retrieved from www.ceps.eu

The Economist. (2013). All eyes on the sharing economy. *Economist, 452*(7184), 137–137. doi:10.1038/452137a

Tukker, A., & Tischner, U. (2006). Product-services as a research field: Past, present and future. Reflections from a decade of research. *Journal of Cleaner Production, 14*(17), 1552–1556. doi:10.1016/j.jclepro.2006.01.022

World Economic Forum. (2013). *Young Global Leaders - Circular Economy Innovation & New Business Models Dialogue.* Retrieved from http://www3.weforum.org/docs/WEF_YGL_CircularEconomyInnovation_PositionPaper_2013.pdf

World Economic Forum. (2014). *Towards the Circular Economy: Accelerating the scale-up across global supply chains.* Retrieved from www.weforum.org

Worldometers. (2018). *World Population Clock: 7.7 Billion People (2018).* Retrieved October 12, 2018, from https://www.worldometers.info/world-population/

Chapter 13
Customer Engagement by Fashion Brands:
An Effective Marketing Strategy

Samala Nagaraj
https://orcid.org/0000-0002-1182-115X
University of Hyderabad, India

ABSTRACT

No matter what changes time and technology bring to the world, fashion has its own way of adaptation. In the present times dominated by advanced technology and information, fashion enthusiasts, marketers, and industry are facing challenges and learning to adapt the new. With the increased options of selecting favorite fashion brands through largely available channels and information, fashion customers are equipped today with greater flexibility and understanding; this challenges brands to retain customers. Marketers are using new ways and platforms to engage customers. The chapter focuses on the effective marketing strategies adopted by fashion brands to engage customers. The chapter elaborately discusses the latest technologies and platforms used to engage customers. The chapter attempts to exemplify the effective engagement strategies followed by some of the successful fashion brands. It discusses new techniques in engaging like gamification and the use of advanced analytics for evaluation.

INTRODUCTION

The fashion industry has evolved significantly in the past few years. With the change in time and technology, the industry has shifted from its normal course. The level

DOI: 10.4018/978-1-7998-2728-3.ch013

of competition has intensified in the industrial setting. It has urged the business participants to employ a wide range of strategies for the purpose of engaging with the market audience. In the technology-driven times, fashion is influenced by technological innovation. The marketers that function in the evolving industry try to adapt to the changing business environment so that they can sustain and survive in the market setting. Some of the top fashion brands such as Louis Vuitton, Gucci, Prada, Ralph Lauren, Chanel, Burberry, and Hermes have continued to survive in the competitive market setting in spite of the evolving nature (Top 10 Best Selling Clothing Brands in The World, 2019). One of the primary reasons for their existence in the fashion industry is the strategies that they implement to interact and engage with the market audience. In spite of facing numerous challenges and obstacles relating to advanced technology and information, fashion marketers operating in the industry are learning to adapt to the new business environment.

The chapter mainly focuses on the effective marketing strategies that are adopted by fashion brands in the market setting. Similarly, the manner in which these market players employ the latest technical elements and platforms to engage with customers has been highlighted. In the prevalent competitive era, the engagement with the audience is the key to the survival of fashion marketers (Moreno-Munoz et al., 2016). The successful and effective engagement strategies that are implemented by successful fashion brands have been explored here. The exact role of engagement has been presented since it has completely transformed the face of the fashion industry. In the digitalized era, social media platforms have played a significant role to change the way fashion brands communicate and engage with the target market audience. The use of social networking sites and online brand communities by fashion marketers has been elaborated. In addition to this, innovative engagement technologies such as Gamification have also been captured as it is being used by a number of reputed fashion brands to enhance the quality of the user engagement (Samala & Singh, 2019). Ultimate, the application of advanced analytical tools and Artificial Intelligence (AI) for the purpose of measuring the effectiveness of engagement has been captured. The chapter would offer a complete picture relating to the customer engagement that is done in the prevailing fashion industry. A number of real-life industry examples have also been captured to simplify the understanding of customer engagement in the fashion industry.

Effective Marketing Strategies Adopted by Fashion Brands

In the cut-throat competitive business setting, fashion marketers employ a wide range of effective marketing strategies for the purpose of engaging with their potential and existing customers. According to the research study by Ashley & Tuten, a number of luxury fashion brands use the online platform for the purpose of interacting and engaging with the target market audience. As per the research findings, the theme of the content plays a key role to influence the relationship that fashion brands establish with their customers (Ashley & Tuten, 2015). In the cut-throat competitive times, a majority of the fashion brands are trying to adopt creative content and marketing strategic models so that the level of engagement can be improved. Instagram is used as one of the most popular technology-driven platforms that are used by luxury fashion brands to communicate with the large market audience. The photo and video sharing social media platform are gaining high popularity in the fashion industry as it allows the marketers to share their image-based and video-based content without any physical barrier.

Andrea Geissinger and Laurell Christofer have stated that at present, social media has been integrated into the marketing strategies so that the ultimate level of consumer engagement can be enhanced (Geissinger & Laurell, 2016). In the Swedish fashion industrial setting, social media is used as a vital tool that helps to strengthen the effectiveness of the marketing strategy. Most of the fashion brands employ strategic approaches so that they can strike a balance between customer engagement, maintaining an exclusive brand and offering valuable products and commodities in the market. One of the main elements that help fashion brands to survive and sustain is creative engagement.

Some of the most common marketing strategies that are adopted by fashion brands to engage potential and existing customers include shoppable videos, shoppable magazines, Instagram stories, interactive campaigns, introducing microsites, and the creation of diverse ads (Geissinger & Laurell, 2016). Many popular fashion names have used such kinds of innovative strategic approaches so that the relationship with the potential and the existing market audience can be strengthened in the process. For example, in the year 2017, the Jigsaw fashion brand designed its print, digital and social marketing campaign around the significance of immigration in the fashion scene.

The 'Love immigration' campaign was a unique marketing strategy which helped the brand to celebrate diversity in the British fashion arena (Gilliland, 2019). Similarly, the Ted Baker luxury brand has also experimented with innovative, inspirational and thought-provoking Instagram stories. In 2017, the fashion brand pushed the boundaries further by introducing a sitcom known as "Keeping up with the Bakers' which was played on the Instagram platform. The objective of the unique marketing strategy was to encourage the users and followers to visit the official page of Ted Baker on a daily basis and take part in the daily challenges. This marketing strategy helped the fashion brand to improve the level of engagement and interaction that the business concern had with its existing customers and the potential customers.

In the 21st century, most of the fashion brands are trying to introduce and share a sleek slice of shoppable content with the target market audience. The intention of the fashion players is to form a connection with the customers in the competitive market environment.

Use of Latest Technologies and Platforms to Engage With Customers

The evolution of the fashion industry scene has given rise to a number of new challenges and hurdles. But at the same time, it has also empowered fashion brands by giving rise to the latest technologies and platforms that can be used for engaging and interacting with the customers. In the digitalized era, numerous fashion brands have combined digital technology with their marketing strategy so that they can easily and effectively engage with their market audience (Gilliam, 2019).

Currently, the most popular technologies and platforms that are being used by marketers to engage with customers include email marketing tools, social media marketing tools, customer relationship management software, and analytical tools and collaboration software (Email Engagement Often talked about, never defined, 2019). The email technology is used so that brands can send frequent updates to the potential customers and existing customers about their offerings. It not only strengthens the level of customer engagement but it also improves the brand awareness. Social media platforms are used to directly interact with the market audience through posts or stories. It enables fashion businesses to establish a long-lasting connection with the audience.

A number of leading fashion brands such as Louis Vuitton and Tiffany & Co. Louis Vuitton has a strong presence in the virtual business setting. The fashion brand has its own official website. In addition to the site, it has its presence on a number of social media platforms such as Facebook, Twitter, Instagram, and YouTube. This unique approach allows the brand to establish an interactive relationship with its existing customers as well as the potential market audience. Similarly, Tiffany & Co. uses social media platforms so that it can blast its marketing message in the vast and dynamic market environment. In the year 2015, it has designed an innovative engagement ring finder application. It basically helped the users to choose the specific ring style and weight of the carat. It even allowed them to take a hand selfie so that they could try the ring in the virtual setting.

Facebook is regarded to be one of the most common and effective platforms that are used by Fashion brands to engage and interact with the vast market audience all around the globe. It is used as a significant part of engagement marketing. Engagement marketing can be defined as the marketing approach that is used by marketers for the purpose of building long-lasting relationships with the customers by engaging with them directly (Harmeling et al., 2017). In the digitalized time Facebook is being used as a key marketing platform which enables marketers to motivate and invite the market audience so that they can play an active part in the evolution process of the brand. According to Harmeling and Arnold, customer engagement marketing has gained high importance in the entire market scene, especially the fashion setting (Harmeling et al., 2017). Numerous platforms are being used by marketers so that they can acquire the new customers and retain the old ones.

Fashion brands are attempting to personalize the customer communication and engagement by using a wide range of interactive tools and techniques. Social media platforms act as the backbone of the engagement marketing strategy. For example, brands are using their respective Facebook pages to retarget their visitors and customers to increase their rate of conversion. Emails are also being used as a major marketing weapon by fashion brands to capture the attention of their buyers (Fashion Digital Marketing: 12 Ideas to Market Your Brand, 2019). Creative style guides are also being introduced by fashion participants that help the market audience to get an idea on how to wear and style the clothes of a particular designer brand. Running campaigns on Instagram has gained high popularity among fashion players as it enables them to expand the size of the online community and increase the brand awareness.

Engagement Strategies of Successful Fashion Brands

In the competitive fashion industry setting a number of selected fashion brands has been able to succeed in the market due to their robust and effective engagement strategic approaches. Nasty Girl is a popular name in the fashion industry, which has added a high level of personality to its micro-content. The choice of tone and language of the fashion brand easily captures the market audience that it intends to target.

Gucci is another well-known name in the fashion market which is known for its effective customer engagement strategic approach. In the current hyper-connected fraught world, the fashion brand has succeeded to expand its annual growth. One of the primary reasons for the successful performance of the brand is the impressive customer engagement strategy. The strategy enables the business firm to enhance the connection, engagement, and interaction in the vast market setting. The way of connecting with people has made it one of the popular fashion brands that have a strong customer base in the global context. It has exploited social media platforms to the core so that it can build a strong engagement on these interactive and technology-driven platforms. On different social media platforms such as Facebook, Twitter, Instagram, and YouTube, the Gucci brand creates and presents innovative content so that it can engage with the new generation of the audience.

Figure 1. Nasty Gal advertisement
Source: (Women's Online Clothes & Fashion Shopping | Nasty Gal UK, 2019)

Gucci has used the technology-driven fashion industry setting as a key opportunity to consume and create social media content to engage and interact with the global community. The fashion brand allowed Diet Prada to take over its Instagram stories for a day and this strategic move was highly fruitful for it. The approach allowed the brand to strengthen the transparency of the business and improve the overall effectiveness of the brand awareness. Over the years, Gucci has used a number of innovative and effective engagement strategies so that it can improve the level of engagement and connection with its market audience all around the world.

Figure 2. Gucci social media engagement
Source: (The day Gucci handed over the keys to Diet Prada - Luxury Highlights, 2019)

According to Jennifer Rowley, the online branding strategies that are employed by fashion brands in the United Kingdom play a vital role to influence the effectiveness of the customer engagement (Rowley, 2009, p 1). Generally, the 'non-value' fashion brands offer transactions via their official websites and other platforms so that they can extend the opportunities relating to customer engagement and consumer experience. The brand knowledge, brand awareness, and brand familiarity have the power to influence the customer engagement and communication to a certain degree (Rowley, 2009, p 5). With the changing times, fashion brands are introducing unique approaches and strategies so that they can have a greater opportunity to interact and engage with the market audience through interactive opportunities, online brand communities, and transaction facilities. For example, the Primark fashion brand enables the customers to download its brochure so that they can get a detailed insight into its offerings (Rowley, 2009, p 3). Similarly, Bonmarche provides limited information pertaining to its offerings. These strategies basically allow the fashion brands to engage with the potential and existing customers and create a long-lasting relationship (Rowley, 2009, p 9).

The Role of Engagement in Changing the Facet of the Fashion Industry

In the current times, technological advancement and innovation have altered the manner in which interaction and communication take place between individuals and business firms. When it comes to the fashion scene, engagement has become an indispensable element that is necessary for fashion brands to survive in the market (Ahmad, Salman & Ashiq, 2015). In the intensely competitive fashion industry, the role of customer engagement cannot be negated. It has, in fact, significantly transformed the face of the fashion industry. As per Ahmad and Salma, the fashion industry is one of the many industries where frequent changes take place. In the highly aggressive market setting, engagement and interaction between a fashion brand and the target market audience is the key to the sustainability and success of the brand.

A transparent engagement is of vital importance as it can help the potential customers as well as the existing customers to establish a long-term relationship with the business concern. Engaging with customers is not a luxury but a fundamental necessity for fashion brands as it enables them to get close to the customers (Ahmad, Salman & Ashiq, 2015). According to Payne, the importance of establishing a transparent and direct engagement has urged fashion brands to use various tools and techniques (Payne, 2016). Many popular fashion brands have started using visual storytelling model to engage through the Instagram social media platform.

According to Zyminkowska, in the current times, fashion businesses are trying to integrate a strong engagement with the market audience so that they can take part in the value creation process (Rupik, 2015). The behavior that is exhibited by the customers is influenced by the kind of engagement that they have with the fashion brand. Their behavior ultimate affects their buying behavior and their fashion brand preference.

Nagaraj Samala in his journal articles has stated that fashion brands have to cautiously design the engagement model while interacting with the millennial generation (Samala & Singh, 2019). These individuals are fashion conscious and they try to establish a personal relationship and association with the brand that they wear. Hence, brand engagement is extremely critical in nature for fashion marketers as it can influence their success or failure in the dynamic and competitive market setting. This shows that the type of engagement that fashion marketers create with the target audience has completely altered the appearance of the fashion industry.

Payne has stated in his research study that engagement refers to the creation of a deeper and more meaningful association between a business undertaking and its customer. In the competitive and dynamic market setting a majority of the fashion brands are trying to use a broad range of interactive tools so that their level of engagement with the target market audience can be strengthened and enhanced (Payne, 2016). The kind of communication that a company establishes with its stakeholders influences its survival, sustainability, and profitability in the competitive fashion industry. In the technology prone era, Instagram has gained high popularity to engage with the existing customers as well as the potential market audience. Ferrer has said that Instagram has enabled fashion brands to engage with the customers by using the storytelling approach. It even provides the public with a detailed and meaningful insight into a fashion brand's functionality which can trigger emotions in the market audience. This form of engagement is vital as it helps fashion brands to create and strengthen a loyal base of customers (Payne, 2016). The Burberry fashion brand is known to post behind-the-scenes images relating to runway shows and photo shoots on its Instagram page. This kind of transparent engagement allows the public to get a sneak peek at the real-life happenings that take place in the glamorous backdrop. Such kinds of interactive and engaging strategies are necessary in the competitive times. This is because it allows fashion business firms to establish a personal interaction with the audience that keeps them wanting more.

The Use of Social Networking Sites and Online Brand Communities

Social networking sites and online brand communities (OBCs) play an extremely vital role in the fashion industry backdrop. According to Guida Helal, in the 21st century, most of the fashion brands have shifted their communication to social media platforms and online brand communities (Helal, 2019). This is one of the new things that can be observed in the modern-day business setting. The use of social networking sites and online brand communities has gained high popularity in the competitive fashion market as these approaches enable firms to form an interpersonal bond with the target market audience. Since brand awareness has become augmented in the current times, the relationship between business undertakings and customers have become extremely critical for the survival of fashion brands (Helal, 2019). Almost all the fashion brands are attempting to foster a sense of community around the brand so that their social identity can be advanced and expanded.

Social networking platforms and online brand communities are considered to be indispensable tools that can foster the level of engagement of fashion brands. This is because they help to have a robust and direct social interaction. This form of interaction and engagement involves the reciprocal exchange as well as response between individuals. It enables fashion brands to produce and distribute quality content that has value for the users. In addition to this, the users and online audience are also empowered as they are able to share the user-generated content that relates to various fashion brands and their offerings (Helal, 2019).

Due to social media websites, fashion brands are able to connect and interact with the regular people. They are not only able to share about their clothing, accessories, and shoes but they are even able to build online brand communities to strengthen their brand awareness. The new technology-driven interactive approaches are very different from the conventional advertising platforms. The digitalized engagement approaches enable fashion brands to have a complete control over their marketing strategy and the brand image that they intend to create. These digital-based tools open a two-way communication path where customers and fashion brands are able to directly have dialogues with each other.

The application of social media platform has gained a lot of popularity in the past decades as it helps fashion brands to expand their loyal customer base in the global market setting. Charlotte Russe has succeeded to establish a strong social media campaign and it has got a strong fan following on various social media platforms such as Twitter, YouTube, Facebook and Instagram. Louis Vuitton entered this technology-driven scene at a later stage as compared to the other counterparts that operate in the fashion industry (Rowley, 2009). But within a short span of time, the global fashion brand has succeeded to build a competitive and advantageous social media campaign. Social media platforms have users from all across the globe and similarly, online brand communities comprise of users that belong to varying regions. These innovative engagement tools allow fashion brands to spread their brand name in the global market setting.

Fashion brands are able to have personalized interactions with the global market audience thanks to social media platforms such as Facebook, Twitter YouTube, and Instagram. Before the emergence of such interactive platforms, fashion designers and emerging fashion stylists were considered to be separate from the entire fashion industry. After the emergence of tools such as YouTube and Facebook, fashion brands have got a voice which allows them to interact with the market audience at the global level. Today, online media outlets and communities serve as a vital interactive source for regular fashion coverage. Fashion brands use these technology-based platforms to make the market audience and customers feel like they are a vital part of a fashion brand's extended family. The interactive elements of social media platforms and online brand communities such as the comment section and the reply section further enhances the relationship between fashion brands and their existing and potential customers.

As per the journal paper by Brogi and Calabrese, just like social media platforms, the online brand communities play an extremely vital role to strengthen the brand equity of fashion brands in the competitive fashion industry (Brogi et al., 2013). Such interactive communities fundamentally allow fashion customers to interact with one another without being restricted due to the difference in space and time. Manu popular fashion brands have created such kind of specialized brand communities in the virtual environment. The online engagement approach is vital for fashion houses as it helps them to expand the customer loyalty, act in a resilient manner towards negative news about the fashion business and showcase the firm's socially responsible behavior to the online masses. Some of the fashion brands with the most effective and successful online brand communities are Gucci and Burberry (The day Gucci handed over the keys to Diet Prada - Luxury Highlights, 2019). The online community of Gucci has a strong fan following. Similarly, Burberry has also succeeded to establish a powerful online community which helps it to strengthen its brand awareness in the competitive fashion industry. Burberry has created a unique online community known as 'Art of the Trench' where users have the liberty to upload images of themselves wearing Burberry apparels. It is a unique approach that the brand has taken by placing the customers in the central position of the brand. It has helped the fashion brand to attract thousands of users from all across the globe. The respective online brand communities of the fashion brands have helped them to capitalize on the dynamic social media revolution of the 21st century.

New Engaging Techniques: Gamification

In the current times, a number of innovative and technology-oriented techniques are being used by marketers in the fashion industry so that they can interact and engage with the market audience in the real time. One of the most innovative engaging techniques is known as gamification. In layman's language, the term gamification can be defined as the application of a number of game principles and game-design elements in the non-game backdrop. It is the process of taking something that already exists such as a website, an online community or an enterprise application and combining gaming mechanics into it. The ultimate objective of the model is to encourage the level of participation loyalty and engagement in the business context.

In the competitive market setting, a number of fashion brands have employed this technique to boost the overall quality of engagement and interaction with the market audience (Samala & Singh, 2019). For example, Victoria's Secret has introduced its Pink Nation App which specifically targets the younger market audience. It is a perfect engagement model that is suitable for the millennial audience. The unique engagement application primarily merges the classic e-commerce experience that is delivered by the brand with unique and fun games and contests. One of the main reasons for the high popularity of the application is that the users get the chance to win an initial offer just by downloading the application.

Gilt is another reputed fashion brand which has introduced a unique engagement technique that is driven by technology. The members of the luxury fashion brand can experience a VIP and high-end shopping experience (Samala & Singh, 2019). The Loyalty program that has been introduced by the business undertaking enables its potential customers and the existing ones to get exclusive deals and offers. The flash sale site provides a tiered loyalty program which is based on the points of the customers. The Gilt members are able to earn points by interacting and engaging with the website, referring their friends, purchasing something and establishing a connection with Gilt's Facebook Timeline.

In the recent years, it has been observed that numerous luxurious fashion brands are trying to leverage the gamification approach so that they can reach nee w market audience such as the Chinese customers. A bevy of key luxury fashion players starting from Dior to Hermes have jumped on board and have started launching fun interactive games on their official 'WeChat' accounts. One of the main reasons for the popularity of the Gamification approach is the rise in the domination of online games. Fashion brands have realized the fact that online gaming provides a way to establish an association with a larger community. In order to exploit the technology-driven times, the Hermes fashion brand has introduced the popular WeChat game known as 'H-pitchhh'. This virtual version of the traditional horseshoe toss game allows the brand and the customers to have a strong interactive relationship.

Similarly, Dior has launched the new O2O loyalty program on WeChat. This interactive game has helped the brand by generating brand awareness for its new fashion store in Shanghai, China. The successful campaign of Dior basically invited its users to collect new items from its latest offerings through an interactive and fun treasure hunt. The individuals who were able to successfully complete the game got the chance to launch a virtual hot air balloon to win a chance to win tickets to the Dior store's opening event. The Guerlain brand has also launched a Tetris-inspired game on WeChat. The game has gained high popularity among fashion enthusiasts.

The addictive game has attracted numerous page views and thousands of players. These real-life examples in the fashion scene show that multiple fashion brands have succeeded to exemplify the art of audience engagement through gamification.

Use of Advanced Analytical Tools and Artificial Intelligence (AI)

The kind of engagement that fashion brands have with their existing customers and the potential customers is vital. Thus brands are taking the additional step to ensure the effectiveness of their engagement strategy by using a number of innovative tools and techniques. As a majority of the customers of fashion brands are found on the digital platform, the marketers have started using social AI for measuring the effectiveness of engagement. This approach basically combines the concept of Artificial Intelligence with social media and it enables them to get a deeper insight into the customer's online activity, buying trend and buying preferences.

According to Ransbotham and Kiron, a wide range of market players spanning various industries are using analytics in order to gain a competitive advantage by improving the effectiveness of customer engagement approach (Ransbotham & Kiron, 2018). A number of tools such as well-devised core analytical capabilities, integration of Artificial Intelligence, and Internet of Things (IoT) have been introduced by business undertakings to measure the effectiveness of the customer engagement approach. As per the research report by MIT Sloan Management Review, analytics can be used to measure the tricky metrics relating to customer engagement such as the ability of a fashion brand to tailor the personalized offerings for the market audience.

The graphical representation that has been presented below shows that analytics can be used to assess various aspects of customer engagement such as the quality of engaging with the customers, the consideration of customer feedback, the level of satisfaction of the customers, tailoring of offerings which is based on the specific desires of the customers and the risk of losing customers that fashion firms face on an ongoing basis (Ransbotham & Kiron, 2018). A wide range of data sources is used so that the exact effectiveness of the customer engagement approach can be captured by fashion brands which can help them to mold the engagement strategy accordingly.

In the digitalized era, AI has gained high popularity to measure the quality of customer engagement and customer experience. AI can be used for various purposes such as it can streamline data, get a detailed insight into the profile of the online consumers and get details pertaining to the real-time engagement approach. A number of tools have come into existence which enables marketers in the fashion industry to measure how effective their engagement strategy is. One of the most popular tools that are available is the IBM customer experience analytics. This simple technical tool allows fashion brands to measure the effectiveness of customer engagement in meaning ways. It facilitates the marketer to visualize and organize the information relating to the customers and it further helps to address the issues associated with poor or ineffective customer engagement.

Figure 3. Graph of customer engagement
Source: (Ransbotham & Kiron, 2018)

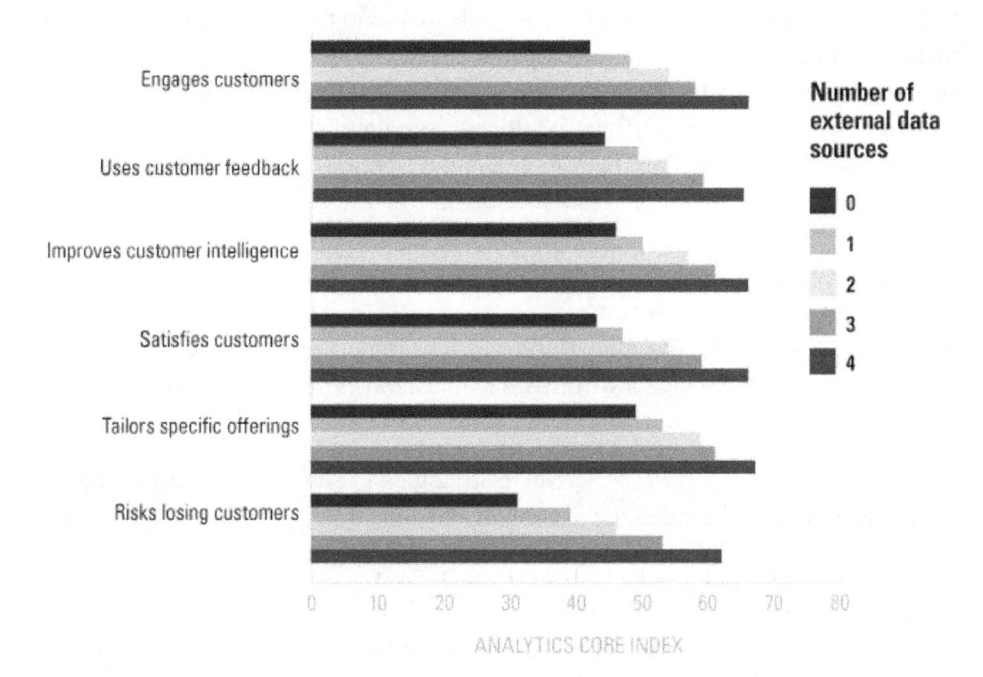

CONCLUSION

In the intensely competitive fashion industry, the majority of the fashion brands are devising various marketing strategic approaches so that the quality and effectiveness of engagement with the customers can be improved. Some of the most popular fashion brands have succeeded to survive in the evolving fashion industry due to the strong engagement and interaction that they have with the market audience at the global level. The real-life fashion industry examples have been used to comprehend the meaning and significance of customer engagement in the fashion arena. With the change in time and technological landscape, renowned fashion houses such as Gucci, Prada, Louis Vuitton, Ralph Lauren, Chanel, and Burberry have modified their customer engagement approach. A wide range of technological-driven tools has entered the scene which is used by the brands to form a long-lasting association with the existing and the potential market audience.

Some of the most popular and effective technology-oriented techniques and approaches that are used by fashion brands to strengthen the effectiveness of customer engagement include social media websites and online brand communities. They facilitate direct and transparent engagement between marketers in the fashion industry and the customers in the global setting. In the current times, they have, in fact, become indispensable engagement tools that help marketers to form deep and meaningful relationships with the customers from all around the globe. In order to survive and sustain in the competitive fashion market, the fashion brands are using innovative tools such as Artificial Intelligence and analytics so that they can keep a tab on the effectiveness on their implemented customer engagement approach.

REFERENCES

Ahmad, N., Salman, A., & Ashiq, R. (2015). The impact of social media on fashion industry: Empirical investigation from Karachiites. *Journal of Resources Development and Management, 7*.

Ashley, C., & Tuten, T. (2015). Creative strategies in social media marketing: An exploratory study of branded social content and consumer engagement. *Psychology and Marketing*, *32*(1), 15–27. doi:10.1002/mar.20761

Brogi, S., Calabrese, A., Campisi, D., Capece, G., Costa, R., & Di Pillo, F. (2013). The effects of online brand communities on brand equity in the luxury fashion industry. *International Journal of Engineering Business Management, 5*, 5-32.

Email Engagement Often talked about, never defined. (2019). Retrieved from https://www.emailmonday.com/wp-content/uploads/2013/02/EngagementDiscussionPaper.pdf

Fashion Digital Marketing. 12 Ideas to Market Your Brand. (2019). Retrieved from https://uhurunetwork.com/fashion-digital-marketing/

Geissinger, A., & Laurell, C. (2016). User engagement in social media–an explorative study of Swedish fashion brands. *Journal of Fashion Marketing and Management*, *20*(2), 177–190. doi:10.1108/JFMM-02-2015-0010

Gilliam, E. (2019). *25 Tools For Your 2019 Marketing Technology Stack - Mopinion*. Retrieved from https://mopinion.com/tools-for-your-2019-marketing-technology-stack/

Gilliland, N. (2019). *10 examples of great fashion marketing campaigns – Econsultancy*. Retrieved from https://econsultancy.com/fashion-marketing-campaigns/

Harmeling, C. M., Moffett, J. W., Arnold, M. J., & Carlson, B. D. (2017). Toward a theory of customer engagement marketing. *Journal of the Academy of Marketing Science, 45*(3), 312–335. doi:10.100711747-016-0509-2

Helal, G. (2019). Social Media, Online Brand Communities, and Customer Engagement in the Fashion Industry. In *Leveraging Computer-Mediated Marketing Environments* (pp. 143–172). IGI Global. doi:10.4018/978-1-5225-7344-9.ch007

Moreno-Munoz, A., Bellido-Outeirino, F. J., Siano, P., & Gomez-Nieto, M. A. (2016). Mobile social media for smart grids customer engagement: Emerging trends and challenges. *Renewable & Sustainable Energy Reviews, 53*, 1611–1616. doi:10.1016/j.rser.2015.09.077

Payne, C. (2016). *Visual Storytelling: Fashion Brands Engagement Through Instagram*. Quinnipiac University.

Ransbotham, S., & Kiron, D. (2018). Using Analytics to Improve Customer Engagement. *MIT Sloan Management Review*.

Rowley, J. (2009). Online branding strategies of UK fashion retailers. *Internet Research, 19*(3), 348–369. doi:10.1108/10662240910965397

Rupik, K. (2015, November). Customer Engagement Behaviour in the Fashion Industry. In *International Conference on Marketing and Business Development* (Vol. 1, No. 1, pp. 338-346). Bucharest University of Economic Studies Publishing House.

Samala, N., & Singh, S. (2019). Millennial's engagement with fashion brands: A moderated-mediation model of brand engagement with self-concept, involvement and knowledge. *Journal of Fashion Marketing and Management, 23*(1), 2–16. doi:10.1108/JFMM-04-2018-0045

The day Gucci handed over the keys to Diet Prada - Luxury Highlights. (2019). Retrieved from https://www.luxury-highlights.com/article/the-day-gucci-handed-over-the-keys-to-diet-prada/

Top 10 Best Selling Clothing Brands In The World. (2019). Retrieved from https://cordmagazine.com/fashion/top-ten-best-selling-clothing-fashion-brands-in-the-world/

Women's Online Clothes & Fashion Shopping | Nasty Gal UK. (2019). Retrieved from https://www.nastygal.com/gb/

Compilation of References

Achabou, M. A., & Dekhili, S. (2013). Luxury and sustainable development: Is there a match? *Journal of Business Research*, *66*(10), 1896–1903. doi:10.1016/j.jbusres.2013.02.011

Ahmad, N., Salman, A., & Ashiq, R. (2015). The impact of social media on fashion industry: Empirical investigation from Karachiites. *Journal of Resources Development and Management, 7*.

Ajzen, I. (1985). From intentions to actions: A theory of planned behavior. In *Action control* (pp. 11–39). Berlin: Springer. doi:10.1007/978-3-642-69746-3_2

Ajzen, I. (1991). The theory of planned behavior. *Organizational Behavior and Human Decision Processes*, *50*(2), 179–211. doi:10.1016/0749-5978(91)90020-T

Allerston, P. (1999). *Reconstructing the Second-Hand Clothes Trade in Sixteenth and Seventeenth Century Venice*. Academic Press.

Amatulli, C., De Angelis, M., Pino, G., Mileti, A., & Guido, G. (2016). *Shame and negative word-of-mouth: The differential effect in individualistic vs. collectivistic culture*. Academic Press.

Amatulli, C., De Angelis, M., Costabile, M., & Guido, G. (2017). *Sustainable Luxury Brands: Evidence from Research and Implications for Managers*. Palgrave Advances in Luxury. doi:10.1057/978-1-137-60159-9

Amatulli, C., & Guido, G. (2011). Determinants of purchasing intention for fashion luxury goods in the Italian market: A laddering approach. *Journal of Fashion Marketing and Management*, *15*(1), 123–136. doi:10.1108/13612021111112386

Andrews, D. (2015). The circular economy, design thinking and education for sustainability. Local Economy. *The Journal of the Local Economy Policy Unit*, *30*(3), 305–315. doi:10.1177/0269094215578226

Anguelov, N. (2015). *The dirty side of the garment industry: Fast fashion and its negative impact on environment and Society*. CRC Press. doi:10.1201/b18902

Anido Freire, N., & Loussaïef, L. (2018). *When Advertising Highlights the Binomial Identity Values of Luxury and CSR Principles: The Examples of Louis Vuitton and Hermès*. Corp. Soc. Responsib. Environ.

Compilation of References

Appadurai, A. (1995). *The social life of the things: Commodities in cultural perspective.* Cambridge: Cambridge University Press.

Aristotle, & Hope, R. (1968). *Metaphysics.* Ann Arbor: University of Michigan Press.

Armitage, C. J., Armitage, C. J., Conner, M., Loach, J., & Willetts, D. (1999). Different perceptions of control: Applying an extended theory of planned behavior to legal and illegal drug use. *Basic and Applied Social Psychology, 21*(4), 301–316. doi:10.1207/S15324834BASP2104_4

Armitage, C. J., & Conner, M. (1999). Distinguishing perceptions of control from self-efficacy: Predicting consumption of a low-fat diet using the theory of planned behavior 1. *Journal of Applied Social Psychology, 29*(1), 72–90. doi:10.1111/j.1559-1816.1999.tb01375.x

Ashley, C., & Tuten, T. (2015). Creative strategies in social media marketing: An exploratory study of branded social content and consumer engagement. *Psychology and Marketing, 32*(1), 15–27. doi:10.1002/mar.20761

Australian Industry Group. (2016, October 3). *Waste Saving Fact Sheet.* Retrieved from http://cdn.aigroup.com.au/Environment/14_Textiles_Waste_Reduction_Factsheet.pdf

Bain and Company. (2017). *Luxury Goods Worldwide Market Study. The New Luxury Consumer. Why Responding to the Millennial Mindset Will Be Key.* Available on line at: https://www.bain.com/insights/luxury-goods-worldwide-market-study-fall-winter-2017/

Bain and Company. (2019). *Bain Luxury Goods Worldwide Market Study.* Available on line at https://altagamma.it/media/source/Altagamma%20Bain%20Worldwide%20Market%20Monitor_update%202019.pdf

Bairagi, N. (2014). Recycling of Textile in India. *Journal of Textile Science and Engineering.*

Balderjahn, I. (2013). *Nachhaltiges Management und Konsumentenverhalten* [Sustainable management and consumer behaviour]. Konstanz: UVK.

Bangladesh factory collapse toll passes 1,000. (2013, May 10). Retrieved from https://www.bbc.com/news/world-asia-22476774

Barreda, A. A., Bilgihan, A., Nusair, K., & Okumus, F. (2015). Generating brand awareness in online social networks. *Computers in Human Behavior, 50,* 600–609. doi:10.1016/j.chb.2015.03.023

Beh, L. S., Ghobadian, A., He, Q., Gallear, D., & O'Regan, N. (2016). Second-life retailing: A reverse supply chain perspective. *Supply Chain Management, 21*(2), 259–272. doi:10.1108/SCM-07-2015-0296

Belk, R. (2014). You are what you can access: Sharing and collaborative consumption online. *Journal of Business Research, 67*(8), 1595–1600. doi:10.1016/j.jbusres.2013.10.001

Bendell, J., & Kleanthous, A. (2007). *Deeper Luxury.* https://www.wwf.org.uk/deeperluxury

Berfield, S. (2015). Making Ethical Chic. *Bloomberg Businessweek,* (4454), 56.

Bertram, R. F., & Chi, T. (2018). A study of companies' business responses to fashion e-commerce's environmental impact. *International Journal of Fashion Design. Technology and Education*, *11*(2), 254–264.

Bhatacharya, A. (2019). *Socail media influencers are the latest obsession among Indian marketers*. Quartz India.

Bhattacharjee, A., Berger, J., & Menon, G. (2014). When identity marketing backfires: Consumer agency in identity expression. *The Journal of Consumer Research*, *41*(2), 294–309. doi:10.1086/676125

Bhattacharya, C., & Sen, S. (2003). Consumer-Company Identification: A Framework for Understanding Consumers' Relationships with Companies. *Journal of Marketing*, •••, 67.

Bick, R., Halsey, E., & Ekenga, C. C. (2018). The global environmental injustice of fast fashion. *Environmental Health*, *17*(1), 92. doi:10.118612940-018-0433-7 PMID:30591057

Binswanger, M. (2006). Why does income growth fail to make us happier?: Searching for the treadmills behind the paradox of happiness. *Journal of Socio-Economics*, *35*(2), 366–381. doi:10.1016/j.socec.2005.11.040

Bly, S., Gwozdz, W., & Reisch, L. A. (2015). Exit from the high street: An exploratory study of sustainable fashion consumption pioneers. *International Journal of Consumer Studies*, *39*(2), 125–135. doi:10.1111/ijcs.12159

BOF, McKinsey & Company. (2018). *The State of Fashion*. Retrieved from https://www.mckinsey.com/~/media/McKinsey/Industries/Retail/Our%20Insights/The%20influence%20of%20woke%20consumers%20on%20fashion/The-State-of-Fashion-2019.ashx

Botsman, R., & Rogers, R. (2010). *What's mine is yours : the rise of collaborative consumption*. Harper Business.

Boucher, J., & Friot, D. (2017). *Primary Microplastics in the Oceans: A Global Evaluation of Sources*. doi:10.2305/IUCN.CH.2017.01.en

Brewer, M. B., & Gardner, W. L. (1996). Who is this 'we'? Levels of collective identity and self representations. *Journal of Personality and Social Psychology*, *71*(1), 83–93. doi:10.1037/0022-3514.71.1.83

Brewer, M. B., & Kramer, R. M. (1986). Choice behavior in social dilemmas: Effects of social identity, group size, and decision framing. *Journal of Personality and Social Psychology*, *50*(3), 543–549.

Brick, C., & Lewis, G. J. (2016). Unearthing the "green" personality: Core traits predict environmentally friendly behavior. *Environment and Behavior*, *48*(5), 635–658. doi:10.1177/0013916514554695

Compilation of References

Brito, M. P. D., Carbone, V., & Blanquart, C. M. (2008). Towards a sustainable fashion retail supply chain in Europe: Organisation and performance. *International Journal of Production Economics, 114*(2), 534–553. doi:10.1016/j.ijpe.2007.06.012

Brogi, S., Calabrese, A., Campisi, D., Capece, G., Costa, R., & Di Pillo, F. (2013). The effects of online brand communities on brand equity in the luxury fashion industry. *International Journal of Engineering Business Management, 5*, 5-32.

Brussels. (2015). *Press release - Circular Economy Package: Questions & Answers*. Retrieved July 29, 2019, from https://europa.eu/rapid/press-release_MEMO-15-6204_en.htm

Burberry burns bags, clothes and perfume worth millions. (2018, July 19). Retrieved from https://www.bbc.com/news/business-44885983

Burgess, J. E., & Green, J. B. (2009). *YouTube: Online video and participatory culture*. Cambridge: Polity Press.

Carrigan, M., & Attalla, A. (2001). The myth of the ethical consumer - do ethics matter in purchase behaviour? *Journal of Consumer Marketing, 18*(7), 560–578. doi:10.1108/07363760110410263

Carrigan, M., Moraes, C., & McEachern, M. (2013). From conspicuous to considered fashion: A harm-chain approach to the responsibilities of luxury-fashion businesses. *Journal of Marketing Management, 29*(11-12), 1277–1307. doi:10.1080/0267257X.2013.798675

Cervellon, M. C., Carey, L., & Harms, T. (2012). Something old, something used: Determinants of women's purchase of vintage fashion vs. second-hand fashion. *International Journal of Retail & Distribution Management, 40*(12), 956–974. doi:10.1108/09590551211274946

Cervellon, M. C., & Wernerfelt, A. S. (2012). Knowledge sharing among green fashion communities online: Lessons for the sustainable supply chain. *Journal of Fashion Marketing and Management, 16*(2), 176–192. doi:10.1108/13612021211222860

Cervellon, M.-C. (2013). Conspicuous Conservation: Using semiotics to understand sustain- able luxury. *International Journal of Market Research, 55*(5), 695–717. doi:10.2501/IJMR-2013-030

Cervellon, M.-C., & Carey, L. (2011). Consumers' perceptions of 'green': Why and how consumers use eco-fashion and green beauty products. *Critical Studies in Fashion and Beauty, 2*(1-2), 117–138. doi:10.1386/csfb.2.1-2.117_1

Challa, L. (2007). *Impact Of Textiles And Clothing Industry On Environment: Approach Towards Eco-Friendly Textiles*. https://www.fibre2fashion.com/industry-article/1709/impact-of-textiles-and-clothing-industry-on-environment

Chamberlain, L. (2018). Gen-Z Will Account for 40 Percent Of All Consumers By 2020. *GeoMarketing from Yext*.

Chen, T. B., & Chai, L. T. (2010). Attitude towards the environment and green products: Consumers' perspective. *Management Science and Engineering, 4*(2), 27–39.

Chen, Y. S., & Chang, C. H. (2013). Greenwash and green trust: The mediation effects of green consumer confusion and green perceived risk. *Journal of Business Ethics*, *114*(3), 489–500. doi:10.100710551-012-1360-0

Choi, T. M., & Cheng, T. C. E. (2015). *Sustainable Fashion Supply Chain Management from Sourcing to Retailing*. Cham, Switzerland: Springer International Publishing.

Choi, T. M., Lo, C. K., Wong, C. W., Yee, R. W., & Chan, T. Y. (2012). The consumption side of sustainable fashion supply chain. *Journal of Fashion Marketing and Management*.

Christopher, M., Lowson, R., & Peck, H. (2004). Creating agile supply chains in the fashion industry. *International Journal of Retail & Distribution Management*, *32*(8), 367–376. doi:10.1108/09590550410546188

Clarewells, D. (2014). *CLARE@BLOG*. Retrieved February 1, 2016, from https://clarewells.wordpress.com/2014/04/14/micro-celebrities-and-social-media/

Claudio, L. (2007). Waste couture: Environmental impact of the clothing industry. *Environmental Health Perspectives*, *115*(9), A448–A454. doi:10.1289/ehp.115-a449 PMID:17805407

Cohen, R. (2007, July 12). Twixt 8 and 12, the Tween. *International Herald Tribune*.

Cone. (2017). *Cone Generation Z Study*. Retrieved at: https://www.conecomm.com/2017-cone-gen-z-csr-study-pdf

Coogan, K & Kangas, S. (2001). Nuoret ja kommunikaatioakrobatia, 16-18-vuotiaiden nuorten k. annykk. a- ja internetkulttuurit. Nuorisotutkimusverkosto ja Elisa ommunications. *Elisa tutkimuskeskus. Raportti*, 158.

Cooley, C. H. (1902). *Human nature and the social order*. New York: Seribner.

Couldry, N. (2004). Teaching us to fake it: The ritualized norms of television's "reality" games. In S. Murray & L. Ouellette (Eds.), *Reality TV: Remaking television culture* (pp. 57–74). New York, NY: New York University Press.

Cowen and Company (2018). *Thrift & Retail Resale Is Major: Understanding thredUP*. Author.

Cross, S. E., Hardin, E. E., & Swing, B. G. (2009). Independent, relational, and collective-interdependent self-construals. In M. R. Leary & R. H. Hoyle (Eds.), *Handbook of individual differences in social behavior* (pp. 512–526). New York: Guilford.

Cultureshop. (2015). *The rise of the micro-celebrity: Why brands should tap into this cultural phenomenon*. Retrieved February 1, 2016, from https://medium.com/@QuantumSingapore/the-rise-ofthe-micro-celebrity-why-brands-should-tap-into-this-cultural-phenomenon886961d37639#.rg17v8yd5

Currás-Pérez, R., Bigné-Alcañiz, E., & Alvarado-Herrera, A. (2009). The Role of Self-Definitional Principles in Consumer Identification with a Socially Responsible Company. *Journal of Business Ethics*, *89*(4), 547–564. doi:10.100710551-008-0016-6

Compilation of References

D'Amico, A., & Scrima, F. (2015). The Italian Validation of Singelis's Self-Construal Scale (SCS): A Short 10-Item Version Shows Improved Psychometric Properties. *Current Psychology (New Brunswick, N.J.), 35*(1), 159–168. doi:10.100712144-015-9378-y

D'Souza, C., Taghian, M., & Lamb, P. (2006). An empirical study on the influence of environmental labels on consumers. *Corporate Communications, 11*(2), 162–173. doi:10.1108/13563280610661697

Dach, L., & Allmendinger, K. (2014). Sustainability in Corporate Communications and its Influence on Consumer Awareness and Perceptions: A study of H&M and Primark. *Procedia: Social and Behavioral Sciences, 130*(15), 409–418. doi:10.1016/j.sbspro.2014.04.048

Danziger, P. (2004). *Why people buy things they don't need: Understanding and predicting consumer behavior.* Kaplan Publishing.

Davies, I., Lee, Z., & Ine, A. (2012). Do consumers care about ethical luxury? *Journal of Business Ethics, 106*(1), 37–51. doi:10.100710551-011-1071-y

De Angelis, M., Adıgüzel, F., & Amatulli, C. (2017). The role of design similarity in consumers' evaluation of new green products: An investigation of luxury fashion brands. *Journal of Cleaner Production, 141*(January), 1515–1527. doi:10.1016/j.jclepro.2016.09.230

De Beers. (2008). *Luxury: Considered.* http://www.debeersgroup.com

Decker, V. (2017, April 26). Vicki von Holzhausen Makes Vegan Leather Luxurious With Her Handbag Brand von Holzhausen. *Forbes.* https://www.forbes.com/sites/viviennedecker/2017/04/22/vicki-von-holzhausen-makes-vegan-leather-luxurious-with-her-handbag-brand-von-holzhausen/#3ddd44a9247d

DEFRA. (2007). *Maximising reuse and recycling of UK clothing and textiles.* London: Department for Environment, Food and Rural Affairs.

Delai, I., & Takahashi, S. (2013). Corporate sustainability in emerging markets: Insights from the practices reported by the Brazilian retailers. *Journal of Cleaner Production, 47,* 211–221. doi:10.1016/j.jclepro.2012.12.029

Doodlage. (2019). *Eco Checklist – Doodlage.* Retrieved from https://www.doodlage.in/eco-checklist/

Ducrot-Lochard, C., & Murat, A. (2011). *Luxe et développement durable: La nouvelle alliance.* Paris: Eyrolles.

Egels-Zandén, N., Hulthén, K., & Wulff, G. (2015). Trade-offs in supply chain transparency: The case of Nudie Jeans Co. *Journal of Cleaner Production, 107,* 95–104. doi:10.1016/j.jclepro.2014.04.074

Egerton-Read, S. (2016). What does the sharing economy mean for a circular economy? *Circulate.* Retrieved July 29, 2019, from https://circulatenews.org/2016/08/what-does-the-sharing-economy-mean-for-a-circular-economy/

Eisenhardt, K. M. (1989). Building Theories from Case Study Research. *Academy of Management Review*, *14*(4), 532–550. doi:10.5465/amr.1989.4308385

Elberse, A., & Verleun, J. (2012). The economic value of celebrity endorsements. *Journal of Advertising Research*, *52*(2), 149–165. doi:10.2501/JAR-52-2-149-165

Elkington, J. (1998). Cannibals with forks: the triple bottom line of 21st century business. New Society Publishers.

Elkington, J. (1994). Towards the Sustainable Corporation: Win-Win-Win Business Strategies for Sustainable Development. *California Management Review*, *36*(2), 90–100. doi:10.2307/41165746

Ellen MacArthur Foundation. (2015, November 26). *Towards a Circular economy: Business rationale for an accelerated transition.* Author.

Ellen MacArthur Foundation. (2017). *A new textiles economy: Redesigning fashion's future.* Retrieved from https://www.ellenmacarthurfoundation.org/publications

Email Engagement Often talked about, never defined. (2019). Retrieved from https://www.emailmonday.com/wp-content/uploads/2013/02/EngagementDiscussionPaper.pdf

Ertekin, Z. O., & Atik, D. (2014). Sustainable Markets. *Journal of Macromarketing*, *35*(1), 53–69. doi:10.1177/0276146714535932

Esposito, M., Tse, T., & Soufani, K. (2017). Is the Circular Economy a New Fast-Expanding Market? *Thunderbird International Business Review*, *59*(1), 9–14. doi:10.1002/tie.21764

Ethitude: A little history of second hand clothes. (2017, January 19). https://medium.com/@ethitudeblog/a-little-history-of-second-hand-clothes

Evans, S., & Peirson-Smith, A. (2018). The sustainability word challenge: Exploring consumer interpretations of frequently used words to promote sustainable fashion brand behaviors and imagery. *Journal of Fashion Marketing and Management*, *22*(2), 252–269. doi:10.1108/JFMM-10-2017-0103

Fashion Digital Marketing. 12 Ideas to Market Your Brand. (2019). Retrieved from https://uhurunetwork.com/fashion-digital-marketing/

Fashion Industry Waste Statistics. (2020, January 8). Retrieved from https://edgexpo.com/fashion-industry-waste-statistics/

Fernandez, C. (2017, December 14). Reformation Raises $25 Million to Fuel Brick-and-Mortar Growth. *Business of Fashion*. Retrieved from: https://bit.ly/2CFA9Fe

Fietkiewicz, K. J., Dorsch, I., Scheibe, K., Zimmer, F., & Stock, W. G. (2018, July). Dreaming of stardom and money: micro-celebrities and influencers on live streaming services. In *International Conference on Social Computing and Social Media* (pp. 240-253). Springer. 10.1007/978-3-319-91521-0_18

Finley, K. (2012). *Trust in the Sharing Economy: An Exploratory Study.* Academic Press.

Flower, G. (2009). Sustainable appeal: The slow fashion movement. *Alive: Canadian Journal of Health & Nutrition.*

Franklin, A. (2011). The ethics of second-hand consumption. In T. Lewis & E. Potter (Eds.), *Ethical Consumption – A Critical Introduction.* New York: Routledge.

Frey, B., & Rudloff, S. (2010). *Social media and the impact on marketing communication.* Academic Press.

Fuentes, C., & Fredriksson, C. (2016). Sustainability service in-store: Service work and the promotion of sustainable consumption. *International Journal of Retail & Distribution Management, 44*(5), 492–507. doi:10.1108/IJRDM-06-2015-0092

Future O. C. Report of the World Commission on Environment and Development. UN Documents. (n.d.). Retrieved from http://www.un-documents.net/ocf-02.html

Gamson, J. (2011). The unwatched life is not worth living: The elevation of the ordinary in celebrity culture. *PMLA, 126*(4), 1061–1069. doi:10.1632/pmla.2011.126.4.1061

Gansky, L. (2010). The mesh - why the future of business is sharing. In Igarss 2010. doi:10.100713398-014-0173-7.2

Gao, S., Jing, J., & Guo, H. (2017). *The Role of Trust with Car-Sharing Services in the Sharing Economy in China : From the Consumers' Perspective.* Academic Press.

Gardner, W. L., Gabriel, S., & Lee, A. Y. (1999). "I" value freedom, but "we" value relationships: Self-construal priming mirrors cultural differences in judgment. *Psychological Science, 10*(4), 321–326. doi:10.1111/1467-9280.00162

Gefen, D. (2000). *E-commerce : the role of familiarity and trust.* doi:10.1016/S0305-0483(00)00021-9

Gefen, D. (2002). *Reflections on the dimensions of trust and trustworthiness among online consumers.* doi:10.1145/569905.569910

Geissinger, A., & Laurell, C. (2016). User engagement in social media–an explorative study of Swedish fashion brands. *Journal of Fashion Marketing and Management, 20*(2), 177–190. doi:10.1108/JFMM-02-2015-0010

Gheitasy, A. (2017). *Socio-technical gaps and social capital formation in Online Collaborative Consumption communities by.* Academic Press.

Gilliam, E. (2019). *25 Tools For Your 2019 Marketing Technology Stack - Mopinion.* Retrieved from https://mopinion.com/tools-for-your-2019-marketing-technology-stack/

Gilliland, N. (2019). *10 examples of great fashion marketing campaigns – Econsultancy.* Retrieved from https://econsultancy.com/fashion-marketing-campaigns/

Giovannini, S., Xu, Y., & Thomas, J. (2015). Luxury fashion consumption and generation Y consumers: Self, brand consciousness, and consumption motivations. *Journal of Fashion Marketing and Management, 19*(1), 22–40. doi:10.1108/JFMM-08-2013-0096

Godey, B., Pederzoli, D., Aiello, G., Donvito, R., Wiedmann, K., & Hennigs, N. (2013). A cross-cultural exploratory content analysis of the perception of luxury from six countries. *Journal of Product and Brand Management, 22*(3), 229–237. doi:10.1108/JPBM-02-2013-0254

Goh, K. Y., Heng, C. S., & Lin, Z. (2013). Social media brand community and consumer behavior: Quantifying the relative impact of user-and marketer-generated content. *Information Systems Research, 24*(1), 88–107. doi:10.1287/isre.1120.0469

Gordon, R., Carrigan, M., & Hastings, G. (2011). A framework for sustainable marketing. *Marketing Theory, 11*(2), 143–163. doi:10.1177/1470593111403218

Gorrell, M. (2008, May 13). When Marketing Tourism, Age Matters, Expert Says. *The Salt Lake Tribune*.

Grappi, S., Romani, S., & Barbarossa, C. (2017). Fashion without pollution: How consumers evaluate brands after an NGO campaign aimed at reducing toxic chemicals in the fashion industry. *Journal of Cleaner Production, 149*, 1164–1173. doi:10.1016/j.jclepro.2017.02.183

Green Strategy. (2019). *Seven Forms of Sustainable Fashion*. Retrieved from https://www.greenstrategy.se/sustainable-fashion/seven-forms-of-sustainable-fashion/

Gregson, N., & Crewe, L. (2003). *Second-hand cultures*. Oxford: Berg. doi:10.2752/9781847888853

Guiot, D., & Roux, D. A. (2010). Second-hand shoppers' motivation scale: Antecedents, consequences and implications for retailers. *Journal of Retailing, 86*(4), 355–371. doi:10.1016/j.jretai.2010.08.002

Ha-Brookshire, J. E., & Hodges, N. N. (2009). Socially responsible consumer behavior? Exploring used clothing donation behavior. *Clothing & Textiles Research Journal, 27*(3), 179–196. doi:10.1177/0887302X08327199

Hair, J. F., Barry, W., Babin, B. R., & Anderson, E. (2013). Multivariate Data Analysis. In Exploratory Data Analysis in Business and Economics. doi:10.1007/978-3-319-01517-0_3

Hair, J. F. Jr, Sarstedt, M., Hopkins, L., & Kuppelwieser, V. G. (2014). Partial least squares structural equation modeling (PLS-SEM). *European Business Review*.

Hamari, J., Sjöklint, M., & Ukkonen, A. (2016). The sharing economy: Why people participate in collaborative consumption. *Journal of the Association for Information Science and Technology*. Retrieved from https://www.researchgate.net/publication/255698095

Hamari. (2015). The Sharing Economy: Why People Participate in Collaborative Consumption. *Communications in Information Literacy*, 1–13. doi:10.1002/asi

Compilation of References

Han, Y. J., Nunes, J. C., & Drèze, X. (2010). Signaling status with luxury goods: The role of brand prominence. *Journal of Marketing*, *74*(4), 15–30. doi:10.1509/jmkg.74.4.015

Harmeling, C. M., Moffett, J. W., Arnold, M. J., & Carlson, B. D. (2017). Toward a theory of customer engagement marketing. *Journal of the Academy of Marketing Science*, *45*(3), 312–335. doi:10.100711747-016-0509-2

Hartmann, P., Ibáñez, V. A., & Sainz, F. J. F. (2005). Green branding effects on attitude: Functional versus emotional positioning strategies. *Marketing Intelligence & Planning*, *23*(1), 9–29. doi:10.1108/02634500510577447

Heath, J. (2001). The structure of hip consumerism. *Philosophy and Social Criticism*, *27*(6), 1–17. doi:10.1177/019145370102700601

Helal, G. (2019). Social Media, Online Brand Communities, and Customer Engagement in the Fashion Industry. In *Leveraging Computer-Mediated Marketing Environments* (pp. 143–172). IGI Global. doi:10.4018/978-1-5225-7344-9.ch007

Hofstede, G. (1980). *Culture's consequences*. Beverly Hills, CA: Sage.

Hook, L. (2016). Review – "The Sharing Economy." *Financial Times*. Retrieved from http://www.ft.com/cms/s/0/f560e5ee-36e8-11e6-a780-b48ed7b6126f

Hou, L. (2018). Destructive sharing economy: A passage from status to contract. *Computer Law & Security Review*, *34*(4), 965–976. doi:10.1016/j.clsr.2018.05.009

Hur, E., & Cassidy, T. (2019). Perceptions and attitudes towards sustainable fashion design: Challenges and opportunities for implementing sustainability in fashion, International Journal of Fashion Design. *Technology and Education*, *12*(2), 208–217. doi:10.1080/17543266.2019.1572789

Inter-Governmental Panel- IPCC. (2000). *Climate Change Special Report on Emission Scenarios*. https://www.ipcc.ch/site/assets/uploads/2018/03/emissions_scenarios-1.pdf

Jacobs, K., Petersen, L., Hörisch, J., & Battenfeld, D. (2018). Green thinking but thoughtless buying? An empirical extension of the value-attitude-behaviour hierarchy in sustainable clothing. *Journal of Cleaner Production*, *203*, 1155–1169. doi:10.1016/j.jclepro.2018.07.320

Jägel, T., Keeling, K., Reppel, A., & Gruber, T. (2012). Individual values and motivational complexities in ethical clothing consumption: A means-end approach. *Journal of Marketing Management*, *28*(3-4), 373–396. doi:10.1080/0267257X.2012.659280

Jaiswal, N. (2012). Green products: Availability, awareness and preference of use by the families. *Indian Journal of Environmental Education*, *12*, 21–25.

Jana, M. H. (2006). Digging for Diamonds: A Conceptual Framework for understanding Reclaimed Textile Products. *Clothing & Textiles Research Journal*, *24*(3), 262–275. doi:10.1177/0887302X06294626

Janssen, C., Vanhamme, J., & Leblanc, S. (2017). Should luxury brands say it out loud? Brand conspicuousness and consumer perceptions of responsible luxury. *Journal of Business Research*, 77, 167–174. doi:10.1016/j.jbusres.2016.12.009

Janssen, C., Vanhamme, J., Lindgreen, A., & Lefebvre, C. (2014). The catch-22 of responsible luxury: Effects of luxury product characteristics on consumers' perception of fit with corporate social responsibility. *Journal of Business Ethics*, 119(1), 45–57. doi:10.100710551-013-1621-6

Jarvenpaa, S. L., Tractinsky, N., & Saarinen, L. (2000). Consumer Trust in an Internet Store: A Cross-Cultural Validation. *Journal of Computer-Mediated Communication*, 5(2). doi:10.1111/j.1083-6101.1999.tb00337.x

Jayson, S. (2009, Feb. 4). It's Cooler than Ever to Be a Tween. *USA Today*.

Jerslev, A. (2016). Media Times| In The Time of the Microcelebrity: Celebrification and the YouTuber Zoella. *International Journal of Communication*, 10, 19.

Jia, P., Govindan, K., Choi, T. M., & Rajendran, S. (2015). Supplier selection problems in fashion business operations with sustainability considerations. *Sustainability*, 7(2), 1603–1619. doi:10.3390u7021603

Jones, B. (2010). Entrepreneurial marketing and the Web 2.0 interface. *Journal of Research in Marketing and Entrepreneurship*, 12(2), 143–152. doi:10.1108/14715201011090602

Joung, H.-M. (2014). Fast-fashion consumers' post-purchase behaviours. *International Journal of Retail & Distribution Management*, 42(8), 688–697. doi:10.1108/IJRDM-03-2013-0055

Joung, H.-M., & Park-Poaps, H. (2013). Factors motivating and influencing clothing disposal behaviours. *International Journal of Consumer Studies*, 37(1), 105–111. doi:10.1111/j.1470-6431.2011.01048.x

Joy, A., Sherry, J. F. Jr, Venkatesh, A., Wang, J., & Chan, R. (2010). Fast fashion, sustainability and the ethical appeal of luxury brands. *Fashion Theory*, 16(3), 273–296. doi:10.2752/175174 112X13340749707123

Kalva, R. S. (2017). A Model for Strategic Marketing Sustainability (Marketing mix to Marketing matrix). *National Conference on Marketing and Sustainable Development*, 7-23.

Kant Hvass, K. (2014). Post-retail responsibility of garments–a fashion industry perspective. *Journal of Fashion Marketing and Management*, 18(4), 413–430. doi:10.1108/JFMM-01-2013-0005

Kapferer, J.N., & Michaut-Denizeau, A. (2015). *Luxury and sustainability: a common future? The match depends on how consumers define luxury*. Academic Press.

Kapferer, J. N. (2010). All that glitters is not green: The challenge of sustainable luxury. *European Business Review*, 40–45.

Kapferer, J. N. (2015). *Kapferer on Luxury: how Luxury Brands Can Grow yet Remain Rare*. London: Kogan Page Publishers.

Kapferer, J. N., & Michaut-Denizeau, A. (2014). Is luxury compatible with sustainability? Luxury consumers' viewpoint. *Journal of Brand Management, 21*(1), 1–22. doi:10.1057/bm.2013.19

Kapila, P., Dhillon, B. S. (2019, March 8). *Management of post consumer textile waste*. Academic Press.

Kaplan, A. M., & Haenlein, M. (2010). Users of the world, unite! The challenges and opportunities of Social Media. *Business Horizons, 53*(1), 59–68. doi:10.1016/j.bushor.2009.09.003

Kara, M. (2017). *400 bin üyeyi geçen ikinci el moda uygulaması Dolap, Morhipo ile iş birliğini duyurdu*. Retrieved October 30, 2018, from https://webrazzi.com/2017/03/10/400-bin-uyeyi-gecen-ikinci-el-moda-uygulamasi-dolap-morhipo-ile-is-birligini-duyurdu/

Khamis, S., Ang, L., & Welling, R. (2017). Self-branding, 'micro-celebrity' and the rise of Social Media Influencers. *Celebrity Studies, 8*(2), 191–208. doi:10.1080/19392397.2016.1218292

Kim, D. J., Ferrin, D. L., & Rao, H. R. (2008). A trust-based consumer decision-making model in electronic commerce: The role of trust, perceived risk, and their antecedents. *Decision Support Systems, 44*(2), 544–564. doi:10.1016/j.dss.2007.07.001

Kim, H. Y., & Chung, J. E. (2011). Consumer purchase intention for organic personal care products. *Journal of Consumer Marketing*.

Kim, J., & Haridakis, P. M. (2009). The role of Internet user characteristics and motives in explaining three dimensions of Internet addiction. *Journal of Computer-Mediated Communication, 14*(4), 988–1015. doi:10.1111/j.1083-6101.2009.01478.x

Kolarova, M. (2018). *# Influencer marketing: The effects of influencer type, brand familiarity, and sponsorship disclosure on purchase intention and brand trust on Instagram* (Master's thesis). University of Twente.

Kopytoff, I. (1986). The cultural biography of things: Commoditization as process. In A. Appadurai (Ed.), *The Social Life of Things: Commodities in Cultural Perspective* (pp. 64–92). Cambridge: Cambridge University Press. doi:10.1017/CBO9780511819582.004

Korhonen, J., Nuur, C., Feldmann, A., & Birkie, S. E. (2018). Circular economy as an essentially contested concept. *Journal of Cleaner Production, 175*, 544–552. doi:10.1016/j.jclepro.2017.12.111

Korotina, A., & Jargalsaikhan, T. (2016). *Attitude towards Instagram micro-celebrities and their influence on consumers' purchasing decisions*. Academic Press.

Koufaris, M., & Hampton-Sosa, W. (2004). The development of initial trust in an online company by new customers. *Information & Management, 41*(3), 377–397. doi:10.1016/j.im.2003.08.004

Kozlowski, A., Bardecki, M., & Searcy, C. (2012). Environmental impacts in the fashion industry: A life-cycle and stakeholder framework. *Journal of Corporate Citizenship*, (45): 17–36.

Kumar, B. (2018). Sustainability Marketing and Its Outcomes: A Discussion in the Context of Emerging Markets. In *Strategic Marketing Issues in Emerging Markets* (pp. 327–341). Singapore: Springer. doi:10.1007/978-981-10-6505-7_30

Kumari, P. (2012). Changing Purchase Behaviour of Indian Customers. *ArthPrabandh: A Journal of Economics and Management, 1*(8), 35-41.

Kumar, P. (2014). Greening retail: An Indian experience. *International Journal of Retail & Distribution Management, 42*(7), 613–625. doi:10.1108/IJRDM-02-2013-0042

Kumar, P., & Ghodeswar, B. M. (2015). Factors affecting consumers' green product purchase decisions. *Marketing Intelligence & Planning, 33*(3), 330–347. doi:10.1108/MIP-03-2014-0068

Kumar, V., Rahman, Z., Kazmi, A. A., & Goyal, P. (2012). Evolution of sustainability as marketing strategy: Beginning of new era. *Procedia: Social and Behavioral Sciences, 37*, 482–489. doi:10.1016/j.sbspro.2012.03.313

Lahti, T., Wincent, J., & Parida, V. (2018). A definition and theoretical review of the circular economy, value creation, and sustainable business models: Where are we now and where should research move in the future? *Sustainability (Switzerland), 10*(8), 2799. doi:10.3390u10082799

Lee, A. Y., & Aaker, J. L. (2004). Bringing the Frame into Focus: The Influence of Regulatory Fit on Processing Fluency and Persuasion. *Journal of Personality and Social Psychology, 86*(2), 205–218. doi:10.1037/0022-3514.86.2.205 PMID:14769079

Lee, M. S. W., & Ahn, C. S. Y. (2016). Anti-consumption, materialism, and consumer well-being. *The Journal of Consumer Affairs, 50*(1), 18–47. doi:10.1111/joca.12089

Leena, K., Tomi, L., & Arja, R. (2005). Intensity of mobile phone use and health compromising behaviors -how is information and communication technology connected to health-related lifestyle in adolescence? *Journal of Adolescence, 28*(1), 35–47. doi:10.1016/j.adolescence.2004.05.004 PMID:15683633

Levi's. (2018, March 22). *Sustainable Clothing & Eco-Friendly Brand Initiatives | Levi's® US*. Retrieved from https://www.levi.com/US/en_US/features/sustainability?ab=aboutusLP_sustainability_031918

Lichtenstein, D., Drumwright, M., & Braig, B. (2004). The Effect of Corporate Social Responsibility on customer Donations to Corporate-Supported Nonprofits. *Journal of Marketing, 68*(4), 6. doi:10.1509/jmkg.68.4.16.42726

Lion, A., Macchion, L., Danese, P., & Vinelli, A. (2016, April). Sustainability approaches within the fashion industry: The supplier perspective. *Supply Chain Forum International Journal (Toronto, Ont.), 17*(2), 95–108.

Luchs, M., Naylor, R.W., Randall, L. R., Jesse, R. C., Roland, G., Sommer, K., & … Weaver, T. (2011). Toward a sustainable marketplace: Expanding options and benefits for consumers. *Journal of Research for Consumers, 19*, 1–12.

Compilation of References

Lueg, R., Pedersen, M. M., & Clemmensen, S. N. (2015). The role of corporate sustainability in a low-cost business model–A case study in the Scandinavian fashion industry. *Business Strategy and the Environment, 24*(5), 344–359. doi:10.1002/bse.1825

Lu, L., Bock, D., & Joseph, M. (2013). Green marketing: What the millennials buy. *The Journal of Business Strategy, 34*(6), 3–10. doi:10.1108/JBS-05-2013-0036

Macarthur, E. (2013). Towards the Circular Economy. *Journal of Industrial Ecology, 1*(1), 4–8. doi:10.1162/108819806775545321

Mair, J., & Reischauer, G. (2017). Capturing the dynamics of the sharing economy: Institutional research on the plural forms and practices of sharing economy organizations. *Technological Forecasting and Social Change, 125*, 11–20. doi:10.1016/j.techfore.2017.05.023

Martin, Upham, P., & Budd, L. (2015). Commercial orientation in grassroots social innovation: Insights from the sharing economy. *Ecological Economics, 118*, 240–251. doi:10.1016/j.ecolecon.2015.08.001

Marwick, A. E. (2010). I tweet honestly, I tweet passionately: Twitter users, context collapse, and the imagined audience. *New Media & Society*.

Marwick, A. E. (2013). *Status update: Celebrity, publicity, and branding in the social media age*. Yale University Press.

Marwick, A., & Boyd, D. (2011). To see and be seen: Celebrity practice on Twitter. *Convergence, 17*(2), 139–158. doi:10.1177/1354856510394539

Marx, K. (1986). *Capital a critique of political economy*. London: Penguin Books.

Mc Kinsey & Co. State of Fashion Report. (2019). https://www.mckinsey.com/~/media/McKinsey/Industries/Retail/Our%20Insights/The%20State%20of%20Fashion%202019%20A%20year%20of%20awakening/The-State-of-Fashion-2019-final.ashx

McCartneyS. (n.d.). *Circularity*. Retrieved from https://www.stellamccartney.com/experience/us/sustainability/circularity-2/

McKinsey. (2019). *The State of Fashion 2019*. Retrieved at: https://mck.co/2twu77j

McKinsey-BoF. (2019). *The State of Fashion 2019 Survey*. The Business of Fashion and McKinsey & Company. https://www.mckinsey.com/industries/retail/our-insights/the-state-of-fashion-2019-a-year-of-awakening

McKnight, D. H., & Chervany, N. L. (2001). *Trust and Distrust Definitions: One Bite at a Time*. doi:10.1177/0734242X05051045

McNeill, L., & Moore, R. (2015). Sustainable fashion consumption and the fast fashion conundrum: Fashionable consumers and attitudes to sustainability in clothing choice. *International Journal of Consumer Studies, 39*(3), 212–222. doi:10.1111/ijcs.12169

Michaelidou, N., Siamagka, N. T., & Christodoulides, G. (2011). Usage, barriers and measurement of social media marketing: An exploratory investigation of small and medium B2B brands. *Industrial Marketing Management*, *40*(7), 1153–1159. doi:10.1016/j.indmarman.2011.09.009

Miller, J. G., Bersoff, D. M., & Harwood, R. L. (1990). Perceptions of social responsibilities in India and the United States: Moral imperatives or personal decisions? *Journal of Personality and Social Psychology*, *58*(1), 33–47. doi:10.1037/0022-3514.58.1.33 PMID:2308074

Mittendorf, C. (2016). *What Trust means in the Sharing Economy : A provider perspective on Airbnb . com.* Academic Press.

Moreno-Munoz, A., Bellido-Outeirino, F. J., Siano, P., & Gomez-Nieto, M. A. (2016). Mobile social media for smart grids customer engagement: Emerging trends and challenges. *Renewable & Sustainable Energy Reviews*, *53*, 1611–1616. doi:10.1016/j.rser.2015.09.077

Morgan, E. (2015). 'Plan A': Analysing business model innovation for sustainable consumption in mass-market clothes retailing. *Journal of Corporate Citizenship*, *2015*(57), 73–98. doi:10.9774/GLEAF.4700.2015.ma.00007

Mun, J. M. (2013). Online Collaborative Consumption: Exploring Meanings. Motivations, Costs, and Benefits. Academic Press.

Nadler, S. (2014). *The Sharing Economy: What is it and where is it going?* Academic Press.

NASA. (2018). *NASA: Climate Change and Global Warming.* Retrieved December 12, 2018, from https://climate.nasa.gov/

Nasties, N. (n.d.). *What is Fair Trade?* Retrieved from https://www.nonasties.in/pages/fairtrade

Naustdalslid, J. (2014). Circular economy in China - The environmental dimension of the harmonious society. *International Journal of Sustainable Development and World Ecology*, *21*(4), 303–313. doi:10.1080/13504509.2014.914599

new circular business models specifically by Ellen MacArthur Foundations Make. (n.d.). Retrieved March 16, 2020, from https://www.coursehero.com/file/p3bs4gu7/new-circular-business-models-specifically-by-Ellen-MacArthur-Foundations-Make

Nikolova, S. N. (2012). *The effectiveness of social media in the formation of positive brand attitude for the different users*(Doctoral dissertation). University of Amsterdam.

Nousiainen, P., & Talvenmaa-Kuusela, P. (1994). *Solid textile waste recycling.* Paper presented at the Globalization–Technological, Economic, and Environmental Imperatives, 75th World Conference of Textile Institute, Atlanta, GA.

Öngel, G. (2018). *Sağlık Çalışanlarının Yaşamış Oldukları İş-Aile Yaşamı Çatışmasının Örgütsel Bağlılık, İş Doyumu Ve İşten Ayrılma Niyetine Etkisi.* Academic Press.

Compilation of References

Owyang, J., Samuel, A., & Grenville, A. (2014). Sharing Is The New Buying: How To Win In The Collaborative Economy. *Vision Critical; Crowd Companies*, 1–31. Retrieved from http://info.mkto.visioncritical.com/rs/visioncritical/images/sharing-new-buying-collaborative-economy.pdf

Palley, T. I. (2012). *From financial crisis to stagnation: The destruction of shared prosperity and the role of economics*. Cambridge University Press. doi:10.1017/CBO9781139061285

Pal, R., & Gander, J. (2018). Modelling environmental value: An examination of sustainable business models within the fashion industry. *Journal of Cleaner Production*, *184*, 251–263. doi:10.1016/j.jclepro.2018.02.001

Park, H., & Cho, H. (2012). Social network online communities: Information sources for apparel shopping. *Journal of Consumer Marketing*, *29*(6), 400–411. doi:10.1108/07363761211259214

Park, H., & Kim, Y. K. (2016). An empirical test of the triple bottom line of customer-centric sustainability: The case of fast fashion. *Fashion and Textiles*, *3*(1), 25. doi:10.118640691-016-0077-6

Pasricha, A., & Kadolph, S. J. (2009). Millennial generation and fashion education: A discussion on agents of change. *International Journal of Fashion Design, Technology, & Education*, *2*(2/3), 119–126.

Payne, C. (2016). *Visual Storytelling: Fashion Brands Engagement Through Instagram*. Quinnipiac University.

Pedersen, E. R. G., Gwozdz, W., & Hvass, K. K. (2018). Exploring the relationship between business model innovation, corporate sustainability, and organisational values within the fashion industry. *Journal of Business Ethics*, *149*(2), 267–284. doi:10.100710551-016-3044-7

Perlacia, A., & Duml, V. (2018). *Collaborative Consumption: Live Fashion, Don't Own It - Developing New Business Models for the Fashion Industry*. SSRN Electronic Journal. doi:10.2139srn.2860021

Perspectives on Retail and Consumer Goods. (2019) https://www.mckinsey.com/~/media/McKinsey/Industries/Retail/Our%20Insights/Perspectives%20on%20retail%20and%20consumer%20goods%20Number%207/Perspectives-on-Retail-and-Consumer-Goods_Issue-7.ashx

Phipps, L. (2018, October 10). *4 companies pioneering the clothing recommerce market*. Retrieved March 16, 2020, from https://www.greenbiz.com/article/4-companies-pioneering-clothing-recommerce-market

Pradiptarini, C. (2011). Social media marketing: Measuring its effectiveness and identifying the target market. *UW-L Journal of Undergraduate Research*, *14*, 1–11.

Prensky, M. (2001). Digital natives, digital immigrants part 1. *On the Horizon*, *9*(5), 1–6. doi:10.1108/10748120110424816

Prieto, M., Baltas, G., & Stan, V. (2017). Car sharing adoption intention in urban areas: What are the key sociodemographic drivers? *Transportation Research Part A, Policy and Practice*, *101*, 218–227. doi:10.1016/j.tra.2017.05.012

Prosperity Without Growth. (2011). *The transition to a sustainable economy*. Sustainable Development Commission. http://www.sd-commission.org.uk/data/files/publications/prosperity_without_growth_report.pdf

Quantis, and Climate Works Foundation. (2018). *Measuring Fashion: Insights from the Environmental Impact of the Apparel and Footwear Industries Study*. Author.

Ramayah, T., Ahmad, N. H., & Lo, M. C. (2010). The role of quality factors in intention to continue using an e-learning system in Malaysia. *Procedia: Social and Behavioral Sciences*, *2*(2), 5422–5426. doi:10.1016/j.sbspro.2010.03.885

Rani, N., Yaduvanshi, R., Myana, R., & Saravan. (2016). Circular Economy for Sustainable Development in India. *Indian Journal of Science and Technology, 9*(46), 1-9. Retrieved from https://www.researchgate.net/publication/312125734_Circular_Economy_for_Sustainable_Development_in_India

Rani, M., & Gupta, R. (2013). Determinants of consumer buying behaviour: A study of readymade garments. *International Journal of Research in Commerce & Managemment*, *4*(4), 49–52.

Ransbotham, S., & Kiron, D. (2018). Using Analytics to Improve Customer Engagement. *MIT Sloan Management Review*.

Rideout, V. J., Foehr, U. G., & Roberts, D. F. (2010). *Generation M 2: Media in the Lives of 8-to 18-Year-Olds*. Henry J. Kaiser Family Foundation.

Rinne. (2013). Circular Economy Innovation & New Business Models Initiative. *World Economic Forum Young Global Leaders Taskforce Circular, 1*, 16.

Ritzer, G., & Stepnisky, J. (2018). Sociological theory (8th ed.). Academic Press.

Rogelj, J., Popp, A., Calvin, K. V., Luderer, G., Emmerling, J., Gernaat, D., ... Krey, V. (2018). Scenarios towards limiting global mean temperature increase below 1.5 C. *Nature Climate Change, 8*(4), 325–332. doi:10.103841558-018-0091-3

Rothman, D. (2016). *A Tsunami of learners called Generation Z*. http://www.mdle.net/JoumaFA_Tsunami_of_Learners_Called_Generation_Z.pdf

Rowley, J. (2009). Online branding strategies of UK fashion retailers. *Internet Research*, *19*(3), 348–369. doi:10.1108/10662240910965397

Rupik, K. (2015, November). Customer Engagement Behaviour in the Fashion Industry. In *International Conference on Marketing and Business Development* (Vol. 1, No. 1, pp. 338-346). Bucharest University of Economic Studies Publishing House.

Samala, N., & Singh, S. (2019). Millennial's engagement with fashion brands: A moderated-mediation model of brand engagement with self-concept, involvement and knowledge. *Journal of Fashion Marketing and Management*, *23*(1), 2–16. doi:10.1108/JFMM-04-2018-0045

Schoorman, F. D., Mayer, R. C., & Davis, J. H. (2007). An integrative model of organizational trust: past, present, and future. In *Academy of Management Review* (Vol. 32). Retrieved from https://pdfs.semanticscholar.org/7aed/d30a40b70ccbadc7c290973d02e8e19b739c.pdf

Schor, J. (2014, Oct.). Debating the Sharing Economy. *A Great Transition Initiative Essay*, 1–19. doi:10.7903/cmr.11116

Schwartz, S., & Bilsky, W. (1987). Toward a psychological structure of human values. *Journal of Personality and Social Psychology*, *53*(3), 550–562. doi:10.1037/0022-3514.53.3.550

Senft, T. M. (2008). *Camgirls: celebrity and community in the age of social networks*. New York: Peter Lang.

Shen, B. (2014). Sustainable fashion supply chain: Lessons from H&M. *Sustainability*, *6*(9), 6236–6249. doi:10.3390u6096236

Shen, D., Richards, J., & Liu, F. (2013). Consumers' awareness of sustainable fashion. *Marketing Management Journal*, *23*(2), 134–147.

Shukla, P., & Purani, K. (2012). Comparing the importance of luxury value perceptions in cross-national contexts. *Journal of Business Research*, *65*(10), 1417–1424. doi:10.1016/j.jbusres.2011.10.007

Singelis, T. (1994). The measurement of independent and interdependent self-construals. *Personality and Social Psychology Bulletin*, *20*(5), 580–591. doi:10.1177/0146167294205014

Smith, A. (1776). *An Inquiry into the Nature and Causes of the Wealth of Nations Book 1*. London: W. Strahan and T. Cadell.

Smith, N., Palazzo, G., & Bhattacharya, C. (2010). Marketing's Consequences: Stakeholder Marketing and Supply Chain Corporate Social Responsibility Issues. *Business Ethics Quarterly*, *20*(4), 617–641. doi:10.5840/beq201020440

Smith, T. W. (2000). *Changes in the generation gap, 1972-1998*. National Opinion Research Center.

Sproles, G. B., Geistfeld, L. V., & Badenhop, S. B. (1978). Informational inputs as influences on efficient consumer decision-making. *The Journal of Consumer Affairs*, *12*(Summer), 88–103. doi:10.1111/j.1745-6606.1978.tb00635.x

State of the media: The social media report 2012. (n.d.). Featured Insights, Global, Media + Entertainment. *Nielsen*. Retrieved December 9, 2012 from http://blog.nielson.com/nielsonwire/social/2012

Statista. (2019). *Value of the global sharing economy 2014-2025*. Retrieved June 25, 2019, from https://www.statista.com/statistics/830986/value-of-the-global-sharing-economy/

Steele, V., & Major, J. S. (2019). *Fashion industry | Design, Fashion Shows, Marketing, & Facts*. Retrieved July 31, 2019, from https://www.britannica.com/art/fashion-industry

Steinhart, Y., Ayalon, O., & Puterman, H. (2013). The effect of an environmental claim on consumers' perceptions about luxury and utilitarian products. *Journal of Cleaner Production, 53*, 277–286. doi:10.1016/j.jclepro.2013.04.024

Sustainability. (1987). Retrieved from https://sustainabledevelopment.un.org/content/documents/5987our-common-future.pdf

Szokan, N. (2016, June 30). The fashion industry tries to take responsibility for its pollution. *Washington Post*. Retrieved from https://www.washingtonpost.com/national/health-science/the-fashion-industry-tries-to-take-responsibility-for-its-pollution/2016/06/30/11706fa6-3e15-11e6-80bc-d06711fd2125_story.html?noredirect=on

Tang, C. M. F., & Lam, D. (2017). The role of extraversion and agreeableness traits on Gen Y's attitudes and willingness to pay for green hotels. *International Journal of Contemporary Hospitality Management*.

Tanz, J. (2008, July 15). Internet famous: Julia Allison and the secrets of self-promotion. *Wired*. Retrieved from https://www.wired.com/2008/07/howto-allison/

Taranic, I., Behrens, A., & Topi, C. (2016). *Understanding the Circular Economy in Europe, from Resource Efficiency to Sharing Platforms: The CEPS Framework*. Retrieved from www.ceps.eu

Taylor, P., & Keeter, S. (2010). Millennials: A portrait of generation next. Pew Research Center.

Taylor, C. (1978). Feuerbach and Roots of Materialism. *Political Studies, 26*(3), 417–421. doi:10.1111/j.1467-9248.1978.tb01307.x

Thamizhvanan, A., & Xavier, M. J. (2013). Determinants of customers' online purchase intention: An empirical study in India. *Journal of Indian Business Research, 5*(1), 17–32. doi:10.1108/17554191311303367

The day Gucci handed over the keys to Diet Prada - Luxury Highlights. (2019). Retrieved from https://www.luxury-highlights.com/article/the-day-gucci-handed-over-the-keys-to-diet-prada/

The Economist. (2013). All eyes on the sharing economy. *Economist, 452*(7184), 137–137. doi:10.1038/452137a

The Worn, the Torn, the Wearable: Textile Recycling in Union Square. (n.d.). Available online at: http://bada.hb.se/bitstream 2320/12345/1NJ2012_Nr2_DG_1209_redigerad%20upp.pdf

Thomas, N. J. (2018). Sustainability marketing. The need for a realistic whole systems approach. *Journal of Marketing Management, 34*(17-18), 1530–1556. doi:10.1080/0267257X.2018.1547782

Thorisdottir, T. S., & Johannsdottir, L. (2019). Sustainability within fashion business models: A systematic literature review. *Sustainability, 11*(8), 2233. doi:10.3390u11082233

ThreadU. R. R. (2019). https://www.thredup.com/resale

Compilation of References

Tipping, M. A. (2012). *Quadruple Bottom Line Reporting – Would You Adopt It For Your organisation.* https://thetippingpoint.me/2012/05/09/quadruple-bottom-line-reporting-would-you-adopt-it-for-your-organisation

Todd, D. (2011). *You Are What You Buy: Postmodern Consumerism and the Construction of Self.* Retrieved: https://hilo.hawaii.edu/campuscenter/hohonu/volumes/documents/Vol10x12YouAreWhatYouBuy-PostmodernConsumerismandtheConstructionofSelf.pdf

Top 10 Best Selling Clothing Brands In The World. (2019). Retrieved from https://cordmagazine.com/fashion/top-ten-best-selling-clothing-fashion-brands-in-the-world/

Torelli, C. J., Basu-Monga, S., & Kaikati, A. (2012). Doing poorly by doing good: Corporate social responsibility and brand concepts. *The Journal of Consumer Research*, *38*(5), 948–963. doi:10.1086/660851

TredUp. (2019). *Resale Report.* Available on line at: https://www.thredup.com/resale

Triandis, H. C. (1989). The self and social behavior in differing cultural contexts. *Psychological Review, 96.*

Triandis, H. C. (1995). *Individualism and collectivism.* Boulder, CO: Westview.

Tukker, A., & Tischner, U. (2006). Product-services as a research field: Past, present and future. Reflections from a decade of research. *Journal of Cleaner Production*, *14*(17), 1552–1556. doi:10.1016/j.jclepro.2006.01.022

Turker, D., & Altuntas, C. (2014). Sustainable supply chain management in the fast fashion industry: An analysis of corporate reports. *European Management Journal*, *32*(5), 837–849. doi:10.1016/j.emj.2014.02.001

Turner, A. (2015). Generation Z: Technology and social interest. *Journal of Individual Psychology*, *71*(2), 103–113. doi:10.1353/jip.2015.0021

Turner, G. (2004). *Understanding celebrity.* London, UK: SAGE Publications. doi:10.4135/9781446279953

Turunen, L. L. M., & Leipämaa-Leskinen, H. (2015). Pre-loved luxury: Identifying the meaning of second hand luxury possessions. *Journal of Product and Brand Management*, *24*(1), 57–65. doi:10.1108/JPBM-05-2014-0603

UN Report. (2013). *World population projected to reach 9.6 billion by 2050.* https://www.un.org/en/development/desa/news/population/un-report-world-population-projected-to-reach-9-6-billion-by-2050.html

UNEP. (2007). *Global Environmental Outlook 4.* http://wedocs.unep.org/handle/20.500.11822/7646

United Nations Sustainable Development Summit. (2015). New York: UN.

United Nations World Commission on Environment and Development. (1987). *Our common future.* Oxford: Oxford University Press.

Upasana. (2015). *About Us*. Retrieved from https://www.upasana.in/pages/about-us

Van Norel, N. D., Kommers, P. A., Van Hoof, J. J., & Verhoeven, J. W. (2014). Damaged corporate reputation: Can celebrity Tweets repair it? *Computers in Human Behavior*, *36*, 308–315. doi:10.1016/j.chb.2014.03.056

Varsha, G. (2012). Value Creation in post-consumer apparel waste: a study of urban-rural dynamics in India. NIFT.

von Holzhausen. (2017). *About our Vegan Technik-Leather*. Retrieved from https://vonholzhausen.com/pages/technik-leather

Walker, S. (2014). *Wasteland: Sustainability and Designing with Dignity*. Academic Press.

Wang, H., Liu, H., Kim, S. J., & Kim, K. H. (2019). Sustainable fashion index model and its implication. *Journal of Business Research*, *99*, 430–437. doi:10.1016/j.jbusres.2017.12.027

Wellner, A. S. (2000). Generation Z. *American Demographics*, *22*(9), 60–65.

Wellner, A. S. (2003). The Next 25 Years. *American Demographics*, *25*, D26–D29.

What is a Capsule Wardrobe? (2019, April 20). Retrieved from https://thefairbazaar.com/blogs/fairblog/capsule-wardrobe

Williams, A. (2015). Move over, millennials, here comes Generation Z. *The New York Times, 18*.

Williams, C. (2003). Explaining Informal and second-hand goods acquisition. *The International Journal of Sociology and Social Policy*, *23*(12), 95–110. doi:10.1108/01443330310790426

Williams, C., & Paddock, C. (2003). The meaning of alternative consumption practices. *Cities (London, England)*, *20*(5), 311–319. doi:10.1016/S0264-2751(03)00048-9

Williams, C., & Windebank, J. (2002). The "excluded consumer": A neglected aspect of social exclusion? *Policy and Politics*, *30*(4), 501–513. doi:10.1332/030557302760590422

Williams, K. C., Page, R. A., Petrosky, A. R., & Hernandez, E. H. (2010). Multi-generational marketing: Descriptions, characteristics, lifestyles, and attitudes. *The Journal of Applied Business and Economics*, *11*(2), 21.

Wilson, J. P. (2015). The triple bottom line: Undertaking an economic, social, and environmental retail sustainability strategy. *International Journal of Retail & Distribution Management*, *43*(4/5), 432–447. doi:10.1108/IJRDM-11-2013-0210

Women's Online Clothes & Fashion Shopping | Nasty Gal UK. (2019). Retrieved from https://www.nastygal.com/gb/

World Economic Forum Annual Meeting 2018. (2018). Retrieved March 16, 2020, from https://www.weforum.org/events/world-economic-forum-annual-meeting-2018

World Economic Forum Annual Meeting 2018. (2020). Retrieved March 16, 2020, from https://www.weforum.org/events/world-economic-forum-annual-meeting-2018

Compilation of References

World Economic Forum. (2013). *Young Global Leaders - Circular Economy Innovation & New Business Models Dialogue*. Retrieved from http://www3.weforum.org/docs/WEF_YGL_CircularEconomyInnovation_PositionPaper_2013.pdf

World Economic Forum. (2014). *Towards the Circular Economy: Accelerating the scale-up across global supply chains*. Retrieved from www.weforum.org

Worldometers. (2018). *World Population Clock: 7.7 Billion People (2018)*. Retrieved October 12, 2018, from https://www.worldometers.info/world-population/

WWF. (2010). *Living Planet Report*. https://wwf.panda.org/knowledge_hub/all_publications/living_planet_report_timeline/lpr_2010/

Yang, S., Song, Y., & Tong, S. (2017). Sustainable retailing in the fashion industry: A systematic literature review. *Sustainability*, *9*(7), 1266. doi:10.3390u9071266

Yan, R. N., Hyllegard, K. H., & Blaesi, L. F. (2012). Marketing eco-fashion: The influence of brand name and message explicitness. *Journal of Marketing Communications*, *18*(2), 151–168. doi:10.1080/13527266.2010.490420

Yin, R. K. (1994). *Case Study Research, Design and Methods*. Londres: Sage Publications.

Zheng, S., Shi, P., Xu, H., & Zhang, C. (2012, June). Launching the New Profile on Facebook: Understanding the Triggers and Outcomes of Users' Privacy Concerns. In *International Conference on Trust and Trustworthy Computing* (pp. 325-339). Springer. 10.1007/978-3-642-30921-2_19

About the Contributors

Archana Shrivastava is presently working at Jaypee Business School, Noida. Her research interest is in the field of e-commerce, online consumer buying behavior and application of blockchain technology in business to achieve sustainability. She has publications in the ABDC indexed A, ABS, Scopus indexed journals. She has been conferred APJ Abdul Kalam award for research excellence and Emerald Highly Commended Paper Award 2018.

Geetika Jain is currently working as Assistant Professor at Faculty of Management Studies, Amity University, Noida, India. She has received her PhD from Dr APJ Abdul Kalam Technical University, Lucknow, (Previously known as UP Technical University, Lucknow) India, MBA in Management from IBS, Hyderabad and B. Tech. degree in Electrical Engineering from Kurukshetra University, Kurukshetra. She has worked in GE- Fleet solutions, IMRS, LINTAS previously. Her research interests include e-commerce, online marketing, and social media marketing. She has published papers in National and International Journals including Scopus and ABDC indexed papers.

***

Adem Akbiyik is an assistant professor of Management Information Systems. His research is focused on consumer analytics and social media analysis. He has taught courses focusing on requirements management, text mining, and IS project management. Dr. Akbiyik completed his Ph.D. at Sakarya University, followed by a post-doctoral fellowship at the McMaster Digital Transformation Research Centre (MDTRC) at the DeGroote School of Business, McMaster University.

Cesare Amatulli is Assistant Professor of Marketing at the University of Bari, Italy. He has been a Visiting Professor at LUISS University, Italy, and Visiting Researcher at the Ross School of Business, University of Michigan, US, and at

About the Contributors

University of Hertfordshire, UK. He has published articles in major international referred journals, such as Journal of Business Research and Psychology & Marketing.

Nagma Sahi Ansari is an Assistant Professor of Communications at National Institute of Fashion Technology, Kolkata. She is a Practice based research scholar at AJK MCRC, Jamia Millia Islamia. Her scholarship revolves around Identity in New Media, Everyday Photographic Practice and Virtual Reality. Trained into filmmaking and cultural studies, she teaches storytelling, applied semiotics, qualitative research paradigms and photographic practice.

Sharmistha Banerjee is a Professor of Business Management at the University of Calcutta. Her teaching and research areas include Management, HRM, OB and Entrepreneurship. The focus of her current research is unique rural enterprises and consequent economic development. Besides Indian public and privately sponsored research, she has received several US fellowships and US India and UK India collaborative interdisciplinary research projects. Her publications spread across core management, multi-disciplinary areas in national and international spaces. In the last 15 years she has been visiting faculty in Bangladesh, South Korea and Japan. She has, for other short term research interactions travelled to England, Sweden, Germany, Switzerland, Turkey, China, Malaysia, Myanmar, Indonesia, Mexico.Dr. Banerjee is a life-long supporter of the girl scouts and follows Lord Baden Powell's credo 'Be Prepared.' She is married and temptations, to which she and her husband surrender, sometimes, are travel opportunities and good coffee!

Matteo De Angelis is Associate Professor of Marketing at LUISS University, Italy, and has been a Visiting Scholar at Kellogg School of Management, US and a Visiting Professor at the University of Wisconsin, US. His articles have been published in journals such as Journal of Marketing Research, Psychological Science and Journal of the Academy of Marketing Science.

Anannya Deb Roy is an Associate Professor in the department of Fashion Management Studies, National Institute of Fashion Technology, Kolkata. He teaches Research Paradigms and Behavioral Psychology for research scholars and post graduate students. His research interest includes triangulation of constructivism and positivism as epistemological inquiry in the field of social and individual psychology. He has done MBA and Doctorate in management from Department of Business Management, University of Calcutta. Loves to discuss avant-garde fashion and philosophy over 'chai' from kaka's roadside tea stall and aspire to return to his native village and teach primary school students.

About the Contributors

Anant Deogaonkar is Assistant Professor, Shri Ramdeobaba College of Engineering & Management at Department of Management Technology. Ex Senior Manager, Tata Communications Transformation Services Limited. He is a seasoned professional with more than 18 years of rich experience in corporate working in different capacities.

Mohamed Elsotouhy is a PhD student in faculty of commerce at Mansoura University. Lecturer Assistant with more than 3 years in Higher Institute of Managerial science in El-Mahalla El-Kubra in Egypt. Having a Master Degree in Business Administration from Mansoura University in 2017.

Ludovica Gallo graduated with honours in Marketing Analytics and Metrics in 2019 at LUISS University. In 2018 she represented her university at the finals of Inside LVMH, a student competition involving 45 European universities awarding the most innovative ideas of the luxury experience of the future. Prior to her graduation she was working for a well known Italian fashion brand in New York.

Floriana Iannone is Professor of "Management of Cultural Organizations" at the Faculty of Economics of the International University of Rome and of "Communication" at the Fashion Academy of Naples. Research Fellow at the University of Naples L'Orientale she achieved a PhD in "Entrepreneurship and Innovation". Her research activity is currently focused on the companies in the creative industry and on the fashion system in general, with particular attention to the issues of sustainability and management of the 'supply chain'.

Rashmi Kaushik possesses a rich experience of more than 13 years in academics. She has done her post-graduation in marketing and IT specialization. She has also completed M.Phil. from Bhartiya Vidya Peeth University Pune. She is pursuing Ph.D. from Ansals University, Gurugram in marketing. She has served in various colleges of NCR. She has published good quality research papers in various national & international journals & conferences.

Samala Nagaraj, PhD, University of Hyderabad. Presently working in the research area of Customer Engagement. Published papers on Customer Engagement in SSCI, ABDC-B & Scopus indexed journals. Having 8+ years of experience in teaching Marketing for Business Management students. Interested research areas are Customer Analytics, Customer-Brand Engagement, Customer Experience, and Mixed Method research methodologies.

About the Contributors

M. K. Nair is working at SGT University, Gurgoan, Delhi-NCR, India as a Professor & Dean. His nineteen years of experience towards the fashion and academics visually appeared and he is not only innovator of fashion products but also a creator of designers. He is a specialist in leather, footwear, accessories, costume design and customer views. Fashion course founder and board of studies members in many Universities in India. Active Member of Fashion Design Council of India. Achiever and motivator in terms of fashion education and innovation.

Sampada Nanoty is graduation scholar in Maharaja Sayajirao University, Vadodara. She is a young researcher and has authored a lot of literature in the field of Human Resource Management.

Chand P. Saini is an Assistant Professor in the area of Marketing Management. He has done his Masters in Business Administration in Marketing as his core area from RBS, New Delhi and also possesses the degree of M. Com. He has completed his doctorate (Ph.D.) in online retailing from IMSAR, MDU Rohtak. He is UGC-JRF/NET qualified in Management. He is having more than ten years of experience in both industry and academia. He has worked with various institutions serving with his core competencies in Retail and Marketing, Consumer Behavior, Advertising Management, Integrated Marketing Communication; Organization Behavior. He has presented many research papers in international and national conferences and seminars. He has also attended faculty development programs and workshops in his field.

Ruchi Sao is currently working as an Assistant Professor at Department of Management Technology, Shri Ramdeobaba College of Engineering and Management. She has completed her degree in law, MBA in human resources, MA in Psychology and PhD from Rashtrasant Tukdoji Maharaj Nagpur University. Her areas of interest are organization behaviour, performance management and psychology. She has more than eight years of teaching and research experience.

K. Tara Shankar is a Dean of Faculty of Commerce and Management, SGT University. He is an IIM Calcutta Alumnus, Doctorate in Management, PGDM and MBA. He has more than 23 years of experience in industry and academics. His area of interest includes Consumer Behavior, Marketing Strategy and Brand Management.

Kanchan Tolani is currently working as an Assistant Professor at Department of Management Technology, Shri Ramdeobaba College of Engineering and Management. She has completed her MBA in Human Resource & MA in Psychology. She is pursuing her PhD in Management. Her areas of interest are human psychology, human resource management and behavioural sciences. She has near about four years of teaching and research experience.

Sana Vakeel is an academician with more than four years of experience including exposure of working with a multinational corporation. She did Masters in International Business (MIB) from Jamia Millia Islamia and secured second rank in the central university. She has qualified UGC-NET (Management) and completed graduation in commerce from the University of Delhi. Before joining the field of academics, she has worked with WNS Global Services as a business research analyst in Gurgaon. Her areas of expertise include various international business and marketing subjects viz., Export Import Documentation, Foreign Trade Policy, International Marketing, Services Marketing and Retail Management. She has attended various faculty development programs and workshops.

Index

A

Agency 33, 75-76, 92
Art of Fashion 80, 82, 84, 86, 88-92, 94-96

B

Branding 27, 32, 68, 112, 167

C

Circular Economy 7, 10, 82-84, 86, 90, 93-94, 130, 142-146
Clothing Sharing Services 142, 144, 147-149, 151, 155
Commodity and Artifacts 85
CSR 99-105, 109, 111-112
Customer Behavior 31, 33-34, 36-37

D

Design Thinking 1

E

Eco-friendly Apparels 41-42, 44-45

F

Fashion Industry 1, 3, 10, 12-13, 15, 17, 19-22, 27-28, 31-34, 36-37, 41, 48-49, 74-78, 81-84, 87, 96, 118, 122, 131-132, 138, 142, 144, 147-148, 156, 161-170, 172-174

Fashion Product 90, 128, 138
Framing 106, 112

G

Generation Z 54, 58-60, 65, 67-68, 92, 118
Green Marketing 112
Green Strategy 2-4

I

Influencer 64, 67
Influences 168
Information Processing 109-110
Innovation 37, 87, 95, 117, 131, 147, 162, 167

K

Kantha 80, 83-84, 86, 88-89, 92-96

L

Luxury Goods 117, 119-120, 122-123, 125, 127-129, 131, 133, 138
Luxury Retailing 120

M

Marketers 25, 31-34, 36, 55-56, 59, 67-68, 87, 161-165, 168, 170, 172, 174
Marketing Strategies 27, 60, 161-163

O

Omichannel Retail Strategies 138
Online Brand Communities 162, 167-170, 174
Overconsumption 47, 86, 148

P

Priming 99, 107-109, 111-112
Purchase Intention 10, 12, 15-16, 40-45

R

Re-Commerce 10-11, 19, 73-78, 117-118, 120, 127, 130-131, 138
Reuse 4, 11, 21, 47, 49, 90, 92-95, 138, 145-148

S

Second-hand Goods 118-120, 123

Sharing Economy 132, 142-149, 151, 155-156
Social Media 54-61, 64, 67, 81, 120, 162-170, 172, 174
Sustainability 2-8, 11-13, 19-22, 24-28, 31-37, 47, 73, 77-78, 80, 82, 84, 88, 99-103, 105-108, 111-112, 117-120, 122-123, 130-133, 138, 142, 148, 167-168
Sustainable Consumption 117, 121, 145
Sustainable Development 2, 20, 32, 84, 103, 118-119, 138, 144
Sustainable Fashion 1-6, 8, 20-25, 27-28, 31, 33-35, 41, 92, 94, 102, 123

T

Textile Waste 11-13, 47-49
The theory of Planned Behavior 40

Purchase Print, E-Book, or Print + E-Book

IGI Global's reference books can now be purchased from three unique pricing formats: Print Only, E-Book Only, or Print + E-Book.
Shipping fees may apply.

www.igi-global.com

Recommended Reference Books

Digital Currency
Breakthroughs in Research and Practice
ISBN: 978-1-5225-6201-6
© 2019; 341 pp.
List Price: $345

Business Transformations in the Era of Digitalization
ISBN: 978-1-5225-7262-6
© 2019; 360 pp.
List Price: $215

Intergenerational Governance and Leadership in the Corporate World
Emerging Research and Opportunities
ISBN: 978-1-5225-8003-4
© 2019; 216 pp.
List Price: $205

Smart Marketing With the Internet of Things
ISBN: 978-1-5225-5763-0
© 2019; 304 pp.
List Price: $205

Breaking Down Language and Cultural Barriers Through Contemporary Global Marketing Strategies
ISBN: 978-1-5225-6980-0
© 2019; 325 pp.
List Price: $235

Green Finance for Sustainable Global Growth
ISBN: 978-1-5225-7808-6
© 2019; 397 pp.
List Price: $215

Looking for free content, product updates, news, and special offers?
Join IGI Global's mailing list today and start enjoying exclusive perks sent only to IGI Global members. Add your name to the list at **www.igi-global.com/newsletters**.

Publisher of Peer-Reviewed, Timely, and Innovative Academic Research

IGI Global
DISSEMINATOR OF KNOWLEDGE

www.igi-global.com | Sign up at www.igi-global.com/newsletters | facebook.com/igiglobal | twitter.com/igiglobal

Ensure Quality Research is Introduced to the Academic Community

Become an IGI Global Reviewer for Authored Book Projects

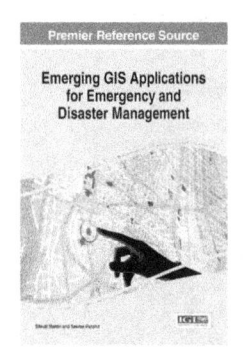

The overall success of an authored book project is dependent on quality and timely reviews.

In this competitive age of scholarly publishing, constructive and timely feedback significantly expedites the turnaround time of manuscripts from submission to acceptance, allowing the publication and discovery of forward-thinking research at a much more expeditious rate. Several IGI Global authored book projects are currently seeking highly-qualified experts in the field to fill vacancies on their respective editorial review boards:

Applications and Inquiries may be sent to:
development@igi-global.com

Applicants must have a doctorate (or an equivalent degree) as well as publishing and reviewing experience. Reviewers are asked to complete the open-ended evaluation questions with as much detail as possible in a timely, collegial, and constructive manner. All reviewers' tenures run for one-year terms on the editorial review boards and are expected to complete at least three reviews per term. Upon successful completion of this term, reviewers can be considered for an additional term.

If you have a colleague that may be interested in this opportunity, we encourage you to share this information with them.

IGI Global Proudly Partners With eContent Pro International

Receive a 25% Discount on all Editorial Services

Editorial Services

IGI Global expects all final manuscripts submitted for publication to be in their final form. This means they must be reviewed, revised, and professionally copy edited prior to their final submission. Not only does this support with accelerating the publication process, but it also ensures that the highest quality scholarly work can be disseminated.

English Language Copy Editing

Let eContent Pro International's expert copy editors perform edits on your manuscript to resolve spelling, punctuaion, grammar, syntax, flow, formatting issues and more.

Scientific and Scholarly Editing

Allow colleagues in your research area to examine the content of your manuscript and provide you with valuable feedback and suggestions before submission.

Figure, Table, Chart & Equation Conversions

Do you have poor quality figures? Do you need visual elements in your manuscript created or converted? A design expert can help!

Translation

Need your documjent translated into English? eContent Pro International's expert translators are fluent in English and more than 40 different languages.

Hear What Your Colleagues are Saying About Editorial Services Supported by IGI Global

"The service was very fast, very thorough, and very helpful in ensuring our chapter meets the criteria and requirements of the book's editors. I was quite impressed and happy with your service."

– Prof. Tom Brinthaupt,
Middle Tennessee State University, USA

"I found the work actually spectacular. The editing, formatting, and other checks were very thorough. The turnaround time was great as well. I will definitely use eContent Pro in the future."

– Nickanor Amwata, Lecturer,
University of Kurdistan Hawler, Iraq

"I was impressed that it was done timely, and wherever the content was not clear for the reader, the paper was improved with better readability for the audience."

– Prof. James Chilembwe,
Mzuzu University, Malawi

Email: customerservice@econtentpro.com   www.igi-global.com/editorial-service-partners

IGI Global
DISSEMINATOR OF KNOWLEDGE
www.igi-global.com

Celebrating Over 30 Years of Scholarly Knowledge Creation & Dissemination

InfoSci®-Books

A Database of Over 5,300+ Reference Books Containing Over 100,000+ Chapters Focusing on Emerging Research

GAIN ACCESS TO **THOUSANDS** OF REFERENCE BOOKS AT **A FRACTION** OF THEIR INDIVIDUAL LIST **PRICE**.

InfoSci®-Books Database

The **InfoSci®-Books** database is a collection of over 5,300+ IGI Global single and multi-volume reference books, handbooks of research, and encyclopedias, encompassing groundbreaking research from prominent experts worldwide that span over 350+ topics in 11 core subject areas including business, computer science, education, science and engineering, social sciences and more.

Open Access Fee Waiver (Offset Model) Initiative

For any library that invests in IGI Global's InfoSci-Journals and/or InfoSci-Books databases, IGI Global will match the library's investment with a fund of equal value to go toward **subsidizing the OA article processing charges (APCs) for their students, faculty, and staff** at that institution when their work is submitted and accepted under OA into an IGI Global journal.*

INFOSCI® PLATFORM FEATURES

- No DRM
- No Set-Up or Maintenance Fees
- A Guarantee of No More Than a 5% Annual Increase
- Full-Text HTML and PDF Viewing Options
- Downloadable MARC Records
- Unlimited Simultaneous Access
- COUNTER 5 Compliant Reports
- Formatted Citations With Ability to Export to RefWorks and EasyBib
- No Embargo of Content (Research is Available Months in Advance of the Print Release)

*The fund will be offered on an annual basis and expire at the end of the subscription period. The fund would renew as the subscription is renewed for each year thereafter. The open access fees will be waived after the student, faculty, or staff's paper has been vetted and accepted into an IGI Global journal and the fund can only be used toward publishing OA in an IGI Global journal. Libraries in developing countries will have the match on their investment doubled.

To Learn More or To Purchase This Database:
www.igi-global.com/infosci-books

eresources@igi-global.com • Toll Free: 1-866-342-6657 ext. 100 • Phone: 717-533-8845 x100

IGI Global
DISSEMINATOR OF KNOWLEDGE
www.igi-global.com

IGI Global
DISSEMINATOR OF KNOWLEDGE
www.igi-global.com

Publisher of Peer-Reviewed, Timely, and Innovative Academic Research Since 1988

IGI Global's Transformative Open Access (OA) Model:
How to Turn Your University Library's Database Acquisitions Into a Source of OA Funding

In response to the OA movement and well in advance of Plan S, IGI Global, early last year, unveiled their OA Fee Waiver (Offset Model) Initiative.

Under this initiative, librarians who invest in IGI Global's InfoSci-Books (5,300+ reference books) and/or InfoSci-Journals (185+ scholarly journals) databases will be able to subsidize their patron's OA article processing charges (APC) when their work is submitted and accepted (after the peer review process) into an IGI Global journal.*

How Does it Work?

1. When a library subscribes or perpetually purchases IGI Global's InfoSci-Databases including InfoSci-Books (5,300+ e-books), InfoSci-Journals (185+ e-journals), and/or their discipline/subject-focused subsets, IGI Global will match the library's investment with a fund of equal value to go toward subsidizing the OA article processing charges (APCs) for their patrons.

   Researchers: Be sure to recommend the InfoSci-Books and InfoSci-Journals to take advantage of this initiative.

2. When a student, faculty, or staff member submits a paper and it is accepted (following the peer review) into one of IGI Global's 185+ scholarly journals, the author will have the option to have their paper published under a traditional publishing model or as OA.

3. When the author chooses to have their paper published under OA, IGI Global will notify them of the OA Fee Waiver (Offset Model) Initiative. If the author decides they would like to take advantage of this initiative, IGI Global will deduct the US$ 1,500 APC from the created fund.

4. This fund will be offered on an annual basis and will renew as the subscription is renewed for each year thereafter. IGI Global will manage the fund and award the APC waivers unless the librarian has a preference as to how the funds should be managed.

Hear From the Experts on This Initiative:

"I'm very happy to have been able to make one of my recent research contributions, 'Visualizing the Social Media Conversations of a National Information Technology Professional Association' featured in the *International Journal of Human Capital and Information Technology Professionals*, freely available along with having access to the valuable resources found within IGI Global's InfoSci-Journals database."

– **Prof. Stuart Palmer**,
Deakin University, Australia

For More Information, Visit: www.igi-global.com/publish/contributor-resources/open-access or contact IGI Global's Database Team at eresources@igi-global.com

CPSIA information can be obtained
at www.ICGtesting.com
Printed in the USA
BVHW092100250620
581832BV00017BA/361

9 781799 827283